Symbian OS Communications Programming

Symbian OS Communications Programming

Michael J Jipping
Hope College,
Holland, Michigan USA

JOHN WILEY & SONS, LTD

Baffins Lane, Chichester,
West Sussex, PO 19 1UD, England

National 01243 779777
International (+44) 1243 779777

Transferred to digital printing, 2005

British Library Cataloguing in Publication Data

A catalogue record for this book is available from the British Library

ISBN 0-470-84430-2

Typeset in 10/12pt Optima by Laserwords Private Limited, Chennai, India

To my wife, Peg.
For her inspiration, encouragement, and
patience ...but mostly for her patience

CONTENTS

Preface

In a recent column in a trade periodical[1], a columnist named Brian Livingston declared that "the future belongs to devices we'll carry around, not boat anchors that must remain tied to our desks." I could not agree more. As I track the development of computers over time, it strikes me that some of the most innovative developments in computers have been done with handheld devices. These devices change the way we view and work with computing. In fact, the convergence of computing, communication, and mobility is one of the most significant innovations in recent years.

I have to agree again with Brian Livingston when he states "I believe the operating systems on the computer we'll soon be using—and taking for granted—will look like a newer, leaner OS named Symbian." Indeed, Symbian OS supports innovations with communication throughout its design. When a company like Nokia states, as it has, that 50% of its 3G devices will run Symbian OS by 2004, there is real recognition of this fact.

This book sets out to describe how Symbian OS supports the convergence of computing and communication. The designers of this operating system have built a strong communications architecture that can flex and adapt. This book covers how this architecture is built and how it can be used to take advantage of the communication capabilities of a device powered by Symbian OS.

Who Should Read This Book?

This book is written for the software developer who needs to design applications in the C++ programming language that harness communication on a Symbian OS device. This book assumes some familiarity with C++ in a Symbian OS environment.

If you are a programmer who needs to know how to write applications to send SMS messages, this book will show you how.

---

[1] Livingston, B., "The next Windows", *Info World*, 24:1 (2002), 30.

If you need to use C++ to access Internet services, this book will show you how. If you want to add infrared or Bluetooth capability to an application to exchange data with other devices, this book will show you how.

The Structure of This Book

This book is organized in three sections.

Section 1: The Basics of Symbian OS Communications

The first section introduces how communications work on Symbian OS.

Chapter 1 introduces the reader to Symbian OS: its structure, its history, and its implementation on various reference designs. It also gives an overview of the book.

Chapter 2 focuses on Symbian OS communications and introduces the Symbian OS communication architecture. The chapter looks at communications in two ways: transport and content. The technologies in each of these areas is discussed and related to support by the operating system. This chapter also discusses techniques used by Symbian OS to implement these technologies.

Chapter 3 looks at the system components that make up the infrastructure supporting communications. The designers of Symbian OS have developed several layered models to address the various aspects of communication and each is examined by this chapter.

Chapters 4 and 5 examine the support Symbian OS gives to transport and content technologies. In these chapters, we get into details about the technologies and discover what is necessary to support them.

Chapter 6 concludes this introductory section by examining issues of security that surround communications. Threats are examined from a Symbian device perspective and the security measures necessary to guard data are introduced.

Section 2: Programming using Symbian OS Communications

This section gets into the meat of writing applications that use the structure we presented in the previous section.

Chapter 7 introduces the programming environment that is used to develop Symbian OS applications. We present the traditional "Hello World!" application here. We also present an example called "TodoX" that will be used in much of the rest of the section. This example application exchanges to-do list items between devices.

Chapter 8 covers the programming interface that is used to work with the serial port. Serial communication is probably the most familiar to programmers and is a good place to introduce the Symbian OS APIs. In this chapter, we introduce some important programming patterns that emerge as we work with communications devices. We also cover the concept of an active object, a special parallel thread of execution that deals with communications.

Chapter 9 is a rather short chapter dealing with serial communications over the infrared port. Its brevity is important: it emphasizes how little an application needs to be altered to move applications between use of the serial port and the infrared port.

Chapter 10 covers sockets, a concept that is used by Symbian OS on almost all non-serial communication. We go into much detail about socket properties and how a programmer would use the socket API. This chapter also covers the host resolver, an object that is used to discover properties of remote devices.

Chapter 11 revisits infrared communication using the socket concept. There are many ways to use the infrared port, and most are implemented using sockets. This chapter examines these new uses for the infrared port and serves as the first real example of socket use.

Chapter 12 examines the TCP/IP suite of network protocols. We start by reviewing TCP/IP and by examining the Symbian OS network manager. Then, using the patterns developed in previous chapters, we examine the many aspects of programming using TCP/IP. The chapter concludes with two examples: one that implements fetching Web pages from Web servers and one that implements a Network Time Protocol client.

Chapter 13 is devoted to programming using Bluetooth. The Bluetooth model is discussed and much space is given to how Symbian OS implements device and service discovery. Symbian OS uses sockets to communicate over Bluetooth, and this use of sockets is covered. The chapter concludes with a new example: sending instant messages over Bluetooth.

Chapter 14 provides a bridge between transport and content and covers telephony. Telephony provides strong evidence of how seriously Symbian OS takes the convergence of computing and communications. Telephony itself is introduced and the Symbian OS ETel programming model is discussed. The chapter discusses each of the ETel components and their APIs.

Chapter 15 switches from transport to content technologies and covers the Symbian OS support for messaging. Messaging is a crucial component in the functioning of communicators and smartphones. The Symbian OS model for messages is covered in detail, as is the API for using this model. The idea of "send-as messaging", which is an easy way to send any kind of message, is also covered.

Chapter 16 is devoted to the "browsable" content of HTML and WAP. The chapter covers the support given by the Symbian OS to HTML and its transport protocol HTTP. It covers in detail the layers in the WAP stack and how Symbian OS addresses them.

Section 3: Miscellaneous Topics

This section covers areas that are useful—but not crucial—to communications programming.

Chapter 17 provides an overview of synchronization issues with Symbian OS. It discusses general issues, and then focuses on two implementations of synchronization. Psion Link Protocol is discussed in detail and SyncML is introduced.

Chapter 18 covers the way applications move data into and out of the communications database. This database is used by Symbian OS to provide nonvolatile storage for communications parameters that would be used by more than a single application. The usage of the database and the API to access it are covered in detail.

Chapter 19 gives a look to the future and the technologies that will be addressed by Symbian OS in upcoming versions. Technologies like Multimedia Message Service and GPRS are coming soon; other technologies like 3G networking are a bit farther away. These future technologies are overviewed.

Foreword

David Wood, EVP, Partnering Evangelism & Research, Symbian

We live in times of tumult and change. In the midst of this excitement, two strong trends are clear. First, software is spreading more widely and more deeply into all aspects of society. Second, communication is becoming pervasive: more objects and gadgets talk to each other all the time, in ever-richer ways.

These two trends collide in the phenomenon of the mobile phone. The next generation of mobile phones uses incredibly sophisticated software to make it easy for their human owners to keep in touch, exchanging voice messages, text messages, pictures, email, and much more besides. These phones also constantly jump in and out of networks, with other phones and larger computers. As a result, they act as connected gaming devices, wicked entertainment devices, precocious pagers, personal and community organizers, mobile information portals, and as 'rich clients' for the forthcoming waves of advanced data services and other compelling add-on software.

The software that lies at the heart of these new phones is Symbian OS. Endorsed by giants of the telecommunications industry—Fujitsu, Kenwood, Motorola, Nokia, Panasonic, Psion, Sanyo, Siemens and SonyEricsson—Symbian OS enables a dramatic leap in the power and utility of mobile phones. Symbian OS is neither a cut-down desktop/server OS nor an extended embedded OS, but a one-of-a-kind mobile operating system. Like all disruptive technologies, it has a challenging learning curve. Thankfully, it also has a flourishing community of software developers and trainers ready to help fellow travelers along this curve—sharing Symbian's motto of 'co-operate before competing'.

Symbian OS Communications Programming is a timely addition to the growing library of books about developing for Symbian OS. Dr. Michael Jipping brings a most welcome new perspective, carefully explaining how Symbian OS deals with communications of all sorts. I commend this book to you as a fascinating read, to help you towards creating your share of the huge market around Symbian OS phones.

Acknowledgments

The fact that you are reading these words means that my family—my wife and three kids—put up with me long enough to enable me to complete it. Their patience and perseverance—and excitement—helped put these words to paper.

Two former students—now computer science colleagues—deserve my thanks. Sarah Dieter and Joshua Krikke read the manuscript, corrected errors, examined the software, and let me know when I did not make sense.

Finally, I am grateful to the folks at Symbian who helped get this book out. In particular, Jonathan Hassell and Phil Northam were instrumental in this book's publication. Their encouragement and editorial skill are greatly appreciated.

Mike Jipping

Section 1

The Basics of Symbian OS Communication

1

Introduction

On February 14, 1946, a group of scientists and engineers activated the world's first general-purpose computer. The Electronic Numerical Integrator and Computer—ENIAC—was a huge computer that took up the equivalent of a small office building. It was built in 30 separate units and used 15,000 square feet of floor space to house 17,480 vacuum tubes and 1,500 relays. At a weight of 30 tons, it consumed 140 kilowatts of power. Its sole purpose was to compute tables of numbers; in its day, it served a crucial purpose by producing trajectory computations for field artillery faster and more precisely than humans could produce the same computations. It could actually compute 5000 additions per second.

Today, computers have evolved from 30-ton behemoths into much smaller machines that can do far more than simple number crunching. Handheld devices and mobile phones are at the leading edge of this evolution. With these devices we are seeing the convergence of communication, computing and mobility.

A Nokia 9210 Communicator is a good example of this convergence. This handheld device combines an ARM 9 processor with 32 MB of memory and digital GSM (900/1800/1900 MHz) communication capabilities in a slim mobile phone size. It can execute over 220 million instructions per second, help manage your personal life, let you make mobile telephone calls, and show videos on a screen that can handle over 32,000 colors. It harnesses the power of a desktop workstation and can fit into your pocket.

The Nokia 9210 is not only a good example of the advanced capabilities that modern computers have, but it is also a good example of the multiple purposes for which such computers are built. While the first computers were designed with one purpose—to calculate numbers quickly and precisely—today's devices have many purposes. They entertain by playing music or games. They manage information by storing files and displaying data. They schedule your day and remind you of appointments. They communicate with each other and the outside world.

In fact, as computers and their operating systems continue to grow and develop, the convergence of this computing power with the ability to communicate becomes an important element that lies at the core of what a computing device does. Along with other facets of computing (such as processor speed and display capability), communication capability is a deciding factor for many people, determining what computer they buy and use. Some current technologies that are key to computer use are messaging—via email or faxing—and browsing the World Wide Web.

In the future, communications will become even more important. This means device-to-device communication, the ability to use the Internet, making phone calls, sending all kinds of messages—email, fax, or SMS (short message service)—and browsing the World Wide Web. The future will bring easy access to information that is stored anywhere in the world, using the Internet as a storage facility. Future communications will feature mobile, wireless connections as well as conventional wired access, and will connect people to each other by way of the devices they carry.

The focus of this book is communication—specifically, on communication using handheld devices. More to the point, this book presents an operational and programming view of communications on handheld devices using Symbian OS. We present Symbian OS in this book and how it can be used to harness the communication power of handheld machines. We will explore the concepts that drive the way Symbian OS implements communication. We will spend a large part of the book examining the interfaces that are used to program communication facilities.

This chapter is an introduction to the book. We will look closely at Symbian OS and at its history; we will examine how Symbian OS is applied to various handheld device designs; and we will conclude with an overview of the rest of the book.

1.1 Introducing Symbian OS

Symbian OS is a *system*: a combination of several different elements that can be applied to several different designs of computing devices. There are six elements that combine to make up Symbian OS:

- the core operating system, commonly called a *kernel*
- a collection of middleware for system services
- a set of resource managers, called *application engines*

- a framework for designing user interfaces
- methods for synchronization with other machines
- a Java virtual machine implementation.

These elements combine to produce software made to control devices from handheld computers to mobile phones. We will overview each element on its own.

Web Sites to Check Out

You can do a lot of research for yourself at Symbian's Web site. There are many white papers on Symbian OS and a large number of practical examples to introduce developers to the Symbian community. The URL is *http://www.symbian.com*.

The Symbian Developer Network is Symbian's developer organization. This site supports developers of software for Symbian OS: it has Symbian OS software development kits, hosts forums for questions and answers, and contains patches and examples of software designs. You will find Symbian DevNet at *http://www.symbian.com/developer*.

Both of these sites provide a growing library of excellent reference material as you develop software for Symbian OS.

1.1.1 The Symbian OS Kernel

The heart of Symbian OS is the core operating system: a collection of device drivers, data tables, and programs that allows the user to work with a computer's hardware. This is the common core of Symbian OS, present in all Symbian OS devices.

Symbian OS is a *kernel-based* operating system. There is one program that runs at all times and manages the services that are provided to the user. This program and its data tables—collectively called the *kernel*—need to be small and efficient. Only the elements of computer operation that need constant attention are placed in the kernel; other functions are moved out to middleware elements or applications. This design makes the kernel very compact and makes the architecture and operation of Symbian OS very modular.

From its beginnings, when it was known as the EPOC operating system, Symbian OS has had an object-oriented design and an efficient, tight structure. It is a 32-bit operating system that supports multitasking and multithreading. Its modular structure supports and encourages a wide variety of communication components and supports the ability to add to and extend core communication elements to adapt to new devices and methods. The communications architecture derives great benefits from this modular design, as we will see.

Symbian OS has seen several releases. The most recent is Symbian OS version 7.0. New devices, such as the Nokia 7650, are using this version to support new technology such as GPRS and Bluetooth.

1.1.2 Middleware

The term *middleware* refers to the collection of elements—libraries, data storage, and programs—that implement system services, but do not need to be in the kernel. In Symbian OS, this includes implementations of services such as data management, communications, and graphics. As an example of middleware, consider the window system in Symbian OS. The window system forms an essential part of how a user interacts with the computer, but management of windows and stylus taps is not essential enough to be built into the kernel. By contrast, management of the display device itself (i.e., the server) is in the kernel. The transformation of a display device into a set of windows is left to middleware.

Symbian OS uses *servers* to implement middleware. The idea it uses is that a server can manage a particular service by accepting requests from many different sources—or *clients*—and coordinating access and implementation by its response to those requests. To follow our example, the window system is not built into the Symbian OS kernel, but rather implemented by a *window server* that receives requests from applications and manages the display. These servers lie in the middle area between the kernel and the user—hence the name *middleware*—and they contribute to the modular design of Symbian OS. By creating a new layer for middleware, Symbian OS designers made it easy to design new system services and to upgrade existing services without rewriting the core of the operating system.

Middleware servers exist for many system services, including the window system, network communication, serial and infrared implementations, multimedia management and database implementation.

1.1.3 Application Engines

User level applications on Symbian OS also benefit from the kind of coordination that middleware provides. Coordination of access to non-essential resources is done through *application engines*.

These form single access points for user level applications as they access resources. Having a single object that coordinates access to an Agenda database, for example, saves memory and processing time by channeling all manipulation of that database through one implementation.

Like middleware, application engines typically take the form of servers. The difference, however, comes from the area being managed. Application engines manage *application* data and services, not *system-oriented* data and services. For example, while Agenda data is certainly crucial to a user for managing her schedule or to-do lists, it is not crucial to the management of the computer. In fact, it is likely that application engines will themselves interact with middleware servers.

The application engines included in the Symbian OS core are:

- the Agenda engine
- the Contacts engine
- the Sheet engine
- the Alarm server and World Time engine
- the Spell engine
- the Help engine

1.1.4 User Interface Framework

Since computers that run Symbian OS are typically small handheld devices that are specifically oriented toward users, the user interface is extremely important. It is important that this interface be easy to use, easy to change, and easy to program. In addition, there are several different device designs that are meant to run the Symbian OS, so this user interface must be adaptable. In the face of these constraints, the Symbian OS designers chose to include a *framework* on which to build user interfaces as part of the core operating system.

By choosing to include a graphical user interface framework rather than one specific graphical user interface, the designers of Symbian OS laid a foundation upon which many different user interfaces can be built. In the current version of Symbian OS, there are two user interfaces that build on the GUI framework. These interfaces use common GUI components, such as controls and dialogs, but the specific look-and-feel of these components is left in the hands of the mobile device manufacturer licensing the Symbian OS so that they control each specific device implementation.

Currently, the core GUI components are Uikon and Standard Eikon. The core libraries of Uikon contain elements that are largely common across all reference designs. Standard Eikon contains starting-point code for modules that occur in most reference designs, but whose functionality typically needs to be altered. A "control factory" element allows the GUI framework to be extended. The intent of this type of structure is to allow the drawing of core and additional controls in such a way that a device manufacturer can change the appearance of the GUI component without affecting the drawing code in individual controls.

1.1.5 Synchronization Technology

In addition to the core technology of Symbian OS, the platform also includes ways to synchronize data with other computers. This type of technology has been the subject of industry-wide cooperation and standards development and Symbian has integrated these developments into the Symbian OS. On Symbian OS, synchronization is implemented in three discrete parts.

- The *connection manager* is a user-initiated process that runs on a Symbian OS Device and detects when another computer wants to connect. It starts a synchronization connection when such an attempt is detected.
- *Connectivity servers* implement the various functions of a synchronization session: simple file browsing, file synchronization, backup, or restoration.
- *File converters* transfer data between formats specific to certain applications. These converters are minimal on the Symbian OS side of the connection; most conversion will probably happen on the connecting computer. However, converters do exist to convert rich text format to HTML and some office-type Symbian OS applications to their Windows counterparts.

Synchronizing is done via a "conversation" between the connectivity servers on two computers. That conversation takes place via a specific protocol or language. Historically, on machines based on Symbian OS, that protocol has been Psion Link Protocol (PLP). This proprietary protocol was invented by Psion Computers and requires a special interface on a PC, which is supplied by Symbian. Symbian OS also uses a more recently developed, and more widely adopted, protocol called SyncML. This protocol was developed in 1999 as a standard for handheld machine synchronization.

1.1.6 Java Virtual Machine Implementation

Symbian OS includes a full Java implementation within what is called the "J2ME" framework. The Java 2 Micro Edition framework is an implementation of the Java Virtual Machine (JVM) as specified by Sun Microsystems for small handheld devices. While this JVM lacks some services and interfaces of the Java 2 Standard Edition, it does include some Java technologies that are tailored specifically for devices that adhere to the Micro Edition specification. Among these are a JavaPhone implementation and an extensive PersonalJava implementation. Coverage of this part of Symbian OS is beyond the scope of this book, and the reader is referred to the many published works of Sun Microsystems, the Java Community, and Symbian to look into this part of the Symbian platform further.

Further Reading on Java

We will not be covering Java in this book. If you want to know more about programming in Java on Symbian OS, I would refer you to a book by Jonathan Allin called *Wireless Java for Symbian Devices*, published by Symbian Press through Wiley. It provides a great reference to using Java on the Symbian platform. You can find out more details at *http://www.symbian.com/books*.

1.2 Symbian OS History

The heritage of Symbian OS begins with some of the first handheld devices. The operating system began its existence in 1988 as SIBO, an acronym for "sixteen bit organizer". SIBO ran on computers developed by Psion Computers, which developed the operating system to run on small-footprint devices. The first computer to use SIBO, the MC laptop machine, died when it was barely out of the gate, but several successful computer models followed the MC. In 1991, Psion produced the Series 3: a small computer with a half VGA size screen that could fit into a pocket. The Series 3 was followed by the Series 3c in 1996, with additional infrared capability; the Sienna in 1996, which used a smaller screen and had more of an "organizer" feel; and the Series 3mx in 1998, with a faster processor. Each of these SIBO machines was a great success, primarily for three reasons: SIBO had good power management, included light and effective applications, and interoperated easily with other computers, including PCs and other handheld devices. SIBO was also accessible by developers: programming was based in C, had an object-oriented design, and employed application engines, a signature part of Symbian OS development. This engine approach was a powerful feature of SIBO; it made it possible to standardize an API and to abstract formats away from the application programmer.

In the mid-1990s, Psion started work on a new operating system. This was to be a 32-bit system that supported pointing devices on a touch screen, used multimedia, was more communication-rich, was more object-oriented, and was portable to different architectures and device designs. The result of Psion's effort was the introduction of EPOC Release 1. Psion built on its experience with SIBO and produced a completely new operating system. It started with many of the foundational features that set SIBO apart and built up from there.

EPOC was programmed in C++ and was designed to be object-oriented from the ground up. It used the engine approach pioneered by SIBO and expanded this design idea into a series of servers that coordinated access to system services and peripheral devices. EPOC expanded the communication possibilities, opened up the OS to multimedia, introduced new platforms for interface items like touch screens, and generalized the hardware interface. EPOC was further developed into two more releases: EPOC Release 3 (ER3) and EPOC Release 5 (ER5). These ran on new platforms like the Psion Series 5 and Series 7 computers.

As EPOC was being developed, Psion was also looking to emphasize the ways that its operating system could be adapted to other hardware platforms. From mobile phones to Internet appliances, many devices could work well with EPOC. The most exciting opportunities were in the mobile phone business, where manufacturers were already searching for a new, advanced, extensible and standard operating system for the next generation of devices. To take advantage of these opportunities, Psion and the leaders in the mobile phone industry—for example, Nokia, Ericsson, Motorola, and Matsushita (Panasonic)—formed a joint venture, called Symbian, which was to take ownership of and further develop the EPOC operating system core, now called Symbian OS.

Symbian OS was explicitly targeted to several different generalized platforms. It was flexible enough to meet the industry's requirements for developing a variety of advanced mobile devices and phones, while allowing manufacturers the opportunity to differentiate their products. It was also decided that Symbian OS would actively adopt current, state-of-the-art key technologies as they became available. This decision reinforced the design choices of object-orientation and a client-server architecture.

1.3 Symbian OS Reference Designs

Symbian OS is intended for a range of devices. To assist in the design of devices that can use the capabilities of Symbian OS, Symbian has developed a series of reference designs for mobile devices and phones.

Keyboard-based mobile phones are device designs that are generally referred to as *communicators*—information devices with communication capabilities. This design most closely resembles the historical line of devices that have used EPOC and Symbian OS. It is a design that reinforces the state of the art: half VGA color screen with a keyboard and a rich application suite derived from previous implementations. Figure 1.1 shows a Symbian concept device and Figure 1.2 shows a Nokia 9210. Both devices feature keyboard navigation, 16-bit color screens, sound, and a rich communication suite. As an example of design customization, the generic concept device specifies a touch screen interface while the Nokia 9210 does not use a touch screen at all. Instead, it implements user interaction through buttons on the right of the display screen.

Single-handed use mobile phones are devices that are typically designed with advanced data capabilities. These are categorized as

Figure 1.1   A Symbian concept communicator design.

Figure 1.2   The Nokia 9210 communicator.

smartphones—communication devices with information capabilities. This design puts browsing content, messaging, and access to entertainment in the forefront and other information management as a secondary goal. A Symbian concept device for a smartphone is shown in Figure 1.3 and a Nokia smartphone—the 7650 phone—is shown in Figure 1.4. Each design includes the integration of a color touch-screen with a communications device. These devices can function as mobile telephones or wireless network nodes. The Nokia 7650 includes technologies like GPRS, Bluetooth connectivity and digital imaging (via a digital camera).

Pen-based mobile phones are communicators without a keyboard. They have a tablet-style form factor that allows additional data inputs, such as a large touch screen (which differentiates it from

Figure 1.3 A Symbian smartphone concept design.

Figure 1.4 The Nokia 7650 phone.

the smartphone above). The Symbian "generic" concept device is in Figure 1.5. An Ericsson concept version is shown in Figure 1.6. This design is built around a quarter VGA sized screen with no keyboard. The device uses handwriting recognition. It is oriented around a browser style interface, and operation of the unit is done completely through a touch screen. This category of device includes the Ericsson R380, the first Symbian OS phone.

Symbian OS allows mobile phone manufacturers to customize the operating system while maintaining an industry-standard common core for all devices. The real-world reference designs

Figure 1.5 The Symbian pen-based mobile phone concept design.

Figure 1.6 The Sony Ericsson P800.

described above derive from generic reference design work done by Symbian. The mobile phone categories above reflect generic Symbian OS reference designs that have been used by Symbian and its licensees in the past.

There are many common components to these device designs and communication plays a strong central role in each. As is the duty of operating systems, Symbian OS provides access to system services; I will focus in this book on the access that is provided to communications. Each reference design provides a different way for the user to access communication methods and Symbian OS integrates different ways of communication. Programming interfaces and the technologies are basically the same across the board. The communications architecture is standard and that is what we will be studying here.

1.4   Who Is this Book For?

The content of this book is targeted at software developers who know something about programming and are looking to expand their knowledge set. The programming in this book will be in the language C++ and will use the software development kits (SDKs) provided by Symbian and its partners.

While software can be designed using other means, the Symbian SDKs are meant to be used with Microsoft Visual C++. Knowledge of this development environment is very helpful.

A Companion Book

There are many good books that can serve as prerequisites or companions to this book. One that I highly recommend as a precursor to tackling this material is *Professional Symbian Programming*, by Martin Tasker, *et al.*, published by Wrox. It provides an excellent introduction to programming using the Symbian platform APIs and is a good way to get started on Symbian programming.

1.5   An Overview of this Book

Aside from this chapter, this book's primary focus is on communication in the Symbian platform. We will cover the communications architecture in three major sections.

- **Communication Basics:** Chapters 2 through 6 will cover the basic concepts and methods used in the Symbian platform's approach to communications. We will introduce the architecture, and then look closely at its infrastructure. We will then go over transport and content technologies in detail, and wrap up with a look at communication security and how it plays in integral role in Symbian platform design.

- **Programming Using the Communications Architecture:** Application programming interfaces (APIs) are the major way that the goals and criteria set up by Symbian are expressed in the design of the communication architecture. Therefore, our examination of APIs and their use will occupy a large part of this book. Chapters 7 through 16 will work through the communication architecture and show how to program using its structures. We will spend time on each of the technology areas—transport and content—outlined above.

- **Miscellaneous Topics:** Before we leave the communications architecture, there are some miscellaneous concepts that are implemented by Symbian that warrant some attention. These include data and device synchronization standards, accessing the communications configuration database built into Symbian OS, and future directions for the platform. Chapters 17 through 19 will overview these topics.

Accompanying Software

All code examples that we will work through in Chapters 7 through 18 can be found on the Symbian Web site at ***http://www. symbian.com/books/socp/socp-info.html***. In addition, throughout this book I will occasionally suggest using software to review some aspects of Symbian OS or its components. You will also find any software development kits from Symbian that you need to get started programming on your own (see Chapter 7). All of this software will be available from this Web site.

I have found examples to be my best resource when learning new programming systems. I have attempted to include as many examples as I could that would illustrate the features we discuss here. I have also included some public domain software and their sources. You will find installation instructions and some tips on using the software at the support site.

2

Introduction to the Symbian OS Communication Architecture

In his book, *Clicks and Mortar*, David Pottruck analyzes the culture of computers and the Internet and applies this analysis to business practices. As one of his observations, he notes that this culture of computers and information we are in is not really the *information age* as it commonly called, but rather it is the *communications age*. Our times do not really focus on information but on the communication that enables us to share and use that information.

Symbian OS reflects this kind of relationship between information and communication. While Symbian devices are indeed information devices, much of the focus of Symbian OS is on a communication-rich environment that is flexible enough to support many forms of connectivity. The organization of the communication layers of Symbian OS should be viewed as more than simply infrastructure; it is in fact an *architecture*: a combination of concept, design, structure, and function.

A majority of this book will be dedicated to the structure and function of Symbian OS communications architecture in the form of tutorials and programming references. This chapter, however, introduces the basics of the communications architecture: the concept and design behind it. In this chapter, we will overview the concepts that comprise the architecture; in the next chapter, we will overview the design that the architecture implements.

Symbian OS was designed for a certain type of computing device; I introduced these devices in Chapter 1. From communicators to smartphones, these devices can vary widely in shape, size, and even function. They all have common needs that are addressed by the various facets of Symbian OS. In this chapter, we will discuss Symbian OS design by outlining the communication requirements of these devices. We will then proceed to discuss the ways that Symbian OS meets those requirements: through a client-server design, through the use of a communications database, and through the use of synchronization. We will complete this chapter by looking at issues that surround the security of information and communication.

2.1 What Is a Communications Architecture?

Architecture is a term used to describe the way that form and function implement design. A building, for example, has an architecture—that architecture is displayed as the way that bricks, girders, and wiring work together to reflect a design that was meant to service the building's inhabitants and the designer's artistic sense. To many, architecture is little more than the shape of the windows or the balance of bricks to glass. But to the architect, there is a set of layers, a collection of facets, a sequence of details for which the final structure is simply the last step.

In the same way, the various communication components of Symbian OS unite together. There is more than simply infrastructure in Symbian OS's communication architecture. It is more than an implementation; it is the combination of concept and design, structure and function into a single expression. There are concepts embedded in the way the pieces work and fit together. There is a design to each component; a structure and a function to each piece. Together, the components form a communications architecture that can serve the needs of each device design and each user in a well-designed and cohesive manner.

The communications architecture is, then, an expression of a specific set of design goals and criteria.

- *The communications architecture must support all user communications applications.* Users of smartphones and communicators expect a level of functionality from their devices. The communications architecture must support this functionality and be able to address future needs gracefully.

- *Communications components must be exceptionally flexible to cope with the mobility designed into these device platforms.* Users of communicators and smartphones are mobile and demand a mix of connectivity methods and communication platforms. The communications architecture must easily adapt itself to the changing requirements of configuration and connectivity. On-the-fly reconfiguration, for example, from a dial-up connection to a wireless network must be easy and straightforward.

- *Communication components must be organized to accommodate the constant restructuring and rebuilding of communication technology.* The communications architecture must be built in a modular fashion so that pieces can be replaced as technology evolves without upsetting the entire structure. In fact, the structure should be able to accommodate the coexisting of old and new pieces.

- *The communication components must adapt to the tight RAM and CPU constraints of their intended target platforms.* While they must do a great amount of work, the components of the communications architecture must not consume a burdensome amount of resources. The resources of a communication device are to be targeted at an application, not consumed by communication methods.

This is a difficult job: support all functionality possible in a flexible, modular fashion in a limited computing environment! Despite the daunting task, the designers at Symbian believe they have achieved an architecture that meets these criteria.

The design of the communications architecture addresses these issues in two parts: *transport* technologies and *content* technologies. Transport technologies address the way data is communicated between devices. Content technologies address the data that is carried by a transport method. For example, in the case where someone is browsing a Web page, the HTML content of the page has been transported to the viewing application over a wired network using TCP protocols.

2.2 Transport Technologies

Transport technologies is an area unseen by most users of communicators or smartphones. It involves *communication media*, or the physical components that convey the signals between devices, and *communication protocols*, which is what we call the structure of the conversation between devices that allows them to move data between them.

There are many transport technologies and Symbian OS addresses several of them. I group these technologies into *point-to-point* technologies, where two devices communicate directly with each other, and *networking* technologies, where the communication medium is shared and devices have the potential to communicate with several other devices over this medium.

2.2.1 Point-to-Point Transport Methods

Serial and infrared communication are the two most widely used point-to-point methods.

Serial transport is one of the oldest communication methods for computers. This transport method typically runs over short distance cables, which conform to one of two standards: RS-232 or RS-432. These cables are comprised of wires in a 9 or 25 wire group. Despite the many wires, only two of them are used to communicate data, one bit at a time, in sequential order, back and forth. One wire transmits data in each direction. The other wires are used as control pins, carrying signals that convey information about traffic flow and data management.

There are liberal interpretations of RS-232 standards in practical implementations. For example, some connections use only three wires: two for data and a signal ground. This three-wire, stripped-down version is still referred to as an RS-232 connection.

Most point-to-point communication methods exchange data between devices in one of three ways:

- *Simplex communication* exchanges data in one direction only. Using this method, one device is a sender and one is a receiver—they never switch roles. Since communication is one-way, the sender never knows if the receiver actually got the information sent and if that information was sent without errors.

- *Half-duplex communication* exchanges data in two directions—both sides can be a sender and a receiver—but data flows in one direction at a time. In half-duplex modes, a single wire can be used to exchange all the data, because the devices involved take turns sending and receiving.

- *Full-duplex communication* is also a bi-directional method, but data can be exchanged between devices in both directions at the same time.

RS-232 communication is full-duplex, using two wires to send data from both sides.

Serial communication is typically controlled on a computing device by a Universal Asynchronous Receiver Transmitter (UART) chip. Currently, UARTs are capable of driving serial transport up to speeds of 115,000 bits per second (115 Kbps).

The infrared (IR) transport method uses light in the infrared spectrum to convey data between two devices. Because it is based on light, IR communication is limited to devices that can directly "see" one another and are within a short, limited range.

There are many standards that infrared communication uses; all of them fall under the umbrella of the Infrared Data Association (IrDA). IrDA specifies that data signaling is bi-directional (however, only one side can transmit at a time) and can operate in speeds from 9600 bps to 4 Mbps. Symbian OS supports IrDA standards that include a serial port emulation protocol (IrCOMM), a multilayered protocol that supports device discovery and data segmentation (IrLMP and Tiny TP), a protocol to exchange digital pictures between devices (IrTranP), and a protocol stack that allows access to wired networks (IrLAN). These standards will be more fully explained in later chapters.

2.2.2 Networking Technologies

To facilitate faster communication, networking technologies address situations when many devices communicate over the same communication medium. Because of their complexity, network implementations are characterized in protocol layers or stacks. The official stack structure (specified by the International Standards Organization (ISO)) is shown in Figure 2.1.

Networks are characterized by *datagram delivery* of data, that is, the delivery of data in the form of small packets that are broken

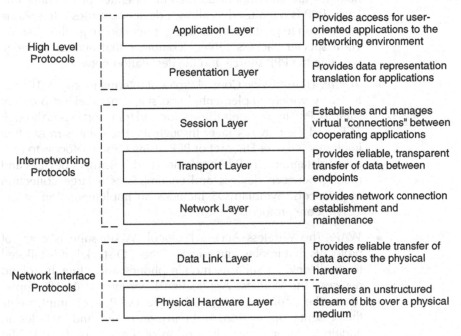

Figure 2.1 ISO protocol stack.

up, passed over the transport medium, and reassembled at their destination. Network data is digital data, and a digital medium is needed to pass that data. While analog methods may be used for transmission (e.g., serial cables or IR), the physical layer will translate the analog data to digital data.

Symbian OS includes support for several networking technologies:

- *Ethernet:* This is by far the most widely implemented and most popular form of networking. Ethernet is a passive form of networking that shares datagrams among all machines that are on the network. It relies on each machine to be well-behaved and to pay attention to only the packets that "belong" to it. Conventional Ethernet technology runs these networks up to 100 Mbps, although most installations of Ethernet are still at 10 Mbps. The newest implementations of Ethernet are currently running at 1 Gbps. Ethernet is a data link layer technology.

- *Point-to-point protocol:* Point-to-point protocol (PPP) is a way of implementing networking protocols between only two machines instead of a multiple machine environment. Networking technologies are still supported, as PPP operates at the data link layer. PPP is often used to allow a device that uses a telephone connection to graft itself into a larger network (e.g., the Internet) via a special "access server" computer that acts as a bridge between the PPP source and the destination network.

- *TCP/IP:* Transmission Control Protocol/Internet Protocol (TCP/IP) is a very widely implemented and stable networking protocol suite. TCP/IP implements the session and transport layers through TCP, and the network layer through IP. The suite is most often implemented over Ethernet or PPP, using these protocols to pass actual datagrams. TCP/IP implements addressing of devices and routing between devices and encompasses a large collection of protocols. Symbian OS includes an implementation of the TCP/IP core protocols.

- *WAP:* The Wireless Access Protocol (WAP) suite is a set of protocols that implements much of the ISO stack but is tailored to small devices such as mobile phones and other handheld devices. The Wireless Application Environment (WAE) implements the application layer, but the WAP stack implements the presentation, session, and transport layers, and includes an additional layer of security on top of the transport layer. The

WAP stack leaves the network, data link and physical layers to wireless transport providers ("bearers" in WAP terminology). Symbian OS has full support for the WAP stack.

2.2.3 Bridge Technologies

There are technologies that bridge the difference between point-to-point and networking technologies. These are technologies that can be used in either setting. Symbian OS supports two of these: Bluetooth and GSM.

Named for a 10th century Viking king, Bluetooth is a short-range, radio-based, wireless protocol suite that is meant to facilitate low power, close-range communication. It was developed as a point-to-point connection strategy that uses the 2.4 GHz radio frequency and allows communication between devices up to 10 meters apart with a gross data rate of 1 Mbps. Much of Bluetooth's appeal comes from its use as a replacement for data cables. Individual point-to-point connections can be tied together to form a personal area network, called a piconet. The Bluetooth specification describes its own protocol stack that includes security protocols as well as those meant for layers in the ISO layer model. The heart of Bluetooth is realtime device discovery and interactive implementation. The Symbian OS implements the Bluetooth stack.

The Global System for Mobile Communications (GSM) is a mobile telephony implementation. It is used by digital mobile devices to exchange information over long or short distances in a wireless fashion. GSM is mostly implemented for mobile phones, and for devices that incorporate mobile telephony as well as voice/data traffic. A central feature of GSM is a messaging service, detailed in the content technology section below. Symbian OS includes support for GSM communication.

2.3 Content Technologies

For the user, it is the content of the communication that matters, not the way it is transported. Thus, the proper implementation of content technologies is very important. Symbian OS addresses several important technologies.

2.3.1 Messaging

The convergence of computing and communication in communicators and smartphones presents some interesting opportunities. One of these is the use of *messaging*: the two-way exchange of various types of messages between devices. Messaging presents several challenges; one of the largest is the sheer variety of the types and technologies of messages currently exchanged between computers. Symbian OS pulls the disparate technologies together and presents a consistent programming interface to the software developer. In addition, Symbian OS is designed to be extensible, i.e., it can incorporate new forms of messaging as they are invented. Among the types of messages that Symbian OS currently supports are these:

- *Email messaging:* One of the most common and widely used forms of messaging is electronic mail. This form was originally invented as an electronic method for sending text-based messages—"mail" for human consumption—between computers. Each message has an "envelope" and a message "body". The envelope contains information about the message—sender, intended recipient, date and subject of message, etc.—in the form of a message header. The message body is typically a textual communication between people, but it can also contain objects, textual or binary data, encoded in special ways so that they can be represented in a text-based message.

- *SMS messaging:* SMS messaging is a form of messaging specific to GSM-based communication. SMS—short for *Short Message System*—uses text messages of 160 characters or less for communication between devices on GSM networks. While textual in nature, these messages can convey special data to devices; specialized data such as graphics or phone ringtones can be encoded in an SMS message.

- *BIO messaging:* BIO messages—short for *bearer independent object*—are messages that are intended for the *system* rather than the *user*. Sending a graphic image contained in a message to a phone for configuration purposes is a good example of BIO messaging. This type of messaging includes configuration information (e.g., system configuration or browser configuration), specially formatted contact and scheduling information (e.g., vCard and vCalendar), and email notification.

- *Fax messaging:* A fax—short for *facsimile*—message is a form of message that contains a digitized image, organized into pages, intended to also convey information about physical paper pages. The support in Symbian OS for faxing includes various methods of fax encoding, multiple recipient outgoing faxes, sending and receiving both standard and fine resolution fax images, and the unattended receipt of fax messages.

- *Other forms of messaging:* Obviously, the designers of Symbian OS could not accommodate all forms of messaging that exist or predict the forms of messaging that will be invented. Therefore, there is also a mechanism built into the platform that can accommodate other messaging forms not designed into it. *Message Type Modules* (MTMs) are implemented by a collection of objects that can be extended to implement any form of messaging that might be needed. An MTM features the receipt, processing, and sending of messages, and is flexible enough to implement many new formats and applications.

2.3.2 HTML and the World Wide Web

As a content platform, the World Wide Web and the technologies that supply its content have been unparalleled in their usefulness and popularity. The heart of the Web is a set of pages, written in *hypertext markup language* (HTML) and rendered by and viewed with applications in various forms, known as Web browsers. These browser applications are clients that contact Web servers—which send pages to the browsers using *hypertext transfer protocol* (HTTP). These pages are connected to each other by hyperlinks on each page that, when followed by clicking the mouse or tapping a stylus on the link, cause the browser to automatically retrieve and display the page referred to by the hyperlink. HTTP uses the TCP/IP protocol suite.

Symbian OS supports Web technologies in two ways.

- It provides support for HTTP and HTML transport in its implementation of networking protocols. HTTP is implemented as a high-level protocol carried by several transport mechanisms. HTML is supported separately and assumed to be carried to a device by some transport means.

- It supplies applications that can be used as Web browsers. There are several Web browsing applications—from Symbian and third parties—that Symbian OS provides and supports.

2.3.3 WML and WAP

Browsing HTML content on the Web has been a great success for desktop and handheld computers. The intent of WAP is to move this success to mobile phone-based platforms. While a great idea, the browsing platform and its content need to be reworked completely for mobile, phone-oriented technology. First, microbrowsers have to be used to reduce the load on the smaller CPU and restricted memory. Then HTML needs to be reduced to fit into these microbrowsers, resulting in *wireless markup language* (WML).

As with technologies surrounding HTML and HTTP, Symbian OS supports WML and WAP in several ways.

- There is native library support for WAP transport and for WML.

- Symbian OS supplies applications for WAP browsing and rendering.

- It supplies tools and interfaces for building separate applications that implement WAP page retrieval.

2.4 Requirements of Communicators and Smartphones

Although there can be many kinds of communicators and smartphones, they have some common requirements that the designers of Symbian OS had to watch. It is difficult to design an efficient communication architecture that meets the needs of the future—especially when the future changes so rapidly. These communication platforms have dictated and directed this design. We will examine their needs, to see how those needs have influenced platform design.

To start with, it is important to mention what are *not* requirements. It is certainly *not* a requirement that these devices all look the same or even do the same things. These devices can come in all shapes and sizes, each implementing different views of computing and communication. Communicators and smartphones do not have to have the same hardware requirements; monochrome screens should be as acceptable as color and many different memory configurations are possible. They do not even need to have the same I/O devices or configuration. In short, Symbian OS places no restriction on hardware design.

However, there are requirements outside of design constraints that Symbian OS devices place on a communications infrastructure. First and foremost, Symbian OS's communication architecture must be one that *supports many device designs* and is *extensible*. As previously mentioned, there is no restriction on size, shape or design. To accommodate many different designs, we do not want to have to completely redesign communications for a new communication method. We want a new method's implementation to fit in with existing implementations, and to be able to take advantage of all the same facilities as the other implementations.

As with most computing devices, these platforms require *robust* implementations. In fact, communicators and smartphones have special needs in this category. While larger computers can perhaps be reset easily or can tolerate errors without affecting other applications, these smaller devices cannot easily accommodate error conditions, nor can they be reset as easily. It does not work to "reboot" your mobile phone to correct a problem, or to restart a data stream or video transmission. These devices often use realtime communication services that charge by the byte or by the connection session. Therefore, restarting equipment or data transfers can cost the user an unacceptable amount of money.

Communicators and smartphones require an *efficient* implementation of communications. By "efficient", we mean both "fast" and "easy on resources". These factors are complicated by the wide variety of designs. No assumptions can be made about speed of processors, amount of memory, or specific communications available. We must have a modular, adaptable implementation, yet one that takes up a small space and runs fast.

Finally, one assumption we can make is that communicators and smartphones will run on batteries. Therefore, implementations must be easy on the resources. Battery power must be preserved, but access to communication ports will utilize power. Therefore, care must be taken to economize access while fully implementing standards.

So, we have a tall order. We must have a general, modular, adaptable infrastructure that supports the implementation of many different communication standards. This general implementation must be robust and efficient, while at the same time being extensible and easy on resources. This is the mandate for Symbian OS.

2.5   Implementation Techniques

As we begin to examine the architecture of Symbian OS, we will notice patterns in the way the architecture is implemented. Certain techniques are used in implementations; understanding these techniques will help to understand the communications architecture.

2.5.1   Client-Server Relationships

The way computers interact—especially in a TCP/IP network like the Internet—can be characterized as a *client-server* type of relationship. The client is the computer taking advantage of the service; the server is the computer providing that service. The client typically utilizes the service by sending requests to the server; the server provides the service typically by responding to these requests. The requests and responses take the form of messages sent back and forth between client and server.

A good example is the microbrowser in a WAP-enabled mobile phone. Figure 2.2 shows how this works. The phone calls up a WML page by sending an encoded request to a computer at the company that provides the service. This computer is called a *gateway server*, because it provides a gateway to the Internet for the mobile phone. This server, in turn, becomes a client by passing the request from the mobile phone on to the actual Internet server that houses the WAP page in question. This server happens to be providing an HTTP service, and answers the request by sending a Web page to the gateway server. The gateway server then translates the HTML page into WML, and encodes the response using the encryption scheme the mobile phone expects. Finally, the gateway server sends the response to the mobile phone, and the microbroswer displays the WML page on the phone's display.

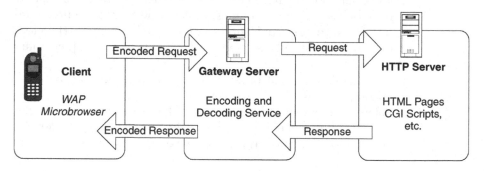

Figure 2.2   Client-server relationships in WML browsing.

Note that in the example, there were two clients and two servers. The gateway server was both a server to the mobile phone and a client to the HTTP server. This is an example of a *proxy server*, a server that represents its client on another network by becoming a client itself.

A variant of this relationship occurs in the Symbian OS kernel to protect and manage resources. In this case, the kernel acts as a server and applications act as clients. The middleware that we discussed in Chapter 1 is an example of this. Applications use a protected resource by connecting to the server that manages that resource. Once connected, applications or clients manipulate the resource through the resource's server (in an application's code, the resource is manipulated by using the server object's functions).

2.5.2 Asynchronous Events

Communications programming requires quite a bit of waiting. As a client, an application might wait for a response from a server. As a server, an application would always be waiting for client requests. An application would be likely to spend time waiting on devices—such as IR ports or Bluetooth chips—to transmit messages or to report back with data.

Because waiting is so frequent, a programming model has been developed for it: *asynchronous, event-driven programming*. This type of programming is asynchronous because responses do not arrive in fixed intervals (if they return at all). We use the idea of an "event" to represent the occurrence of something that an application might be waiting for in a communications exchange. In Symbian OS, there are many events that are specified to represent communications. We will discuss these in later chapters.

With asynchronous programming, there is an event defined as a timeout. A timeout is a good example of the care a programmer has to take with communications. Assuming, for example, that all communications will result in a response would be a mistake. Programmers must plan and design for the event that nothing happens when communications is attempted. We will discuss ways to build timeout exceptions in the way we approach communications.

This asynchronous event model is useful in several ways. It keeps applications from freezing while they wait for some event. It allows the system to interleave instructions more efficiently from concurrent processes/threads. It also allows the system to put the entire device to sleep in certain cases (e.g., all processes are waiting for events) to conserve battery power.

2.5.3 Active Objects

To accommodate the constant waiting imposed by the asynchronous nature of communications, Symbian OS uses the idea of *active objects*. An active object is a thread—a parallel object that executes alongside the main code—that makes communications requests and handles the event that is generated when the request gets a response. By building into the Symbian OS the concept of an active object as a thread, the designers of Symbian OS built an object that can handle waiting for responses from devices and not prevent other code from running.

An example of how an active object might be used is an email application. Email can be collected by sending a request to a POP3 (Post Office Protocol, version 3) server. A response is rarely immediate, however, especially if there are many messages to pick up. If an application were not to use active objects, the application would quite likely freeze up while waiting for all the messages to download. This situation would occur because the application would be concentrating on the data exchange with the POP3 server, and not on listening for stylus taps or updating the screen. However, if the application used an active object for communicating with the POP3 server, then it could respond to the user at the same time it was waiting for messages. Active objects enable more interaction with applications and a clean interface for handling situations that might arise during communication.

2.6 Summary

This chapter opens a section of this book on the basic concepts and design of Symbian OS's communication architecture. Specifically, we covered the following:

- What a "communications architecture" actually is
- What technology is supported by Symbian OS—from a *transport* and a *content* perspective
- What requirements communicators and smartphones make on Symbian OS's communications architecture
- What implementation (or programming) techniques are used by Symbian OS: client-server relationships, event-driven programming, and active objects

The next chapter will introduce the communications structure of Symbian OS from several different perspectives, taking a close look at the elements that form its foundation.

3

Several Introductions to the Architecture Infrastructure

In Chapter 2, we had an introduction to the communication architecture of Symbian OS. We stated in that chapter that this architecture "is more than simply infrastructure". While this is certainly true, the infrastructure of communication in Symbian OS is a foundational part of the architecture and we need to discuss it. This chapter takes a look at the concepts that comprise the infrastructure of Symbian OS's implementation of communication from several different perspectives.

The communication infrastructure weaves several common themes through the various interfaces and layers of its implementation. We look at these common themes in this chapter. We will begin with an overview of the infrastructure by looking at the components used to build it. Then we will take a close look at the client-server model in Symbian OS, which is at the center of the infrastructure. Next, we will overview the communication database, which is at the heart of accessing peripherals. We will conclude by examining two issues tied closely to the infrastructure: synchronization and security concerns.

3.1 Basic Infrastructure Building Blocks

A good way to start looking at the infrastructure is by examining its basic components. This will also serve as an introduction to the implementation.

Let's start by considering a very generic form of the communications infrastructure. Figure 3.1 contains a generic diagram of the infrastructure. Consider this diagram as a starting point for an organizational model. At the bottom of the stack is a physical device, connected in some way to the computer. This device could be a

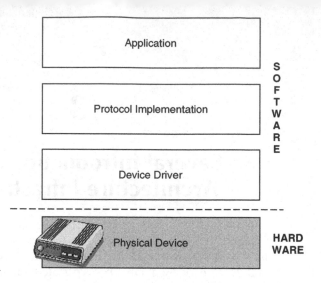

Figure 3.1 A generic API diagram.

mobile phone modem or a Bluetooth radio transmitter embedded in a communicator. Since we are not concerned with the details of hardware in this book, we will treat this physical device as a "black box", an abstract unit that responds to commands from software in the appropriate manner.

The next level up—actually the first level we are concerned with—is the *device driver* level. The software at this level is concerned with working directly with the hardware via a fixed, standardized interface to the upper software layers. The software at this level is hardware-specific, and every new piece of hardware requires a new software device driver to interface with it. Symbian OS comes with a set of device drivers for commonly used pieces of hardware (e.g., internal modems and printers). Different drivers are needed for different hardware units, but they all must implement the same interface to the upper layers. The protocol implementation layer will expect the same interface no matter what hardware unit is used.

Standards play a major role with device drivers. Hardware is becoming increasingly standardized, and sometimes one device driver can manage several pieces of hardware because they all abide by the same standard. For example, many modems can be controlled by a single device driver. In addition, protocol implementations are increasingly assuming device driver standards. Standards such as IrCOMM, for instance, are becoming widely supported and therefore must be incorporated in the device driver layer.

The next layer up is the protocol implementation layer. This layer contains implementations of the protocols supported by Symbian OS. These implementations assume a device driver interface with the layer beneath and supply a single, unified interface to the application layer above. This is the layer that implements the Bluetooth and TCP/IP protocol suites, for example, along with the other protocols discussed in Chapter 2.

Finally, the top layer is the application layer. This layer contains the application that must utilize the communication infrastructure. The application does not know much about *how* communications are implemented—however, it does do the work necessary to inform the operating system of which devices it will use. Once the drivers are in place, the application does not access them directly, but depends on the protocol implementation layer APIs to drive the real devices.

3.2   A Closer Look at the Infrastructure

Now let's take a closer look at the layers in Symbian OS communication infrastructure. Figure 3.2 contains a diagram based on

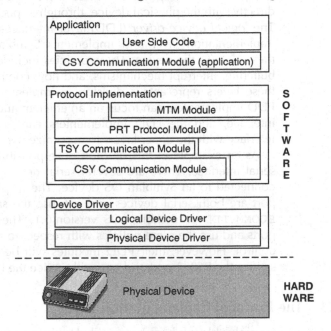

Figure 3.2   More detailed API diagram.

the generic model in Figure 3.1. The blocks from Figure 3.1 have been subdivided into operational units that depict those used by Symbian OS.

3.2.1 The Physical Device

First, notice that the device has not been changed. As we stated before, Symbian OS has no control over hardware. Therefore, it accommodates hardware through this layered API design, but does not specify how the hardware itself is designed and constructed. This is actually an advantage to Symbian OS and its developers. By viewing hardware as an abstract unit and designing communication around this abstraction, the designers of Symbian OS have ensured Symbian OS will handle the wide variety of devices that are available now and that it can accommodate the hardware of the future.

3.2.2 The Device Driver Layer

The device driver layer of Figure 3.1 has been divided into two layers in Figure 3.2. The *physical device driver* (PDD) layer interfaces directly with the physical device, through a specific hardware port. The *logical device driver* (LDD) layer interfaces with the protocol implementation layer and implements Symbian OS policies as they relate to the device. These policies include input and output buffering, interrupt mechanisms, and flow control. The division of these layers represents a division in implementation, where the PDD implementers can focus on an efficient and correct hardware interface, and the LDD implementers can work to perfect the interface with the upper layers to maximize performance.

As an example of this division of responsibilities, consider the serial interface. There are several serial device types that can be connected to an Symbian OS device. The IR port and the RS232 port are both serial devices and can use the same LDD—called ECOMM.LDD on Symbian OS version 6.1. These ports are serial ports and use the same policies with respect to issues such as flow control. However, their PDD modules will be different: one will service the RS232 port and one will service the IR port.

3.2.3 The Protocol Implementation Layer

Several sublayers have been added to the protocol implementation layer in Figure 3.2 from Figure 3.1. Four types of modules are used for protocol implementation; these are itemized below:

- *CSY Modules:* The lowest level in the protocol implementation layer is the *communication server* or CSY, module. A CSY module communicates directly with the hardware through the PDD portion of the device driver, implementing the various low-level aspects of protocols. For instance, a protocol may require raw data transfer to the hardware device or it may specify 7-bit or 8-bit buffer transfer. These "modes" would be handled by the CSY module.

  Note that CSY modules may use other CSY modules. For example, the IrDA CSY module that implements the IrCOMM interface to the IR PDD also uses the serial device driver, ECUART CSY module.

- *TSY Modules:* Telephony comprises a large part of the communications infrastructure, and special modules are used to implement it. *Telephony server–*or TSY—modules implement the telephony functionality. Basic TSYs may support standard telephony functions, e.g., making and terminating calls, on a wide range of hardware. More advanced TSYs may support advanced phone hardware, e.g., those supporting GSM functionality.

- *PRT Modules:* The central modules used for protocol implementation are *protocol modules* or PRT modules. PRT modules are used by servers to implement protocols. A server creates an instance of a PRT module when it attempts to use the protocol. The TCP/IP suite of protocols, for instance, is implemented by the TCPIP.PRT module. Bluetooth protocols are implemented by the BT.PRT module.

- *MTM Modules:* As Symbian OS has been designed specifically for messaging, its architects built a mechanism to handle messages of all types. These message handlers are called *message type modules* or MTMs. Message handling has many different aspects, and MTMs must implement each of these aspects. User Interface MTMs must implement the various ways users will view and manipulate messages, from how a user reads a message to how a user is notified of the progress of sending a message. Client-side MTMs handle addressing, creating and responding to messages. Server-side MTMs must implement server-oriented manipulation of messages, including folder manipulation and message-specific manipulation.

These modules build on each other in various ways, depending on the type of communication that is being used. Consider Figure 3.3, which depicts some example module relationships. Implementations of protocols using Bluetooth, for example, will use only PRT

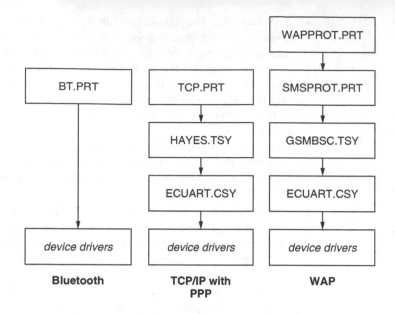

Figure 3.3 Example communication module relationships.

modules that communicate directly to device drivers. Certain IrDA protocols will do this as well. TCP/IP implementations that use PPP will use PRT modules and both a TSY and a CSY module. The WAP protocol stack uses a WAP PRT on top of an SMS PRT, which in turn is built on a GSM TSY and some kind of CSY (ECUART, IrCOMM, or RFCOMM).

Look for Yourself

See for yourself which modules are installed on your emulator or Symbian device. You need to look on the Z: drive, which Symbian OS uses to designate the ROM. To do this, use the Web browser in your emulator or Symbian device and activate its main menu. Choose File, then Open, then Open Web Page (on the Quartz emulator, you must choose Web, then Open Web Page). In the file dialog that opens, type Z: in the text field under the Open URL Address label (Location, for Quartz). When you press the Enter key or choose the Ok option, the Web browser will present you with a display that holds the contents of the ROM.

On the Quartz emulator, there is an easier way. The Symbian OS 6.1 Quartz emulator comes with a file browser interface. It is called "QFileMan". Tapping the icon brings up the interface.

You can browse the Z: drive by tapping the righthand menu and choosing the correct drive.

Use the interface to explore the ROM. In particular, look under Z:\System\LIBS. Look for the CSY, TSY, PRT, and MTM modules that are delivered with your emulator or device.

3.2.4   Infrastructure Modularity

We should take a moment here to appreciate the modularity of the communication infrastructure design. The "mix and match" quality of the layered design should be evident from the examples just given. Consider the TCP/IP stack implementation. A PPP connection can go directly to a CSY module or choose a GSM or regular modem TSY implementation, which in turn goes through a CSY module. When the future brings a new telephony technology, this existing structure still works, and we only need to add a TSY module for the new telephony implementation. In addition, fine tuning the TCP/IP protocol stack does not require altering any of the modules it depends on; we simply tune up the TCP/IP PRT module and leave the rest alone. This extensive modularity means new code plugs into the infrastructure easily, old code is easily discarded, and existing code can be modified without shaking the whole system or requiring extensive reinstalls.

3.2.5   Application CSYs

Finally, Figure 3.2 has added sublayers to the application layer of Figure 3.1. There are CSY modules that applications use to interface with protocol modules in the protocol implementations. While we can consider these as parts of protocol implementations, it is a bit cleaner to think of them as assisting applications. An example here might be an application that uses IR to send SMS messages through a mobile phone. This application would use an IRCOMM CSY module on the application side that uses an SMS implementation wrapped in a protocol implementation layer. Again, the modularity of this entire process is a big advantage for applications that need to focus on what they do best and not on the communications process.

3.3   Client-Server Relationships

Another way to examine the communication infrastructure is by looking at the client-server relationships built into it. This section will examine the servers; the next section will look at the clients.

3.3.1 Kernel Servers

In general, Symbian OS uses kernel servers to protect and manage shared resources and services. Servers form a gateway that processes must go through to access communication functionality. If the operating system was only able to run one program at a time, run that program until it was done, and move on to the next one, servers would not be necessary because only one access at a time would be possible. But Symbian OS is a multitasking operating system, allowing multiple processes to run at the same time. And Symbian OS is also multithreaded, allowing multiple threads of control to run in parallel within a single process. All this concurrency could wreak havoc on communication resources. Imagine three Web browsers, each using the TCP/IP stacks and each fighting for the communication ports at the same time.

The use of servers, then, cuts down on the amount of memory and CPU resources needed by supplying access to resources that applications do not have to implement. Using servers also correctly channels the accesses from multiple processes and threads into proper usage of resources.

In Symbian OS, servers are accessed by clients in the following way:

- Servers must first be started if they are to serve their gateway function. Only a few servers are started when the operating system initially boots, to prevent slowing down a system with rarely used servers. The other servers must be started explicitly before an application may use them. To help application programmers, Symbian OS allows the starting of servers that are already started (only one copy will be left running); this means applications can blindly start servers without checking if the one they need is running.

- To use a server, clients must establish a connection to the server they need. Within the communications infrastructure, this client-server connection is facilitated by a *socket*. Servers listen for socket connections, and have the option to accept or deny connections. Most of the time, servers will accept socket connections. Decisions to deny connections can be based on information that comes with the connection request (e.g., the identification of the sending computer) or on local information (e.g., the number of connections already open).

- Once a socket is open, the server waits for requests to arrive over that socket. Requests are simple bytes of data, interpreted by the server in special, designated ways. The server then services those requests and sends responses back to the client, again in the form of bytes of data written to the socket.

- When the exchange is done, the socket is closed. Either side can close the socket, but Symbian OS notifies both sides of the closure no matter which side initiates it.
- A server might stay active for a time to service other requests or might terminate immediately to preserve resources.

There are several servers used throughout the communication infra-structure. These servers include:

- *Serial communications server:* The serial communications server provides clients with a consistent interface that manipulates serial devices. The serial communications server manages the built-in serial ports and the IR port, using the ECUART and IrCOMM communication server modules to interface with lower layers.

- *Telephony server:* The telephony server manages services for initiating and terminating voice, fax, and data calls. It provides an API for accessing telephony services implemented through either GSM mobile phones or landline modems (using Hayes standard AT modem commands).

- *Socket server:* The socket server manages socket connections and provides a programming interface for a variety of protocols to clients. It also allows new protocols to be inserted into the socket framework. Standard interfaces are provided for Internet and IR protocols, as well as for the Psion Link Protocol (PLP) which is used for PC synchronization.

- *Communications database server:* As the central repository for information regarding configuration settings for devices, the communications database server serves an important function. It guards the source of information for devices and manages access to this information set. This information set includes data pertaining to phones, modems, protocols, and Internet service provision information (network access phone numbers, Internet addresses and physical locations). In addition, details of device drivers available to the system servers and the Symbian OS kernel are available through this server. This server is an instance of the Symbian OS DBMS server (see Section 3.4 below).

- *Other servers:* There are other communications servers that Symbian OS uses that serve a less common, but important, role. These servers include the fax server, which is used to send and receive faxes, and the resolver server, a service that resolves names of Internet sites to IP numbers. The concept behind these is the same as with all servers; one must connect to the server, then use the connection object's API to access the information being protected.

You might have noticed that each of the descriptions above use a phrase something like "...this server provides an API for accessing...". This might seem strange, as we have talked about "connecting" to servers rather than using a server's API. It is, however, the duty of a server to provide a standard interface for the usage of the services it manages. Most times, even though a client sets up a socket to the server, the real interaction with the server takes place through function calls to a server object, not by explicitly constructing requests for the server. This will come through when we discuss the details of programming.

You might also have noticed that there seem to be a few things missing from the above list. For example, Bluetooth, which is featured quite prominently on Symbian OS, is not implemented via its own server. It is generally the case that the above servers are all that Symbian OS needs. If the technology you are looking for is not in the above list, it is likely implemented by other servers. Bluetooth, for example, is implemented using its own serial communication module (look for btcomm.csy) but using the serial communications server.

3.3.2 Clients

Clients are the users of the resources that servers are built to protect. They contend with each other to use resources. Any process or thread can be a client of a server; in fact, because threads can be clients, a process might even contend with itself for a resource. It is the server's role to manage this contention for resource access.

To become a client, a process or thread needs to go through the following steps:

- Clients must first make sure the drivers—both the LDD and the PDD parts—are loaded by Symbian OS kernel. Different drivers will be loaded, depending on how a client wants to access a particular resource.

- Next, a client needs to start a server in order to communicate with it. Remember that the number of running servers is typically carefully planned, and that a client's server may not be running when it is needed.

- A client must then connect to a server. This is through a call in the socket object's interface (typically, a call to Connect()). A socket is opened to the desired server and data may flow between the client and the server.
- Once the connection is made, interaction occurs in a request-response cycle. The client makes requests to the server by

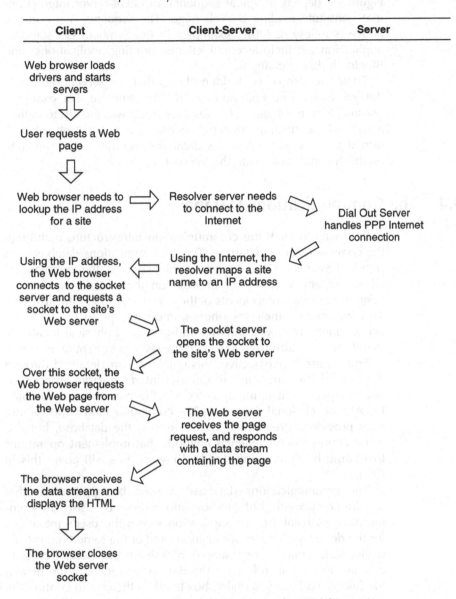

Client	Client-Server	Server

Web browser loads
drivers and starts
servers

⇩

User requests a Web
page

⇩

Web browser needs to ⇒ Resolver server needs ⇒ Dial Out Server
lookup the IP address   to connect to the   handles PPP Internet
for a site   Internet   connection

Using the IP address,   ⇐ Using the Internet, the ⇐
the Web browser   resolver maps a site
connects to the socket name to an IP address
server and requests a
socket to the site's
Web server ⇘
                        The socket server
                        opens the socket to
                        the site's Web server ⇙

Over this socket, the
Web browser requests
the Web page from
the Web server ⇘
                        The Web server
                        receives the page
                        request, and responds
                        with a data stream
                        containing the page ⇙

The browser receives ⇐
the data stream and
displays the HTML

⇩

The browser closes
the Web server
socket

Figure 3.4 A client-server interaction for a Web browser.

sending it messages (in the form of data); the server reads the request and sends the responses back.

- Eventually, the client will complete its use of the server and will close the connection.

An obvious example of a client is a Web browser application. Figure 3.4 depicts a typical sequence of client-server interactions that constitute reading a Web page. The sequence we outlined above is followed. Other examples in the Symbian OS standard application set include email clients, printing applications, and Bluetooth data exchanges.

There are also other, hidden clients that use servers hidden in the internals of the communications infrastructure. For example, consider Figure 3.4 again. The resolver server was the first to initiate a network connection, thereby becoming a client itself when it turned to the communications database and the socket server to establish connections with the Internet.

3.4   The Communications Database

A third way to view the communication infrastructure is through the communications database. The communications database is a standard Symbian OS database, manipulated by the Symbian OS DBMS system. It stores all information that should need to be referenced about components of the communication infrastructure. This information includes phones, modems, protocols, network access phone numbers, Internet addresses and physical locations. The database is also used to record the settings current at any time.

From a user's perspective, this database is maintained through the Control Panel in Symbian OS user interface. From an application perspective, it is manipulated via the conventional Symbian OS API for relational databases. The communication infrastructure does provide a streamlined way to access the database, but this API amounts to convenience methods that implement operations that could be done using standard means. We will cover this in Chapter 18.

The communications database is used by applications that require component configuration information. By using the communications database, an application shares the user's intentions for the device with other applications and at the same time is truly device independent. For example, a program that needs access to a serial service can reference the database to identify the default module to load, using a dialog box to allow the user to confirm the setting.

Browse the Database

A good way to become familiar with the common components of Symbian OS is to examine this database. While browsing the actual database itself entry by entry is probably not too informative, the Quartz emulator includes a tool that allows you to browse and edit the database by categories of use.

To start this tool, you need to execute the command `setup-comms` in the DOS command shell. This will bring up a window like the one shown in Figure 3.5. This window will allow the browsing of categories that are used in the communications database. Beware, however, that changing anything using this interface will have an effect on the way applications work in the emulator.

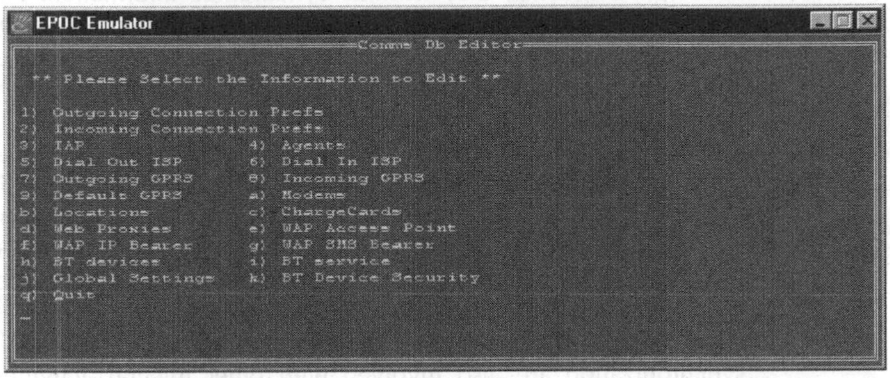

Figure 3.5 Browsing the communications database using `setupcomms`.

3.5 Infrastructure Issues

As we look through the infrastructure, a few global issues crop up that should be examined. Other issues will come up and we will deal with them later; synchronization and security matters are so woven through the infrastructure that we should deal with them now.

3.5.1 Synchronization

Many Symbian devices are commonly used in connection with other computers—whether desktops, laptops, or other handheld computers. It is typical in these situations for the two computers to share information. The Symbian platform was designed from the ground up with this type of cooperation in mind. For example, sharing agenda information between a handheld Symbian device and a larger desktop computer running Microsoft Outlook is an everyday event for many people. This synchronizing of information is such a common event that it is accommodated in the communication infrastructure.

In a different environment, we might share information by simply accessing the same files over a network. Two applications on two different machines might share one file and each manipulate that file. In this case, a server would probably be involved, with the two machines wanting to share information acting as clients to a third machine acting as the server.

The situation we are focusing on, however, is fundamentally different. We do indeed have two computers, but these computers are disconnected from each other most of the time. They do not need to *share* a file; they need to *synchronize information*. File sharing would imply that the two computers are running the same application and therefore need the same file. In our case, we cannot assume that the two computers are running the same application; in fact, we assume that they are not. In this case, we need to synchronize information, i.e., we need to make sure that both sides have equivalent information as specified by their specific applications. To do this, we need to (a) transfer files between the two computers, (b) determine if files are up-to-date, and (c) convert files from one format to another. Therefore, synchronization implies file transfer and file conversion.

In Symbian OS, because many of the actions involved in synchronization are also involved with other integral activities, synchronization was implemented using a new protocol. The Psion Link Protocol (PLP) was implemented to transfer files and to enable remote control of a Symbian device. PLP works over serial media—the serial port or IR port—and requires an application on the other computer that implements PLP as well. Psion, for example, provides a program called "PsiWin" to provide synchronization and other browsing tools to its devices. Symbian provides a set of tools to implement this remote application.

To incorporate this new protocol into Symbian OS communications infrastructure, we simply need a PLP protocol module. Since PLP uses serial communication, no new device drivers are needed. PLP is implemented by the `PLP.PRT` protocol module.

3.5.2 Concerns over Security

By definition, communications move data between two computing devices or phones. Any time this transfer happens, there is opportunity for that data transfer to be observed or even disrupted by a third party. We can control the computers themselves and can even watch them at all times, but once the data leaves the computer en route for a new one, control is lost. We can make very few assumptions about the data as it makes its way to its destination: Is it being observed? Is it being changed in some way?

Consider how insecure various media are. Serial cables are by nature point-to-point connectors, and it is difficult to discern the data transferred by somehow "listening" to the outside of a cable. The nature of serial communication is for the devices to be relatively close to each other, so any tampering with the connection media would be noticed. Infrared communication, however, allows snooping of at least one side of the communication without big changes to the environment. A machine could certainly be situated within the infrared transmitter range and pick up one side of the conversation. Networks are inherently insecure. Because of the passive, multipoint nature of networks, all network data is accessible to all network nodes. Low level network protocols, like Ethernet, are based on the fact that a node will ignore data unless that data is targeted at the node. But all Ethernet cards have a "promiscuous" mode, where all data can be read and analyzed. Wireless data transfer and data networks are extremely insecure. While a machine must be physically connected to a wired network in order to snoop it, the requirements for snooping wireless data are simply that a machine has a receiver that can read the wireless data. Such data—from mobile telephone traffic to network data to Bluetooth conversations—can be read and analyzed from a hidden location or using small reader equipment.

So now that we are convinced that our data transmissions can be intercepted, read, and changed, how do we protect our data? It is important to first realize what we *cannot* do. For most data transmissions, we cannot control the transmission's course or the eyes that view the transmission. It is simply not feasible to know how the data is transmitted every step of its journey. Data over the Internet, for instance, will move through many different pieces of routing equipment before they will reach their destination. Each piece of routing equipment might be in a secure location, or might be out in a public area. The sender cannot control where or how the data gets transmitted.

What we do have control over is the data itself. Most methods to ensure the secure transmission of data utilize *encryption*, a method of data encoding that renders the data unreadable for those readers that do not know how to decode it.

Encryption can occur at different levels in the protocol stack. Encryption can be implemented, for example, by applications themselves. The data is encoded before transmission by the sender and decoded after it reaches its destination. An example of this is the Secure Hypertext Transfer Protocol (SHTTP), a protocol used by Web servers and browsers to pass important data (like credit card information). A Web server that uses SHTTP will encode the data, then send it to the Web browser it is connected to. The Web browser will receive the information, then decode it and display it. Data that goes to the Web server follows the reverse route.

Another kind of implementation encrypts the data in lower protocol layers after it is transmitted. In this approach, the application really does not know if the transmitted data has been encrypted or not. Lower layers encrypt and decrypt the data. An example of this is the stack of protocols that make up WAP. In the middle of the protocol stack is the WAP Transfer Layer Security (WTLS) layer. This protocol layer encodes any data it receives from the upper layers, passing that encrypted data on to lower layers, and decodes any data it receives from lower layers, passing that data on to upper layers. The advantage to inserting a new layer in the protocol stack to do this encryption is that *any* application can use encrypted data, not just those that have encryption built in.

While encrypting data is the most secure method of protecting that data, it is not the only method used. Most other methods rely on a form of *identification* of the user through *authentication* methods. Identification involves a way for the user to identify him- or herself, for example, by having the user type in a user name. Authentication involves verification of an identity by some unique information included with the username—say, a password—that can be stored and known only by the user and the authentication source. This type of security method is woven into protocols—PPP uses forms of authentication in its protocols, for instance—and is typically used to guard the entrance into time-shared computer systems. (Many Symbian devices use password protection upon power-up to prevent unauthorized access to the device.)

Using authentication as a security measure has been problematic. With the powerful computers that we have today, passwords can be easily attacked and discovered. Systems can be compromised by attempting to gain access repeatedly with different passwords. Many "canned" programs exist on the Internet for just this kind of entry. Some systems compensate by not using passwords and relying on other forms of unique information, such as fingerprints or retinal scans.

Therefore, most communications protocols and even system access programs are turning to data encryption for their security. Encryption will feature in many parts of the communication infrastructure, and we will point it out through this book as we encounter its use.

3.6   Summary

This chapter serves as an introduction to the infrastructure of the Symbian communication architecture. In this chapter, we looked at the infrastructure from four different angles:

- We looked at the building blocks—the basic components—of the infrastructure. In successively closer looks, we overviewed what the components are, how they fit together and what they do.
- We looked at the server side of the client-server relationships built into the infrastructure. We looked at the client side of the architecture's client-server relationships.
- We finished by overviewing the communications database used by Symbian OS and by applications to store information about the communications system.

We finished the chapter by introducing two issues that are important to the communication's architecture: data synchronization and system security.

Now that we have introduced the communications architecture, the next two chapters will examine the technologies that the architecture supports. This is broken down into *transport* technologies, covered by Chapter 4, and *content* technologies, covered by Chapter 5.

4

Transport Technologies

I do not particularly like to use the word "technologies" to describe the applications built on top of the communication infrastructure. It has become a buzzword, and has almost graduated from useful, everyday speech to marketing talk. However, Webster's dictionary defines this word as

> the practical application of knowledge especially in a particular area

or, in another way,

> a manner of accomplishing a task especially using technical processes, methods, or knowledge

Both of these definitions make sense. In this chapter, we will take the second definition: we will use technical methods to accomplish moving content data between machines. So I will use the term, but I will make every attempt to be descriptive, and steer clear of buzzwords.

In the last chapter, we looked at the communication infrastructure of Symbian OS from several different perspectives. The infrastructure is very important; it provides the foundation for the support of communication technologies. These technologies, of course, are what most people end up using and are the reason a Symbian OS device exists in the first place. So now that we have established the infrastructure, let's take a look at the technologies that make up the communications architecture.

As I have stated before, communication technologies fall into two categories: transport and content technologies. These are the technologies of moving data between machines and those that provide the useful information and applications on a Symbian device. We deal with transport technologies in this chapter and content technologies in the next.

Different technologies exist because there are several different media used to transmit information. We will start this chapter by looking at the various media in use by Symbian OS (this will be brief; we have already seen this information in previous chapters). Then we will spend time on the details of communication transport methods. Along the way, I hope to dispel some myths about each technology and set expectations about its capabilities.

4.1 A Review of Communication Media

Communication media—the various hardware conduits that convey information—influence the software methods that are used to convey information. Transport technologies evolve in ways that both exploit and circumvent the hardware. So it will serve us well to review the communication media and look at their uses as well as their restrictions. Communications occur using both wired and wireless methods.

4.1.1 Wired Media

Wired media—cables, to be specific—have a long history by computer standards. The first cabled communication using computers goes back to the first computers. While the ENIAC did not have components, the UNIVAC—the first commercial computer, produced in 1951–contained components that communicated with each other using cables. Wired media take several forms: serial, parallel, telephony, and network media.

The concept of serial communication is simple. The serial port sends and receives information one bit at a time. Although this may seem slower than sending bytes all at once, it is simpler, less error-prone, and can be used over longer distances. Serial cabling, for example, can extend as much as 1200 meters, while parallel communication should only go for 20 meters. Serial communication is asynchronous, and data can be sent and received over the same cable at the same time (this is full-duplex communication, as we defined in Chapter 2).

In its simplest form, a serial communication cable needs only three wires. One wire receives data; one wire sends data; and one wire is an electrical ground. The two signal wires are crossed so that the sending wire becomes the receiving wire at the other end and vice versa. This kind of cable is called a "null modem" cable, from the fact that this kind of cable is meant to emulate the signaling of a line without a modem. The serial cable used to connect a modem to a serial port, on the other hand, is wired "straight through"—meaning that the wires are not crossed as the wires in a null modem cable would be.

While only three wires are necessary, a few others are typically included. Two wires for synchronizing the exchange of data (hardware "flow control") are typically used, and four more for indicating readiness to send or receive data (see Section 4.2.1 below). The result is a set of nine wires. These wires are packaged in several different ways; a 9-pin configuration was popularized because it is used on PCs; a 25-pin configuration is also very widely used because it was the first generalized standard (although it does contain unused pins). Many different configurations are possible, because the standards that govern serial communications specify what types of signals should be used, not a specific pin configuration.

The Psion Data Port

The serial cable that Psion chose to use on many of their devices (e.g., the Series 5mx and the netBook) has a 9-pin connector on the PC side and a unique configuration on the Psion device side. This type of connector is called a *fast serial* "Honda" connector—Psion claims that it complies with the RS232 standard. While implementing serial communications, it has a different pin configuration than the 9 or 25 pin specifications for serial cables.

To find out more about this connector, check out information from the Web and the references in the bibliography. As you discover more, it might be helpful to draw a diagram of the Psion data cable, using a null modem cable as a base point.

The medium for parallel communication moves data bytes at a time. Because of this, there are many more wires in the cable. Parallel communication requires eight data wires, eight grounds for the eight data wires, and several more wires, including power for the data transfer. The result is between 25 wires (parallel printer cable) and 36 wires (Centronics parallel cable). Because of this complexity and the power requirements, parallel communication is not typically implemented on handheld devices.

Telephony requires only two wires: a sender and a receiver. These wires are housed inside a standardized connector, which has room for several wires and allows multiple telephone lines to be included in the same connector for multi-line telephones. For our purposes, modems use only one telephone line, and therefore only two copper wires.

Wired network media take several forms. While past networks have used many different media types, currently there are three forms that are used. Two older forms are called "thicknet" and "thinnet". Thicknet is a 50 ohm coaxial cable, 0.4 inches in diameter. Thinnet is 0.2 inches in diameter, with the same impedance measure. Both cables are coaxial, a type of cable that includes one wire that carries a signal surrounded (after a layer of insulation) by metal braiding that carries another signal, effectively forming two channels. The outer channel also serves as a ground. Both of these forms of network cabling have fallen from grace, since they are inflexible and difficult to use in many situations. Thicknet is still used in enterprise network backbones.

The most popular wired medium for networks is called "10baseT" or "twisted pair" cables. Twisted pair is comprised of two ordinary insulated copper wires, twisted around each other to eliminate crosstalk interference. The cabling can be made of standard wiring (called "category 5"), and is normally terminated with standardized jacks. This makes connecting and disconnecting cables very easy. With this type of cabling, network hubs are needed. Cables connect the computing device to the hub, and the hub serves as the conduit for network data to move between cables or on to a larger network.

Thicknet, thinnet, and 10baseT cabling can handle network data that transfers at conventional speeds up to 100 Mbits/second. The newest technology has achieved Ethernet speeds of 1 Gbps.

4.1.2 Wireless Media

There are two alternatives we can choose from if we want to communicate without wires. The first is to use infrared; the second is to communicate by radio.

Infrared technology uses light with wavelengths longer than those of visible light, but shorter than those of radio waves. To compare it to other wireless technology, we would look at the frequency of this medium, measured in terms of terahertz, or trillions of cycles per second. They are just above radio-based wireless, which operates in the gigahertz (GHz) range.

Infrared devices can operate between two devices within a line of sight over a maximum distance of 5 meters. This has more to do with the transport technology than the medium, however. We will say more on this later.

All wireless technology other than infrared sends its data via radio. The main differences between the radio-based wireless technologies are the radio frequency they use and how they use that radio frequency. They operate at either 2.4 or 5.0 GHz. As the frequency increases, the bandwidth capability increases, but the range decreases. These are unlicensed bands, and many different technologies operate in them. For instance, cordless telephones, wireless networks, and Bluetooth devices all operate in the 2.4 GHz range and can easily interfere with each other.

4.2 Serial Technologies

4.2.1 Serial Standards

Several standards have been developed which use serial cables for serial communications. By far, the standard that has proved most versatile and durable is the RS-232 standard. Developed in 1960 by the Electronics Industry Association, the RS-232 standard was adopted by PC manufacturers and, because of this, will be around for a very long time. Symbian OS has always supported the RS-232 standard.

Sending an 8-bit word in a serial sequence requires both sides of the communication to agree on a way to figure out where the word starts and ends. One solution is to use *synchronous* communication, where bits are sent on specific clock intervals, with a brief interval between each word. Once both sides agree on what the word size is, synchronous communication makes it easy to determine where the word is in the data stream. Missing or extra bits can be detected; the word separator can be used to determine this. Synchronous communication has problems, however, in a generalized environment where different computers from different manufacturers are used. Timing can easily fall out of sync, and if either end loses a clock signal for any reason, the communication stops dead.

Asynchronous communication is much more dependable in general situations. In asynchronous mode, we do not use the clock to determine where the word markers are or where the bits are. We need to mark the ends of a word sequence, and allow each side of the communication to synchronize on these marks. The only requirement is that both sides use the same bit transmission speed. This speed is called the *baud rate*, and is measured in bits per second.

We can now construct a *data frame* out of markers for the beginning and ending of a word and the word itself. We surround the data bits by special bits called the *start* and *stop bits*.

In asynchronous communication, errors are harder to detect and correct. We need a way to encode the data so that we can detect an error, because we cannot depend on timing. Serial communications uses a *parity bit* added to the frame to signal the presence of errors. This bit is set to make the number of 1s in the frame even or odd, thus making bit flips somewhat easier to detect (although even numbers of bit flips would go undetected).

As an example, consider sending the letter "A" between two computers using even parity with one start bit. The ASCII encoding for an "A" is 7 bits: 1000001. The number of 1s is even, therefore the parity bit must be set to "0". Using a 1 as a single start bit gives us the data frame in Figure 4.1. Note the empty bit position. This "space" is allowed since the next data frame synchronizes when a 1 bit is sent.

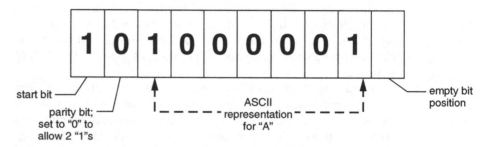

Figure 4.1 Serial dataframe using ASCII.

The RS-232 standard specifies a specific signal sequence for data exchange. The two sides of the transmission are called the Data Terminal Equipment (DTE) side and the Data Carrier Equipment (DCE) side. DTEs are typically originators of the communication, e.g., PCs or terminals. DCEs are typically communication devices like modems. A typical data exchange sequence might go like this:

- To indicate that it is initialized and ready, the DTE asserts the Data Terminal Ready (DTR) signal. To indicate a similar state, the DCE asserts the Data Set Ready (DSR) signal.

- When the DCE has a good carrier signal (e.g., a telephone connection to another modem), it asserts the Data Carrier Detected (DCD) signal.

- When a station wants to send data, it asserts the Request To Send (RTS) signal. When the receiver is ready, it asserts the Clear To Send (CTS) signal.

- The sender sends data using the Transmit Data (TD) signal; the receiver will receive over the Receive Data (RD) signal.
- So the sender will only send data when the DSR, DCD, and CTS signals are set. Likewise, dropping any of these signals will stop the data transmission.

It is important to note here that one side of the data transmission might be able to process data at a faster rate than the other side, even though the communication channel can deliver the higher baud rate. Therefore, we need a way to control the transmission, to tell one side to slow down or to stop while the other side catches up. This is done in one of two ways. One way is to use software, by sending special characters that are signals to stop and restart the data flow. In the ASCII character sequence, these characters are called XOFF (ASCII character number 19, a Ctrl-S) and XON (ASCII character number 17, a Ctrl-Q). While this is effective most of the time, it can be slow, and the characters can be lost or ignored. A more effective way is to use hardware flow control by manipulating the RTS and CTS signals. The signal on these lines must be asserted to send data; dropping the signal will stop the data flow. This is an effective and speedy method to control the data flow. This exchange of control signals is known as *handshaking*.

Debugging Hardware Signals

While software has its SDKs and debugging environments, there is very little that you can use if you are interested in debugging or examining hardware signals over a serial line. The most readily available tool is a *breakout box*.

Breakout boxes are small boxes about twice the size of a serial connector. The simplest models have a row of lights that turn on or off to indicate the state of one of the pins in the serial connector. Other models offer the capability to rewire the serial connection from inside the breakout box. This allows you to try various wiring configurations.

If you are interested in examining or experimenting further with serial signals, breakout boxes provide an easy method to do this. These are available at most places you would purchase serial cabling.

4.2.2 IrDA

RS-232 serial communications are relatively straightforward to understand. The data frame is simple and there is one function for serial connection (i.e., to pass bytes to a receiver). Most other transport mechanisms are quite a bit more complicated. As a way to manage the complexity of the technology, these other mechanisms are designed in layers. Each layer focuses on a specific aspect of transport functionality.

IrDA technology is a good example of this effort to hide complexity. Although there is a physical device that communicates with other infrared devices via light, there is a protocol stack in Symbian OS that isolates this layer from other functionality. This stack is shown in Figure 4.2. Let's briefly consider each protocol layer.

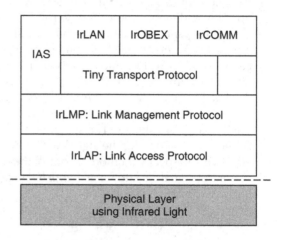

Figure 4.2 IrDA protocol stack.

The physical layer

The physical layer starts with an optical transceiver and deals with aspects of manipulating optical signals. Because the transmission medium is through optical signals, information is relayed in a serial manner, one bit at a time. And as with RS-232 serial communication, we must be concerned here about framing issues: start and end frame flags and encoding of data bits. The IrDA framing techniques are based on those used in networking standards, and therefore are more complicated than those used with RS-232 serial communication. A seven-bit sequence is used as the start and stop sequence, and a value is included with each frame that is computed from the bits in the frame and allows multi-bit errors to be caught.

As with RS-232 serial communication, IrDA communication can be either synchronous or asynchronous. Unlike RS-232 serial communication, either mode is used for different situations. Synchronous communication is faster, but is more prone to errors; asynchronous communication is slower, but more flexible and adaptable to a variety of infrared equipment.

The physical layer is primarily a hardware layer, but a portion of it is usually implemented in software. To isolate issues of framing and protocol from physical issues of infrared light, a software layer is typically used here called the *framer*. The primary responsibility of the framer is to deal with framing issues, encoding and decoding outgoing and incoming frames and interfacing with layers above the physical layer. The framer also deals with hardware interface speeds and follows instructions from the IrLAP layer. The framer is included in the physical layer because the interface to the actual hardware is not standard, so changing speeds or reading and writing through the infrared device is still specified by the infrared manufacturer.

Using a Symbian OS Device as a Remote Control

A common question Symbian OS device users have is about the relationship between its infrared functionality and the infrared capability included on a remote control device. Both devices have infrared ports. Using your Symbian OS phone as a programmable remote control seems rather appealing. Unfortunately, the IrDA standards specify a different modulation frequency for IrDA compliant devices than the frequency remote controls use. So a program that implements a remote control device must bypass most APIs and reprogram the infrared driver outside of IrDA standards. This is a daunting task for all but the hardiest of programmers.

IrLAP: The Link Access Layer

The first all-software layer in the IrDA stack is the IrLAP layer, the Link Access Protocol Layer. The duty of the IrLAP layer is to provide reliable data transmission over the physical layer. By dealing with reliability at this layer, the upper levels in the stack are freed from dealing with it. We define *reliable data delivery* as delivery that is guaranteed either to happen or to fail with notice. No data will go undelivered without an error being generated and upper layers notified.

To ensure reliability, the IrLAP layer uses three mechanisms. First, it employs error detection by generating and monitoring the cyclical redundancy check (CRC) checksum. This value is computed, using an algorithm called "cyclical redundancy", based on the current string of bits that make up the data frame. If the

CRC checksum computed for the transmitted data frame does not match the checksum that accompanies the data frame, then an error occurred in transit.

The second mechanism used by IrLAP to ensure reliability is to establish a primary/secondary relationship between the sender and the receiver of an infrared transmission. The primary device initiates the connection/transfer, is responsible for the organization and control of the data flow, and deals with the errors that occur. The secondary device is only responsible for sending acknowledgement frames for data received. The primary in an IrLAP relationship obviously has much more work and management to do. Because of the acknowledgement-based protocol, the exchange occurs by turns, with each side taking a turn in the exchange of data. Neither side can talk for more than 500 milliseconds at a time before allowing the other side to take a turn (even if there is nothing to say).

The third reliability mechanism used by IrLAP establishes two modes of operation, based on the establishment of a connection between two machines. One mode, called Normal Disconnect Mode (NDM), is the default state of devices when they are disconnected. A device in NDM must check whether other transmissions are occurring before transmitting. If no IR activity is detected for more than 500 milliseconds, a device is free to try to establish a connection. Communication from the NDM state always follows the same serial configuration parameters: asynchronous communication at 9600 baud, using 8 bit frames with no parity bit set. By establishing this rule, each initial connection is made with the same parameters. Once an initial connection is established, the two sides often exchange different capability information, and they alter their configuration to the best one for both sides.

The other mode IrLAP establishes is Normal Response Mode (NRM). This is the normal mode of operation for connected devices. Once both devices are communicating and have exchanged configuration information, this mode allows the upper layers to assume the connection exists.

The IrLAP layer uses different framing techniques based on the speed of the IR connection. Three different framing methods are used for three different situations:

- Asynchronous connections can run from 9600 bps to 115 Kbps.

- Synchronous connections that use a network style of framing (synchronous data link control or SDLC) can run from 576 Kbps to 1.152 Mbps.

- Synchronous connections using a "retooled" network framing technique (known as pulse position modulation or 4PPM) can run up to 4 Mbps.

One final note should be made here about the functionality of IrLAP. It is possible to share the IR port between several different applications, each sending their own data to companion applications on a remote device. The IrLAP layer enables this by establishing an address for each data stream. Because IR connections are point-to-point, the connected devices do not really need addresses. However, by tagging data streams with addresses, a single IrLAP connection can be multiplexed between upper layer applications.

IrLMP: The Link Management Layer and IAS

The Link Management Layer in the IrDA stack assumes the reliable connection established at the IrLAP layer, and is responsible for the connections between applications on different machines. By multiplexing the IrLAP link, implementing device discovery, and managing connections between applications, the IrLMP layer connects applications to one another.

The connections at the IrLMP layer are made between Logical Service Access Points (LSAPs). Each service—think of each as a data stream—is assigned a one-byte number, called an LSAP Selector (LSAP-SEL). These selectors are assigned dynamically, but are assigned from specific ranges to indicate the nature of the data connection (a service ID lookup from a directory, for example, is different from a "connected" service). LSAP-SELs are "recycled" and reassigned when the data stream that used one is terminated.

The IrDA specification demands a minimum set of services from an IrLMP implementation:

- *Device Discovery:* This service exchanges information with the other IrLMP layer to discover information about the other device.
- *Connection:* This service establishes a data connection over the IrLMP layer, setting up the service IDs and recording them.
- *Data Delivery:* This service exchanges data between the two sides.
- *Disconnection:* This service closes the IrLMP layer connection, including resetting the service ID and erasing table entries about the stream.

Service IDs and applications waiting for connections must be recorded so that data streams can be run through the same IrLAP layer and still make it to their appropriate destinations. This recording service is called the Information Access Service (IAS). IAS acts like a "yellow pages" service for a device, allowing for fixed services with pre-assigned IDs or ones that are dynamically registered with temporary IDs.

TinyTP: Tiny Transport Protocol

The Tiny Transport Protocol (TinyTP) layer is an optional layer in the IrDA stack specification. It is so important, however, that it is provided as a layer in most implementations (including Symbian OS). TinyTP provides two essential functions to the IrDA stack: flow control and data stream segmentation and reassembly.

Flow control is the most important use of TinyTP. Recall that flow control is available at the IrLAP layer, and that IrLAP sees one stream of data flowing between two devices. If one application were to require a data stream to stop briefly, the only alternative is the IrLAP layer, which would have to stop the entire stream, not just the stream for the application. The advantage that TinyTP provides is the ability to regulate data flow on a per-IrLMP-connection (i.e., per application) basis, allowing the other applications on the device to continue using the IR data stream.

The other function TinyTP performs is the segmentation and reassembly of data. Here, the TinyTP layer will receive a data stream from an upper layer, and break that stream into pieces. These pieces are numbered and then sent to the other side. The TinyTP layer on the recipient's end will then reassemble the stream based on the numbering and present the original data stream to the upper layer application. The pieces are called Service Data Units (SDUs) and the size of these SDUs is negotiated when the TinyTP connection is made (actually, the negotiation is done by the IrLMP layer and passed up).

This segmentation and reassembly is important for two reasons. First, it helps in the interleaving of various application data streams. The more pieces we have, the better we can interleave them. Second, it enables error control. In one long data stream, even a tiny error can cause the entire stream to break down and be re-sent. When that stream in broken into pieces, one error results in only one SDU re-sent. Error recovery is easier and much more efficient.

Programmer API: IrCOMM, IrOBEX, IrTranP and IrLAN

At the top of the IrDA stack are three protocols that Symbian OS ties together to form the layer that applications will interface with. These are IrCOMM for serial and parallel port emulation, IrOBEX for data object exchange, and IrLAN for local area network attachment.

IrCOMM was designed as a "legacy" protocol; existing applications were supposed to be able to use this protocol as an emulator for standard wired serial and parallel communications. The reality is that, because IR is so different from wired communications, the IrCOMM standard requires changes in existing applications to use it. However, these changes are minimal and, for the most part, IrCOMM meets its design goals. Actually, new applications would be better served if they avoided IrCOMM and used IrOBEX or IrLAN, or even TinyTP directly. IrCOMM hides some of the useful features of the lower protocols; for example, parameter negotiation is not available (all traffic runs at 9600 bps!).

IrOBEX, or Infrared Object Exchange Protocol, is designed to allow flexible, rapid exchange of data objects in a very abstract manner. Applications that use IrOBEX are those that simply need to ship an object to the other side of the connection, with little or no concern for how it gets there. IrOBEX is a simple and compact protocol, yet it is flexible enough to handle any data object. The protocol sets up a session with the other side, negotiates an acceptable set of parameters, exchanges data objects as an abstract bit stream, then gracefully closes the session. It has some extra features that allow connections to stay alive even if data transfer is terminated prematurely.

Infrared Transport Protocol (IrTranP) is an optional protocol used to transport images from devices that can capture digital images (e.g., the Nokia 7650 phone or a digital camera). While this protocol is a standard, its limited application means that programs that use it and research work to extend it are slow to develop. Because of its specific application, it is a protocol with low overhead. Like IrOBEX, it sets up its own session with the remote imaging device, negotiates an acceptable set of parameters, exchanges images as a bit stream, then shuts the session.

IrLAN is a protocol that allows the originating device to connect to a local area network. In most uses, the "sender" in this case is a device that wishes to connect to a network; the "receiver" is an access point or adapter that is IR-enabled, and is connected directly to a network. In this mode, the receiving device becomes a gateway to the network in question. A second mode can be used with IrLAN where two devices establish a LAN between them, communicating as if the two devices were on a larger network. In either mode, IrLAN allows devices to use network protocols as if they were directly connected.

For Further Reading

IrDA protocols have an extensive set of standards defined for them. Most computers that have an infrared port—handheld or otherwise—abide by these standards. You can read more about these standards at the Infrared Data Association's Web site: *http://www.irda.org/standards/standards.asp*.

4.2.3 PLP

Psion Link Protocol (PLP) is the protocol currently used to synchronize data between a Symbian device and a personal computer. It allows the PC to manipulate files on the attached device and manage software installation. It was developed by Psion Computers and is still used in Symbian OS.

We cover PLP in this section because it was designed to run over serial transport mechanisms, and is itself a transport protocol. It will run over serial or IR connections.

PLP is designed in three layers in addition to the physical layer, as shown in Figure 4.3. The physical layer is either the serial or the IR port. PLP uses hardware handshaking and has a frame format of 8 bits, 1 stop bit, with no parity. Any data rate supported by the physical layer can be used. Communication is asynchronous.

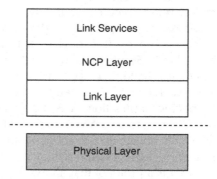

Figure 4.3   PLP protocol stack.

The link layer implements reliable transport of the data stream between the Symbian device and the PC. The data frames from the upper levels are encapsulated in a data frame with a CRC checksum at this level. Upon receipt of a data frame, the receiver recomputes a CRC checksum and compares it to the one in the data frame. It implements error recovery by implementing retransmission of data frames.

The Network Control Protocol (NCP) layer assumes a reliable transport mechanism and implements data stream multiplexing over the link layer. As with IR transmission, multiple services can be carried over one link layer data stream, and the NCP layer implements this. In addition, the NCP layer implements flow control over each service's data stream.

The final layer is the Link Services layer. This layer implements the various services used by the PC: software management, file manipulation and synchronization of files. This is accomplished as a client-server relationship, where the PC becomes the client and the Symbian device works as the server.

SyncML

PLP is a Symbian proprietary protocol. Most handheld manufacturers have their own proprietary protocols for synchronizing with desktop PCs. Because of this, each handheld device needs different software to run on a PC for synchronizing or file management.

A new standard called SyncML will help with this problem. It is a synchronizing protocol standard that most handheld manufacturers—including Symbian as a sponsor—have agreed to adopt. This would enable several things—including using one program to synchronize several devices and using networks as well as serial cables for synchronization.

SyncML is covered in more detail in Chapter 17. The Web site for SyncML technology is *http://www.syncml.org*.

4.3   Network Technologies

As a transport technology, serial communication works well, but has several constraints. It is point-to-point only, and is *fixed* point-to-point. Once connected, two computers must (in the wired case, physically) break their connection to connect to another device. It is relatively slow. While in certain cases, IrDA communication can reach 4 Mbps, most connections attain a maximum of 115 Kbps.

Networking technologies overcome these constraints. They use multipoint communication that employs a different medium to give networked devices access to multiple machines at a time using very fast speeds. Ethernet, for example, can give access to over 2^{48} machines at one time (or 2.81×10^{14}), at speeds up to 1 Gbps.

As we examine these technologies, we need to pay attention to *addressing*. Since multiple devices can coexist on a network medium, there must be a way to identify each one. A device is typically assigned an *address* to identify it to the rest of the network. While addressing schemes vary across networking technologies, they are usually made up of numbers arranged in a special way (significant to the networking scheme). Also, if one networking method supports another (e.g., Ethernet supporting TCP/IP), then multiple addressing methods will be used across one network.

4.3.1 Ethernet

Many networking implementations have been developed over the years, the most popular and stable of which is Ethernet. Standardized in 1981, Ethernet technology implements the data link layer from the ISO network layer diagram in Figure 2.1. Several features of the Ethernet standard characterize it.

- *Ethernet uses a bus-oriented, passive medium.* The medium that conveys Ethernet data is passive, that is, it accepts all data and broadcasts that data to all machines connected to it. As on any bus-oriented medium, all machines connected to the Ethernet can access all data broadcast over it. Each machine on the Ethernet must be well-behaved and ignore data not meant for that machine.

- *Ethernet uses a collision detect mechanism.* The method used by Ethernet to access the network medium is called Carrier Sense Multiple Access with Collision Detect (CSMA/CD). This method uses a carrier signal to convey the status of the transmission medium. When that signal implies that no one is sending information, the sending machine will send data. If there is a machine using the medium, the sender waits. If however, two machines send at the same time—i.e., a collision occurs—then both machines will detect that collision and employ a resolution algorithm to resend their data at a future time.

- *Ethernet uses special addressing.* One of the requirements of a multipoint access medium is that each machine accessing that medium needs to have a unique address. Ethernet addresses are in the form of 6 8-bit quantities. These 6 octets are typically written in hexidecimal with colons to separate them, as below:

```
12:40:bc:f2:55:10
```

- *Ethernet implements the data link layer of the protocol stack.* As with other protocol stacks we have seen, the protocol just above the physical medium—i.e., the data link layer—has some specific responsibilities. As such a protocol, Ethernet must provide a reliable transfer of the data stream, and a method for error detection and recovery. Ethernet is specified as asynchronous, and its data frame has a sequence to start and stop it. It includes a CRC checksum on the data frame so the receiver can detect errors, and error recovery is based on retransmission of data frames.

Ethernet looks quite a bit like many of the other transport protocols we have seen in the chapter. The biggest difference is the broadcast nature of the medium and the resulting need for addresses.

Symbian OS supports Ethernet by providing drivers for various Ethernet hardware devices and the CSY module for the communication server.

Wireless Ethernet

Although Ethernet was invented as a wired technology, it has been adapted to be wireless. Three standards carry wireless Ethernet. The IEEE 802.11b standard is the most widely used at the present time. It operates at a radio frequency of 2.4 GHz and has a maximum data rate of 11 Mbps. IEEE 802.11a is a wireless standard that operates at 5.0 GHz and has a maximum data rate of 54 Mbps. Obviously, 802.11a seems more inviting. However, 802.11b has a greater reception range and is more flexible. In addition, the two protocol suites are incompatible; equipment that uses one standard will not work with equipment that uses the other.

The most recent standard tries to bridge the gap between these two. IEEE 802.11 g is a standard that works at 5.0 GHz, has the high data rate of 802.11a, and can adapt itself to work with both 802.11a and 802.11b.

More information on these protocols can be found at the IEEE WLAN Standards Working Group Web site at *http://grouper.ieee.org/groups/802/11*.

4.3.2 TCP/IP

Ethernet implements the data link layer in the ISO stack model. Other protocols work on top of Ethernet to make a complete set of network protocols. The most widely used of these is Transmission Control Protocol / Internet Protocol or TCP/IP. IP implements the network layer in the ISO stack; TCP implements the transport layer. Both protocol suites include an implementation of a set of protocols that implement each ISO stack layer. Because of its stability and open availability, TCP/IP is the de facto standard for linking networks that use computers with a variety of different operating systems.

TCP/IP is known for the services it defines over its transport layers (e.g., Ethernet). Services like remote access via telnet, file transfer via FTP, email delivery via SMTP, and Web page services via HTTP are well known. There are many services in existence, with more added all the time. Each service at the TCP level is assigned a *port number*. On the server computer, these port numbers are connected to an application or server program. Therefore, connecting to a machine on port number 23 will probably start a telnet server program that will accept a telnet connection and will perform telnet services.

TCP/IP was originally designed to run over wired network media, to support both local area networks and wide area networks. The intent of its designers was to be a communications protocol suite that would tolerate multiple failures (its original design was for wartime communications) and would accommodate new protocols and expanded usage. Because of its flexibility, TCP/IP is an extremely stable protocol suite whose functionality has been expanded over new media and new computing innovations.

In order to link many different networks together, the IP layer needs to be able to route data frames between various networks. To allow routing, IP introduces its own set of addresses, ones that are organized in a manner that will assign machines on a local network addresses from the same address group. So the IP layer makes addresses that are four integers (8 bit quantities, less than 256) separated by periods:

```
192.168.112.32
```

IP addresses have a *network* ID portion and a *host ID* portion. The network ID is used to identify the network to which the address belongs; the host ID identifies the computer on its home network (the one given by the network ID). The IP address is broken down into these two pieces by a *subnet mask* that is ANDed bitwise with the address to reveal the network ID. For example, a subnet mask of 255.255.255.0 will extract a network ID of 192.168.112.0 from the above address.

In addition to a new form of addressing, the IP layer implements a new form of datagram exchange between machines. It uses its own form of datagrams, separate from whatever format datagram is used by the data link protocol that supports it.

TCP is mainly concerned with adding reliability to the transport of the application data stream. As is done with other protocol stacks, TCP breaks the data stream into pieces, building its own datagram from each piece. Each datagram is numbered and is sent to the IP layer with a CRC checksum. Once they arrive at their destination, the datagrams are checked for errors and reassembled.

In addition to these features, TCP adds the idea of *connected sessions* between machines. Data exchange sessions are data exchanges that remain active for the exchange of many datagrams at a time, without the need to reopen or reconnect the data path between two machines. This results in a more reliable interface that is easier to program.

Two examples of the flexibility of TCP/IP are Point-to-Point Protocol (PPP) and IrLAN. PPP is a data link layer protocol that runs underneath TCP/IP and supports its operation (replacing Ethernet). PPP is implemented across two machines, building a data link layer in the point-to-point manner (hence the name). While PPP has been implemented for many point-to-point situations, its most effective use has been in hooking up dial-up users to the Internet. A typical dial-up scenario is shown in Figure 4.4. Here, a user at home dials up an Internet Service Provider (ISP) via a modem. An access server at the ISP authenticates the user and gives the user access to the ISP's local network by assigning the dial-up computer an IP address for duration of the phone call. The ISP's local network has a gateway to its Internet connection, and that gives the dial-up computer access to the Internet. When the dialup connection is severed—either by the user (hanging up) or the ISP—the PPP connection is terminated and the IP address is recycled and given to another dial-up user.

PPP provides three main features:

- *Option negotiation:* As with other protocols we have seen, PPP engages in a series of negotiations with the access server that grants access to its local network before completely establishing a data link layer connection. Configuration options such as an IP address, error correction methods, and framing protocols are decided in these negotiations.

- *Framing method:* PPP uses asynchronous communication, and because of this, establishes a special framing method. This framing method looks much like those we have seen before. It uses special character sequence to start and end frames, and includes error control information (including CRC checksums).

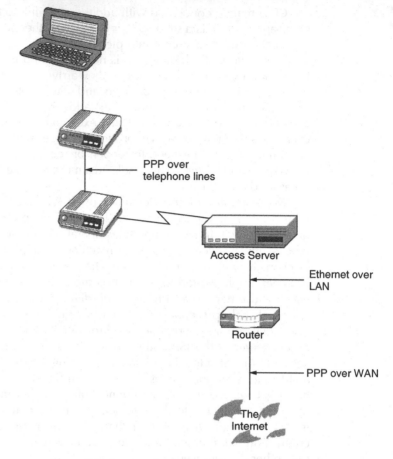

PPP over
telephone lines

Access Server

Ethernet over
LAN

Router

PPP over WAN

The
Internet

Figure 4.4 An example of using PPP to connect to the internet.

- *Link control protocol:* PPP implements the data link layer across its asynchronous connection, including: data frame transport, measurements of line status (e.g., if a connection is up or down), and frame error detection and correction.

Symbian OS has complete support for PPP, most often used for mobile dialup to the Internet.

IrLAN is another data link layer protocol that supports TCP/IP. We have already discussed IrLAN briefly. Basically, IrLAN looks very much like PPP; they both use configuration negotiation, they construct similar data frames, and they implement a similar link control protocol. Instead of modems, IrLAN uses a network access adapter that has an infrared port and is connected directly to a LAN. The IrLAN protocol works between the computing device and the IR network access point.

Snooping

Networks are notorious security holes. One side effect to the open standards of Ethernet and TCP/IP is that it is easy to discover and decode data frames. And because Ethernet implements a passive medium, network traffic is easy to snoop without detection. This means that these networks are intrinsically insecure and more steps need to be taken if data is to be protected from prying eyes. Chapter 6 deals with security and with snooping in various forms.

4.4 Wireless Access Protocol

It is tempting to view Wireless Access Protocol (WAP) as exclusively a content technology. It is, after all, focused on content for small devices. However, underlying the content technologies is a transport and delivery platform that we should overview in this chapter. The WAP architecture is shown in Figure 4.5.

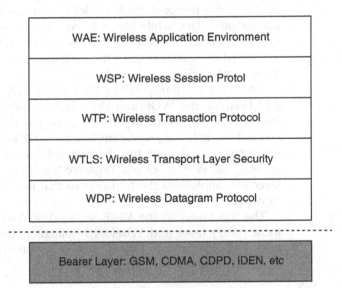

Figure 4.5   The WAP stack.

At the base of the WAP stack is the bearer layer. This corresponds to the physical layer in other protocol stacks but is not specified for WAP. The designers of WAP assume that there will be "bearers" that will support the upper WAP structure and will be able to interact with the upper structure through a specified API. This bearer layer can be implemented by any digital carrier, and is currently implemented over many mobile phone protocols, including GSM, which is supported by Symbian OS.

The Wireless Datagram Protocol (WDP) layer provides network and certain transport functions to the rest of the WAP stack. It provides the upper layers with datagram transport between stacks, implementing port level addressing. It provides for datagram segmentation and reassembly, supporting selective retransmission of datagrams, and for error recovery.

The Wireless Transaction Protocol (WTP) layer provides the rest of the transport layer functions. It provides both connection-oriented and connectionless transactions between WTP layers that use the segmentation and reassembly functions of the WDP layer. It directs the retransmission of datagrams and can concatenate data packets into larger packets for efficiency.

The Wireless Transport Layer Security (WTLS) layer lies between the WDP and WTP layers. This layer provides encryption of data between client and server and provides methods for authentication. It ensures the integrity of the data exchanged. It exploits the modularity of the protocol stack model to provide upper layers with unencrypted data, while lower layers see only an encrypted data stream. It has facilities for detecting when data is sent repeatedly or unverified (e.g., attacks on system security) and can reject data in these cases.

Note how the transport functions in the WAP stack have been split between the WDP and WTP layers. This is to facilitate the insertion of the WTLS layer. For example, the WTP layer will coordinate packet segmentation, but the WDP layer will implement the segmentation *after* the data packet has been encrypted. In general, the WTP layer will organize the transport and the WDP layer will implement the transport so that the WTLS layer can do its work.

The top layers in the WAP stack—the Wireless Session Protocol (WSP) layer and Wireless Application Environment (WAE) layer—implement the content of WAP data transmission. We will overview these layers in the next chapter.

4.5 Bluetooth

We have discussed several kinds of connections between machines—from point-to-point connections to wide area multipoint connections—using cables, infrared, and radio communication. The focus of these connections has been to connect independent computing devices to each other, where clients take advantage of services offered by servers. Also, we have specifically made the concept of *distance* to be irrelevant; as long as there are enough computers that will link networks together—either wired or mobile—we can dismiss the distance between two computers.

The Bluetooth model of connectivity zeroes in on these two areas: it allows *components* as well as independent computers to use wireless connectivity, and it specifically makes distance a factor, focusing on short range wireless connectivity. For example, a headset can be connected to a mobile phone via Bluetooth. The headset is designed as a component of a mobile phone system (i.e., it cannot function on its own) and will not work when it is separated by more than 10 meters from the phone. By broadening the possibilities of connections and restricting those connections to short distances, Bluetooth makes many new communications innovations possible. In contrast to wide area networks (a regional network called a WAN) and local area networks (often restricted to a building), it establishes the idea of a "personal area network" (PAN), also called a "piconet". In a piconet, a network of computers and components connect to each other over a small (personal) area. Bluetooth also addresses the connection of piconets to each other, forming an ad-hoc "scatternet" that communicates over network gateways.

Consider a few Bluetooth scenarios. A piconet could be a computer system, where the components are connected to each other without cables. A mouse, a keyboard, and a printer could all be Bluetooth enabled and work together. A wireless phone that senses its proximity to a base station could dynamically choose to use landline or mobile communication. A headset could be wireless and connected to a mobile phone stored in a briefcase.

The Bluetooth model spans the layers of our ISO stack model from Figure 2.1. The model reuses existing protocols as much as possible and substitutes only those layers that are necessary for radio transmission and accompanying management needs. Therefore, protocols such as PPP and OBEX can run over Bluetooth protocols, and Symbian devices implementing Bluetooth can reuse many protocol modules.

The Bluetooth protocol stack is given in Figure 4.6. Symbian OS supports this protocol stack from version 6.1. We will discuss each of the components in turn.

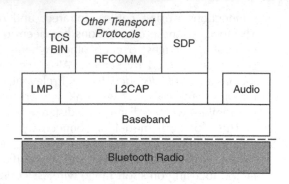

Figure 4.6 The Bluetooth stack.

4.5.1   Bluetooth Radio

This layer is the physical layer of the Bluetooth stack. Bluetooth uses radio frequencies in the Industrial, Scientific, and Medical (ISM) band allocated at 2.4 GHz. This ISM band is unregulated, therefore no license is needed to operate in it (actually, the ISM band varies a bit from country to country, so Bluetooth takes care to stay out of the way of applications that use out-of-ISM frequencies). Bluetooth is designed to operate in very low power situations; the specifications give power requirements from 1 mW to 100 mW.

This gives components the ability to send and receive Bluetooth signals at low power. This also helps manufacturers keep both the size of the Bluetooth chip and the power supply to the chip small.

> ## Further Reading on Bluetooth Radio
>
> Further details about the Bluetooth Radio layer are beyond the scope of this book, but you can read more about the specifications on the Web site of the Bluetooth Consortium. Technical specifications on the Bluetooth standard—including information on the radio layer—can be found at *http://www.bluetooth.com/developer/specification.core.asp*.

4.5.2 Baseband

Baseband serves as the software complement to the radio hardware and straddles the physical and data link layers. The services at the baseband layer regulate the radio hardware so that the device abides by the Bluetooth standards. Data encoding, transmitter management, frequency hopping, security, error detection and correction, and framing are all covered by the services specified at the baseband layer.

The baseband layer uses a frequency hopping, spread spectrum system. Data frames are transmitted in defined time slots through synchronized transmission. By using a combination of several frequencies and a wide range of hopping sequences, Bluetooth transmissions can be reliable and can avoid collisions with transmissions on physically adjacent piconets.

The baseband layer implements two types of link. Synchronous Connection-Oriented (SCO) links are made on a point-to-point basis between one primary and one secondary device. These links are used to acquire fixed, reserved allocations of bandwidth between the two devices involved in the link. Through this reserved bandwidth, the baseband layer transmits audio or a mix of audio and data (see Section 4.5.7 below for Bluetooth audio). Asynchronous Connectionless (ACL) links are used in a more flexible fashion. They can implement point-to-multipoint connections and are asynchronous. ACL links are used for data only.

The Bluetooth standard requires that up to three SCO connections can be transported in a single piconet, and ACL traffic is limited primarily by the transmission quality and data rate of the underlying RF transport. The ACL traffic flow is managed by the primary station, with secondary stations speaking only when spoken to.

The baseband layer is usually provided as a hardware implementation. It accompanies the radio transmitter chip on a Bluetooth card.

4.5.3 LMP: Link Manager Protocol

The Link Manager Protocol (LMP) is used to establish, secure, and control the links between devices. LMP is defined at the data link layer.

LMP is not used by upper layers. It provides the establishment of links, which get handed off to the L2CAP layer. The devices involved in the link are authenticated first, and the data streams may be encrypted. LMP also controls transmission power on the Bluetooth device, sometimes at the request of the remote host (a device may request that the connected device increase or decrease its transmission power based on the signal strength from that device). In addition, this layer is responsible for monitoring the link between devices and watching for link quality.

4.5.4 L2CAP: Logical Link Control and Adaptation Protocol

The Logical Link Control and Adaptation Protocol (L2CAP) Layer is also a data link layer protocol, implemented alongside the LMP. The L2CAP layer provides the following services to upper protocol layers:

- *Connectionless and connection-oriented data services:* The L2CAP layer connects upper layers to the baseband layer through two types of connections. Connectionless sessions send data frames that are not tied to each other; connection-oriented sessions send data frames that are sequenced and numbered, and that must be delivered in order. The L2CAP layer provides reliability through connection-oriented service.

- *Protocol multiplexing:* Because the baseband layer does not distinguish between data streams from separate upper layers, the L2CAP layer must multiplex between the various types of upper layer protocols. It gathers all upper protocol types and presents one data stream to the baseband layer.

- *Data stream segmentation and reassembly:* This function provides the freedom for upper layers to make packets that are larger than the baseband layer will handle. L2CAP makes this possible by segmenting large upper layer data frames into frames that the baseband can handle. L2CAP also reassembles frames from the baseband into the appropriate frames for upper levels.

This allows upper layer flexibility and efficiency in protocol interleaving.

- *Group abstractions:* L2CAP manages protocol groups, allowing a mapping of the protocols onto the piconet concept defined by the baseband. This is an abstraction of a multicast. Protocols from upper layers may want to address all devices in the local network. Since upper layers do not know which devices are in the local network at any given time, they rely on the L2CAP layer to keep track of this. The upper layer will refer to a group of devices; the L2CAP layer will map this group into the currently defined piconet.

The L2CAP layer is defined only through ACL connections to the baseband layer, and therefore is used only for data transmissions.

4.5.5 SDP: Service Discovery Protocol

Bluetooth devices operate by participating in a Bluetooth piconet or scatternet. Maintaining a stable list of these services can be quite difficult, however, given the dynamic nature of Bluetooth networks. So a Bluetooth device must *discover* the services that are available instead of being configured with a static list of them. Service Discovery Protocol (SDP) allows a Bluetooth device to do this.

SDP allows Bluetooth devices to *discover* services, to *search for* services, and to *browse* services. This applies to new devices joining a piconet and for devices already part of a piconet that are exposed to newly offered services. We can think of this like a client in a client-server model; the device offering the service is like an SDP server and the devices looking for or discovering the service are like SDP clients. We should also note here that SDP is a distributed protocol. When a service discovery needs to be made, there is no central place where this information is stored. Rather, SDP must broadcast queries and field the responses to find out which device offers specific services.

So as to be transport independent, SDP is implemented on top of the L2CAP layer.

4.5.6 RFCOMM

The RFCOMM layer is not a "core" Bluetooth layer. Rather, it is a layer built on top of the core layers to allow an interface between existing services and the Bluetooth stack. RFCOMM emulates an RS-232 serial line.

To upper layers of existing protocols, e.g., OBEX, RFCOMM presents an interface that looks exactly like an RS-232 connection (remember IrCOMM?). It provides all the transport capabilities that upper level services expect. It interfaces with the L2CAP layer and implements a point-to-point transport method. Up to 60 connections can be made between devices.

4.5.7 Other Stack Components

There are a few other components of the Bluetooth stack that warrant attention.

Telephone Control Protocol—Binary (TCS BIN) is an optional bit-oriented, call control protocol that enables Bluetooth devices to establish speech and data "calls" with other Bluetooth devices. The idea here is to allow Bluetooth-enabled mobile devices to make calls to each other—both voice and data. TCS BIN enables devices to make calls between two devices or from one device to many devices. It also allows connectionless calls, one-time messages or data drops to one device or a group of devices. TCS BIN works above the LMP and L2CAP layer.

There is a set of "AT" commands defined for Bluetooth. "AT" commands are used to give control commands to modems. The specification of Bluetooth "AT" commands defines how Bluetooth devices could fit into a standard computer-to-modem scenario. It is an attempt to allow Bluetooth devices to work with legacy equipment and software. The "AT" command set is defined for Bluetooth mobile phones and modems, and works for data calls as well as fax calls.

Finally, a note should be made about Bluetooth audio. Figure 4.6 shows that Bluetooth audio bypasses LMP and L2CAP and interfaces directly with the baseband layer. Audio data is transferred between Bluetooth devices as raw data routed directly to and from the baseband layer. The Bluetooth audio model is very simple; while devices exchange data tagged as audio data by opening a special link, each application is free to manipulate the data as it sees fit.

4.6 Telephony

The last communications technology that we will cover in this chapter is telephony. Loosely defined, telephony is the technology usually associated with the transmission of voice, traditionally associated with telephone communication. It is, however, a point-to-point communication medium that can be viewed in much the same way we view other data networks. Although voice transmission was the first—and is still the foremost—use of telephony, data can also be exchanged using most telephony methods. In fact, the units that use telephony can be addressed by their phone number.

We can use two dimensions through which to view telephony. The first way to view telephony is in two broad categories: analog and digital services. Analog services are those provided using traditional telephone equipment, which alters the telephone line signal's amplitude or frequency to reflect the transmitted voice quality or intensity. Digital services are those provided using media that can transmit the bit states of digital data—1s and 0s provided by changing the state of the signal into one of two states (or three, using the third state to indicate a carrier signal).

A modem provides a good example of the difference between these two categories. When a computer transmits a data frame of bits to another computer, each side expects the data as digital data. However, if telephone lines are between them, then the data must be transferred in an analog fashion. A modem is a digital-to-analog converter, taking the digital data from a computer, and converting it to sound for transmission over telephone lines. The sound has three distinct types, each representing a digital state. On the receiver side, the modem "hears" the sounds on the telephone line, and converts it to bits for the receiving computer.

The second dimension focuses on the telephony signal and defines wired and wireless signal carriers. These categories need little elaboration; wired telephony has a long history while wireless telephony is a more recent invention.

Figure 4.7 provides a good look at how these two dimensions interact. For example, traditional telephone service has been carried over wires. The interface between the computer and the phone line has taken on much of the terminology of a human using a telephone. Each analog line has two states: on-hook, which describes a disengaged line (think of the telephone handset as on its cradle or hook), and off-hook, which describes an engaged line (with the handset removed from its hook). Computers connect to each other by dialing phone numbers—sometimes referred to as "addresses"—and interpreting responses humans usually get, such as busy tones or phone ring tones. A computer should be aware of services the telephone service provider puts on a phone line, such as call-waiting or call-forwarding. These are configured by hand for each phone line.

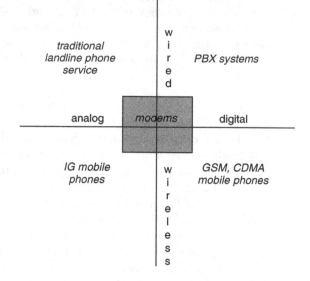

Figure 4.7 The two dimensions of telephony.

A mobile GSM phone is a good example of digital wireless. Just as we have seen in other digital implementations, GSM is based on data packets in a specific format. GSM uses time division multiplexing (TDM), which is a way to have up to 8 separate connections to one device over any of 124 frequencies at any one moment. Sharing that device is based on synchronous communication and depends on fixed-time slots in which 148-bit data frames are sent. The data rate can be high—32,500 bits are sent every 120 milliseconds—but the overhead on each data frame is also very high. Because it is digital, a GSM phone can receive messages as well as phone calls, and can act as both a telephone and a modem. As a telephone, GSM phones convert analog voice to digital data. Because of aspects like high overhead, the modem data rate is not fast, typically a maximum of 19,200 baud. This will change soon, however, as new protocols and faster transmission technology is implemented.

Notice in Figure 4.7 that modems span all four quadrants. Modems can be connected to analog, wired phone lines as well as wireless digital lines. When used with digital technology, the actual "modem" functions—the modulation and demodulation of the digital signal—are blurred. The connection of one computer to another through a phone service is still the primary use and so the "modem" term sticks.

4.7   Summary

This has been a swift (but not brief), rather sweeping survey of the transport technologies supported by Symbian OS. We should take a moment to get our bearings and re-examine the protocols. Figure 4.8 contains a good diagram comparing the various protocol stacks. The comparison is to the ISO stack model, shown in Figure 2.1.

Serial transport methods address a portion of the data link layer. Implementations of serial transport implement enough of the data link layer to let applications at upper layers talk to each other. There is no reliability and very little error correction. The maximum speed of this technology is 115 Kbps, using primarily asynchronous communication.

IrDA-based transport methods are the most comprehensive and most specific. They specify implementations from the physical layer up through the session layer and work through tight integration of all protocols. The top asynchronous speed of this protocol set is 115 Kbps; a top speed of 4 Mbps can be reached using synchronous implementations.

PLP methods are synchronization protocols. These protocols implement only the data link and network layers, but offer very effective services as applications on top of these two layers. Because PLP is implemented on top of asynchronous serial transport—either cabled serial or IrDA methods—the top speed of PLP is 115 Kbps.

The networking and TCP/IP suite of transport methods implements a very complete set of protocols. While it does not specify a physical layer, its various data link layer implementations require specific physical layer connections. It offers many different protocols and services from the data link layer up through applications. This suite implements what most would consider to be network protocols. Speeds for TCP/IP can range from 115 Kbps for serial PPP to 10 Mbps and 1 Gbps for Ethernet.

The WAP protocol stack mimics TCP/IP, but customizes it for small devices and mobile phones. It lacks both physical layer and data link layer specifications, assuming that bearers—that is, device manufacturers—will provide these layers in hardware or firmware. There is an additional security layer added for security that provides data encryption, authentication, and denial of service detection. Speeds for WAP depend on the speed of the bearer, currently not over 38.4 Kbps.

Bluetooth transport methods are the most recently developed methods and, like IrDA specifications, are tailored for a specific

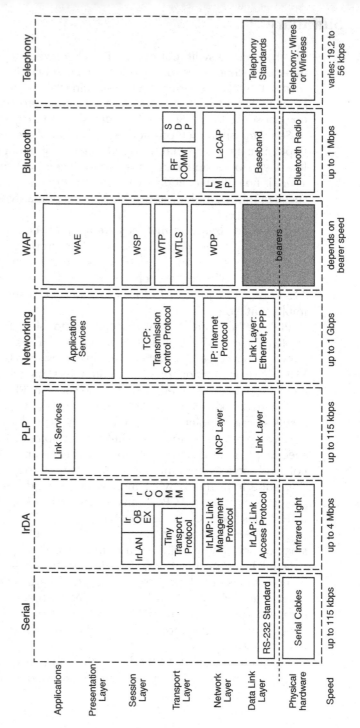

Figure 4.8 Comparing the protocol stacks.

physical medium. Bluetooth specifies the physical layer, and tailors the rest of its stack to work with this physical layer. Speeds of Bluetooth methods range up to 1 Mbps.

Telephony transport methods are much like serial methods. They typically comprise only the data link layer, and allow applications to be connected to each other with no other promises. The relay of data is unreliable, and error detection is minimal. Speeds are comparable to serial communication, and can range up to 56 Kbps, depending on the implementation.

5

A Look at Content Technologies

In the last chapter, we overviewed many different transport technologies. From RS-232 serial communication to Bluetooth protocols, the common thread that drew these technologies together was that each was used to transport data between Symbian OS devices. In this chapter, we take a look at the kinds of content that Symbian OS supports in the data that is transported. We will overview content technologies along with the content itself.

Content is, after all, the most important aspect of communication. It is very important to understand the transport methods used, but once you have spent hours poring over details about those transport methods, those details fade into the background as we discuss content issues like messaging and how to use WAP. It is very easy to take the transport for granted as we start to depend on the content.

In this chapter, we will overview messaging on Symbian OS in its many forms: email, SMS, fax, and BIO messages. We will also review HTTP and WAP, two of the important content-providing technologies.

5.1 Messaging

Messages are self-contained data objects sent between two devices. They are *self-contained* in the sense that they do not depend on the sender's or the receiver's environment. They are *data objects* because they may take one of a number of forms, and their definition is open-ended. Messages are typically used to relay specific pieces of information between machines, as well as humans.

Messages have several common characteristics:

- *A sender:* Each message originates from somewhere, either from a person or a computing device. The identity of the sender is usually included with the message, although that identity can rarely be trusted. Messages can be original person-to-person communications, or can be generated by a computer.

- *An intended destination:* Although this may seem obvious, a message is always sent *somewhere*. Messages can be sent to a single destination, to a group, or to any device that will accept it. At some layer in the transport system, messages are always sent device-to-device. The final destination, however, can be a human reader or an application.

- *Timestamps:* Messages are typically timestamped, that is, given time and date information about when an operation is performed on it. A message can receive many timestamps, and can have many operations performed on it. An email message, for example, may travel through several relay points before arriving at its final destination, and will then bear timestamps from each relay point.

- *Content:* A message always carries information to its intended destination. While that content could be empty, it is still considered to be part of the message's definition.

- *Format:* Naturally, different types of messages take different forms. However, messages tend to have a common organizational format: a *header* and a *body*. The message header contains information about the message itself, such as sender, destination, delivery options, timestamps, and the like. The body of a message contains its content, that is, the information the message was meant to convey to its recipient. Beyond this general structure, messages vary widely in how they represent or format each message section.

Consider the example found in Figure 5.1. This figure displays an email message in the form that gets exchanged between two devices (not necessarily the final form a person might read). This message has a typical format. The header is separated from the body by a blank line (about two-thirds the way down the message). You can easily spot the sender and destination by the "From:" and "To:" lines. The header contains several timestamps; the "Received:" fields display information about the relays the message went through. Note that there is a lot of information in the header, more information than is typically useful. In this case, the body of the message is an ASCII-based textual message.

Message sending and receiving typically involves both servers and clients. A typical scenario is depicted in Figure 5.2. The sender composes the message on his or her local device. The message is then "sent"—which means it is uploaded to a server, either over

```
Received: from mail.brainshareproject.com (mail.brainshareproject.com)
       by smaug.cs.hope.edu (8.9.3+Sun/8.9.1) with ESMTP id AAA09235
       for <jipping@cs.hope.edu>; Wed, 27 Jun 2001 00:33:11 -0400 (EDT)
Received: from debian (dialup-209.Dial1.Level10.net [192.245.239.242])
       by mail.brainshareproject.com (EL-8_9_3_3/8.9.3) with ESMTP
       id VAA14057
       for <jipping@cs.hope.edu>; Tue, 26 Jun 2001 21:32:46 -0700 (PDT)
Received: from jjones by debian with local (Exim 3.22 #1 (Debian))
       id 15F70M-0000UR-00
       for <jipping@cs.hope.edu>; Tue, 26 Jun 2001 23:32:42 -0500
Date: Tue, 26 Jun 2001 23:32:42 -0500
From: John Jones <jjones@brainshareproject.com>
To: jipping@cs.hope.edu
Subject: Infomercials.org
Message-ID: <20010626233241.A1876@brainshareproject.com>
Mime-Version: 1.0
Content-Type: text/plain; charset=us-ascii
Content-Disposition: inline
User-Agent: Mutt/1.3.18i
X-StarTrek-Quote: Make it so.
Sender: John Jones <jjones@brainshareproject.com>
Content-Length: 701

I want to bounce this site off of you:
       http://www.infomercials.org/
and hear any opinions you have on the material it presents.   They seem
to have a very well-thought-out approach to managing large (or small)
numbers of customers.

John J.
```

Figure 5.1   An example email message.

a network or wirelessly. This server, known as a message center or
relay server, must now deliver the message.

There are also delivery methods that work on a peer-to-peer
basis. These methods allow local message composition and deliver
the message directly to the recipient. The message relay server is
removed from the loop.

In general, then, there are two models for mail delivery:

- *The "push" model:* If it can, the server will deliver the message
  directly. This means that it must contact the destination device
  and "push" the message to it. This requires that the destination
  is powered on and can receive messages.

- *The "pull" model:* When a device is not usually connected to a
  network or mobile service, the server will store the message for
  the recipient. The receiving device then must contact the server
  and "pull" its messages from the server. Often, in this model,
  the message relay point is not the message storage point. The
  storage server receives the message from the message relay and
  keeps it for the recipient.

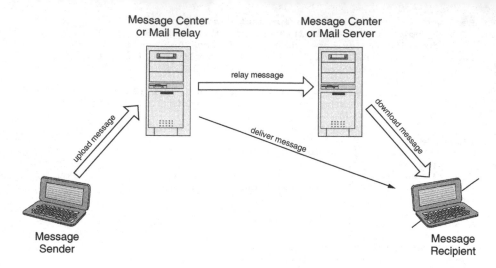

Figure 5.2 A typical message delivery scenario.

Note that the pull model could involve the push model. A device might pull its messages by simply notifying a server that it is online and ready. The server then uses push model mechanisms to deliver content to that device.

The Symbian platform supports four specific message types as well as the ability to extend the platform to embrace new ones. It also supports both models of message delivery. We will cover the message types in this section, as well as the technologies that support them. We will cover message delivery later when we discuss programming with messages.

5.1.1 Electronic Mail

Electronic mail is one of the most common and widely used forms of messaging. It was originally developed as an electronic means to send text-based messages—textual "mail" for human consumption—between computers. As the value of sending messages was realized, people began to send other things as well. Email has evolved to encompass all types of objects, for example, programs, spreadsheets, or word processing documents.

The format of an email message is exemplified in Figure 5.1.* As we have stated, email messages have a header and a body. The

---

*The most widely used format for email messages is specified by the Internet Engineering Task Force by a document called RFC 821.

header is comprised of a sequence of lines or fields, each of which is composed of a key and a value, separated by a colon. Each field relays information about the message to the receiver. The sender is required to insert a "From" field, a "To" field, and a "Posted-Date" field into the message header, and is free to insert other defined fields. In addition, any field whose key value begins with the string "X-" may be inserted by the user (note the "X-StarTrek-Quote" field in Figure 5.1).

The body of an email message contains the message content. This content is typically composed of a message in ASCII or UniCode text. However, the message body can also have *attachments*, which are data objects that accompany the message. These objects are included using a standard called Multipurpose Internet Mail Extensions (MIME). Objects included using MIME are each included in a message type format, with a header to identify the type of the data object and a body that contains the data object itself. Many objects can be included in a message.

Even when it includes MIME objects, an email message has a text-based representation. All email is sent using readable (ASCII/UniCode) characters. If a message contains attachments that are not comprised of text, then those attachments are encoded in a special way to derive text from them. The encoding method used, e.g., base 64, is included in the header for the data object, so the receiving software can decode the object.

The delivery of email messages to the end user follows the "pull" model of mail delivery.

There are several protocols that are used to send and receive email. By far, the most widely used sending protocol is Simple Mail Transfer Protocol (SMTP). There are two protocols used to receive or read email: Post Office Protocol (POP) and Internet Message Access Protocol (IMAP). These are TCP/IP, network-based protocols.

Look at Your Email

Look at your own email messages to verify the format I specify here. Save your email to a file and examine the file's contents. If you can, find a mail message with attachments and look at the contents. You may have to specify a "save headers" or "save all headers" property to your mail reader; often mail readers will save only those header fields that it deems interesting. Use these headers to track the path your email message has gone through to reach you.

SMTP is a protocol that is used to upload email from applications, and to exchange email between servers. Message senders will use SMTP when exchanging messages with relays or storage servers and relays and storage servers will use SMTP when exchanging messages between them. As its name implies, SMTP is a simple, textual protocol.

SMTP has three phases. The first is an *identification phase*. In this phase, the sender sends an "HELO" message, which includes its name. The receiver accepts this name and both sides move to the exchange phase.

In the *exchange phase*, the sender can make some general queries or can send messages to the mail server. Address verification is a good example of a general query. Sending a "VRFY" message with an email address will cause the mail server to send back an acknowledgement or an error message that tells the sender if the email address is valid on the server's system. Mail exchange is initiated by the "DATA" message and terminated by a line with only a "." character on it.

The final phase is a *termination phase*. This happens when the sender issues a "QUIT" message.

You can see how simple this protocol is. It is easily understandable and easily implemented. It is also easily broken and can be a major security risk. There is no authentication and verification of identification. Those who snoop networks can easily read and figure out what email is being exchanged.

Experiment with SMTP

It is easy to experiment with SMTP because it is a simple protocol. Identify an SMTP server—perhaps the one that receives your email. Follow these steps:

1. Telnet to this server on port 25. Use a command line like:

    ```
    telnet smtp.server.com 25
    ```

2. You should get a response from the connection that identifies the SMTP server, the version of the server software, and the current date and time. Your response should be to identify yourself by giving the HELO command, like this:

    ```
    HELO my.computer.com
    ```

    You give your computer name—fully qualified with a domain.

3. The response should be a greeting ("pleased to meet you"). You are then free to enter SMTP exchange commands. One easy one is to use "VRFY" to verify an email address:

```
vrfy jipping@cs.hope.edu
```

Experiment with other commands. With many SMTP servers, you can issue a "HELP" command, and the server will give you assistance for using the commands that it accepts.

4. Terminate the connection with the server by using the "QUIT" command when you are done.

POP3: Post Office Protocol

SMTP is a protocol for mail uploading and exchanging, but applications do not use it for mail receipt. Post Office Protocol Version 3 (POP3) is a popular protocol used to receive and download messages.

Like SMTP, POP3 has three phases: authorization, transaction, and termination. The *identification phase* uses a username and a password, which is verified by the mail server. This means that the receiver typically has an account on the server's system, so that the username and password can be verified. Once verification has been achieved, both sides move to the message delivery, or transaction, phase.

The *transaction phase* allows some information and maintenance messages, and allows for message download. Information messages such as how many email messages are waiting to be picked up or the size of those messages are very useful. Maintenance messages include the ability to delete messages from the server's storage. Download messages allow the receiver to download only message headers or entire messages.

Termination is initiated by the sender through the "QUIT" command. The protocol connection between client and server is severed by this command.

The POP3 protocol was designed for situations where messages are delivered to the receiver client. It is assumed that clients will manipulate and store messages on their own devices and not on the server and the default delivery mode is to delete messages from the storage server after delivery. However, most email receiver clients offer the option of leaving copies of email messages on the mail server in the user's mailbox.

POP3 uses authentication while SMTP does not. We have assailed SMTP for being insecure, but the use of authentication does not make POP3 much better here than SMTP. POP3 still uses plain and unencrypted text characters for communication between server and client. This means that the username and password are available to snoopers and that each email that is downloaded is potentially readable by those who are watching the network traffic.

IMAP4: Internet Message Access Protocol

Internet Message Access Protocol Version 4 (IMAP4) is a mail download protocol very much like POP3. There are four states with IMAP4: non-authenticated, authenticated, selection, and termination.

The *non-authenticated state* is the initial state a client enters when it contacts an IMAP4 server. This is where the client will identify itself with the username and password of its user. Upon verification, both sides enter the authenticated state.

When it enters the authenticated state, the client must then select a mailbox to access, and the server checks if the client has permissions to this box (by checking against the username). Both sides then move to the selection state.

In the *selection state*, a user has been identified and has selected a mailbox to review. Now, the user has information, maintenance, and downloading choices much like those with POP3. However, there are more possibilities for maintenance, because IMAP allows messages to stay on the server and to be placed in folders for storage. IMAP does not assume that the messages are going to remain on the receiver's device.

The termination phase is initiated by the client. The server updates its tables and severs its connection with the client.

IMAP is an improvement over POP3 in two ways. First, it allows the client to have choices over the mailboxes it opens, allowing multiple mailboxes for a single client. Second, it allows storage of messages on the server in an organized manner. Security is not improved, however, over POP3. Plain text passwords and messages are still used and can easily be snooped and stolen.

Experiment with IMAP4

You can experiment with IMAP4 as easily as you did with POP3. Identify a IMAP4 server. This could easily be the one you use to download email from. Follow these steps:

1. Telnet to this server on port 143. Use a command line something like this:

    ```
    telnet pop.mailserver.com 143
    ```

2. You should get an identifying response from the mail server. You then identify yourself like this:

    ```
    sessionID LOGIN jipping jipspassword
    ```

    The "sessionID" is a string to identify the IMAP4 session you are engaging in. Substitute your username for "jipping" and your password for "jipspassword".

3. Once you have moved into the authenticated state, you must select your mailbox. The INBOX will do:

    ```
    A001 SELECT INBOX
    ```

4. If you are successful, you should get a list of mail attributes along with an "...OK...SELECT completed" response, and you are in the selection state. In this state, you can manipulate the mailbox you have selected by using selection commands. There are many of these, but you can play with some:

```
A001 FETCH <msg#> (RFC822)
```

This will fetch a message in RFC822 format—normal Internet email format—from the server. Another is

```
A001 SEARCH FLAGGED SINCE 1-Feb-2001 NOT FROM "Smith"
```

This will find the messages since 1 February 2001 that are not sent from "Smith".

5. When you are done using the IMAP4 session, you can quit the session by issuing the LOGOUT command:

```
A001 LOGOUT
```

5.1.2 SMS Messaging

Email messages are meant to be in a general form that adapts to most computer systems. They are text-based, so most devices can read and relay them. They are flexible enough to accommodate many different types of data objects. By contrast, SMS messages are very specific and targeted by their nature to a specific carrier technology.

SMS messages are short messages, 160 characters or less, and are specifically targeted for mobile phones and devices that use a GSM phone service. They are data messages, not intended to be viewed by humans until they are decoded and displayed. The sending of SMS messages adheres to the "push" model of message delivery. Messages are sent to a service center that relays the message and delivers it to its destination. The service center contacts the device—and keeps trying until it finds the device powered on and receiving messages.

An SMS message follows the standard message format in that there is a message header and a message body. The header contains information about the message and the body contains the message itself. The SMS message below contains the message "hello":

```
07917283010010F5040BC87238880900F10000993092516195800AE83229BFD46
```

Note that the data is actually a stream of bits and written above in hexadecimal. If this message were to be received on a GSM phone, chances are that the phone would display "hello". It is fairly obvious that we are dealing with a different type of message than we dealt with for email.

Let's examine this message and by this example examine the SMS standards for messaging. The table below analyzes the pieces of the example SMS message above.

Data Field	Description
07	The length of the service center information. In this case, the number is 7 octets.
91	The type of service center address. In this case, 91 means the phone number has an international format.
72 83 01 00 10 F5	The service center address in "decimal semi-octets". Although formatted like octets, the number reads in decimal digits. Because the service center address has an odd number of digits, it is padded with F (all ones) to pad out the octet. Here, the number is +27381000015.
04	Type of message. This is an SMS-DELIVER message.
0B	Sender address length. Here, 0B means the sender address is 11 digits.
C8	The type of the sender's address
72 38 88 09 00 F1	The sender's address, in decimal semi-octets. Note the padding. Here the address is +27838890001
00	A protocol identifier, establishing the way we will send the rest of the messages.
00	The data coding scheme. SMS messages can be sent in many encoding; the most popular, used here, is 7-bit data.

Data Field	Description
99 30 92 51 61 95 80	This is the sending time stamp in semi-octets. The first 6 octets represent the date, the next 6 represent the time, and the last two represent the time zone.
0A	Length of the message, in this case 5 octets.
E83229BFD46	The actual message, where 8-bit octets are used for 7-bit data.

Let's take note of a couple of things about this message. First, the semi-octet format of the addresses and the timestamp is odd, but readable. Note that the octets are swapped in this representation. Second, this message is in 7-bit "default alphabet" format. This is an alphabet of 127 characters that contains many of the most often used international characters. This is a GSM standard. Finally, to compress as much as possible, the 7-bit representation is encoded in the 8-bit quantities in a special way.

SMS messages can have many forms. In the GSM standard, the messages can, for example, be faxes or pages. The standard also allows email messages to be sent to GSM phones by way of SMS. In this latter case, the mobile device is able to treat the message as an email message and perform email operations on it (like replying to the message, for example). Adapting SMS messages to these other forms requires both a service provider that can perform such conversions and software on both the sender's and receiver's devices that can handle these adaptations. For example, the service provider will probably have to provide an email-address-to-phone-number mapping and software must be used to cut large messages into smaller messages that can be sent over SMS.

5.1.3 BIO Messaging

BIO messages are messages meant for the receiving device, not the user. These messages contain structured data objects of a known, predetermined format. They can be delivered using various transports: for example, email, SMS, and IR can be used.

Various data objects can be sent as BIO messages, including SMS configuration messages, configuration settings for various applications, and application data objects.

A good example of a BIO message is one that contains ringtones. A ringtone is a tune that a mobile phone will play to alert its user of some condition—say, a call coming in. While mobile phones have many unique tones, many phone manufacturers also provide the ability to program ringtones and send them to the phone. So you can have your favorite movie theme song play when you get a phone call. Ringtones are programmed using a textual "language" that can be encapsulated in an SMS message and sent to a mobile device. Because of special settings in the message header, the phone would process the message itself rather than display the message on its screen. Processing a ringtone means decoding the specification, storing the resulting tone, and incorporating the tone in its list of tones.

Another good example of BIO messaging is the exchange of vCards. vCards are electronic versions of business cards, containing names and contact information. The specification of a vCard is textual and can be included as an object, for instance, in email. By sending a device your vCard, by IR, for example, your contact information can be automatically inserted into the device's directory. This is accomplished by sending a message containing the textual specification of a vCard. By indicating in the message header that the vCard message is a special message, the device intercepts the vCard and records it, rather than displaying it.

vCard and vCalendar Objects

Virtual business cards and virtual calendar objects are a standardized way to exchange information about contacts and agenda items between devices. These can be attached to email or sent to another device via methods like IR or Bluetooth. They are textual specifications and, as such, are flexible and adaptable to many different transports and devices.

The Internet Mail Consortium governs the maintenance of the standards on these objects. The IMC is a group of computer companies that includes Symbian. Their Web site is at *http://www.imc.org*.

Further information about the format of these objects can be found in later chapters. We will be using these objects in examples; they are supported directly by the Symbian platform.

5.1.4 Fax Messaging

As a messaging technology, facsimile transmission—that is, the electronic transmission of images over phone lines—developed in parallel with computer communication. As standards were developed regarding digital messages and their transmission, fax standards were developed independently. In order to integrate a fax standard with the messaging standards we have discussed, some adaptation has been required.

A fax message is actually an image. Before computers were used to send faxes, fax machines were developed to scan a piece of paper into an image in the machine's memory, to transfer this image to other machines via a modem, and finally to print the image from memory back to paper. As computers got involved in this process, they eliminated the need for paper, and the fax image could be converted from its native format to one of the more standard image formats that computers use (e.g., GIF or JPEG formats). Modems have been adapted to include fax capability.

The faxing model is compatible with the messaging models we have discussed. Sending a fax follows the "push" model of messaging, where the sender keeps trying to send the fax until the intended recipient fax machine can receive it. As a message, a fax transmission has a body: it is the image that gets transmitted. We have to stretch the model a bit to find a message header, however. For a fax message, implementations typically consider the cover page of the fax transmission to be its header. It contains information typically found in a message header—send and destination information, for example—and it precedes the message body.

The data format of a fax transmission is specified by the Comité Consultatif International Téléphonique et Télégraphique (CCITT), now known by its parent organization, the International Telecommunication Union (ITU). The actual format of the graphics image that gets transferred is specified but is outside the scope of this book. It is the job of the sending machine to convert any text or images to that graphics format, to use the fax mode of an attached communications device, and to push the graphics data stream through to the recipient.

Sending a fax is typically done through a modem with fax capability. There is also faxing capability built into the GSM standard. Mobile devices that use GSM therefore have the capability of sending fax messages through the GSM service.

The Fax Image Format

You can find more information on the fax image format on the Web. However, CCITT Group 4 standards are a bit hard to find, because fax images are specified as TIFF class F images. More information on TIFF class F can be found in "The Spirit of TIFF

Class F'', 1990, available from Cygnet Technologies, 2560 9th., Suite 220, Berkeley, CA USA.

5.2 World Wide Web Technologies

It is fair to say that when Tim Berners-Lee started to build a system of "distributed hypermedia" (as he called it) in 1992, no one suspected that the eventual result—the World Wide Web—would be as large or as important a system as it is today. As it has currently evolved, the Web is a gigantic collection of interconnected documents that use the ideas of hypertext and multimedia to link documents to each other and to convey information. The Web contains many different forms of content, mostly distributed via the Internet.

The Web is a collection of hypertext documents. These documents contain text and images, formatted according to certain rules. The hypertext nature of Web pages is what has made them such a useful tool; buried in the text and graphics of a Web page are hypertext "links" to other documents and multimedia data on the Web. Links can reference Web pages, sounds, documents of any format; any downloadable data can be linked in this way. In a hypertext document, if you want more information about a particular subject that contains a link to another document, you can click or tap on the link to load the new page or to access the referenced data.

Using the Web is a classic example of client-server interaction. To access documents on the Web, you run a Web browser application as a client. The browser requests and downloads documents from Web servers, which serve up pages and other information. Web browsers can, in addition, access files by other protocol methods, for example, file transfer protocol (FTP), Internet news services (via Network News Transfer Protocol (NNTP)), and email (via POP3 or IMAP4). On top of these, if the server has search capabilities, browsers can enable searches of files and databases.

Pages on the Web are addressed by their Uniform Resource Locator (URL) address. This address is in the form:

```
<protocol>://<host>[:<port number>]/<file location>
```

The standard values for "<protocol>" are "http" for Hypertext Transfer Protocol, "ftp" for File Transfer Protocol, and "mailto" for access to SMTP email servers. This set has been expanded by various browsers for certain uses (e.g., "about" and "file" are popular). The "<host>" field specifies the returned address of the computer (either name or IP address) and the "<file location>"

field specifies the path to the file on that host. The <port number> is optional and gives the TCP port number on the <host> server to use to initiate the connection and to send the request. Most Web service is done over port 80.

Web servers implement many different services, usually accessed through some kind of dynamically generated Web page interface. A common way to access the dynamic features of the Web is through the Common Gateway Interface (CGI). Via CGI, the Web server implements a gateway to its execution capabilities. Using CGI, a Web page reference will cause a separate program to be run on the server side and that program's output will be channeled through the Web server to the browser as the Web page. Dynamic Web pages are also implemented using other methods:

- Web pages can reference Java programs, which can be executed by a Java-enabled browser right in the Web page.

- JavaScript, a Java-based scripting language, can be included in a Web page and can be used to make the display of the page programmable.

- Active Server Pages (ASPs) are pages generated dynamically by the Web server, which uses scripts contained in the Web page to build the page that is sent to the browser. ASP files can contain HTML (including related client-side scripts) as well as calls to Windows components that perform a variety of tasks, such as connecting to a database or processing business logic. ASPs represent a streamlined alternative to CGI for Windows servers.

So Web browsing and Web service can access static pages and can work together to implement dynamic interfaces. On the Symbian platform, our focus is on the client side of the Web—browsing and accessing pages. Therefore, two important parts of using the Web that warrant closer attention are HTTP—the Web page transport protocol—and HTML—the language used to specify Web pages.

5.2.1 HTTP: Hypertext Transfer Protocol

HTTP is the protocol used to send pages from a Web server to a Web browser. HTTP is, in fact, two different protocols. It specifies the interaction of machines to transfer the data that makes up a Web page. It also specifies the format of the Web page data. The Web page itself is augmented in HTTP to give the data stream some extra meaning for the Web browser.

HTTP was designed as a simple, text-command-based protocol that could transfer Web pages and adapt to many situations. In its current version (the Symbian platform supports HTTP version 1.1), HTTP is a very stable protocol that works over a variety of connection strategies in a number of different network configurations.

HTTP was designed to work within a TCP/IP network framework, using a client-server model. In the simplest case, this can be accomplished with a single connection between the browser client and the Web server.

More complicated situations develop when intermediaries are present in the client-server relationship. Three forms of intermediary are possible: proxy, gateway, and tunnel. A *proxy* is a forwarding agent that receives requests for a Web resource, rewrites all or part of the request, and relays the reformatted request to the server in the original request (i.e., the URL). A *gateway* is a receiving agent, acting as a layer above some other server(s) and, if necessary, translating the requests to the underlying server's protocol. A *tunnel* acts as a relay point between two connections without changing the requests or responses; tunnels are used when the communication needs to pass through an intermediary (such as a firewall) even when the intermediary cannot understand the contents of the messages.

Any party to the request chain which is not acting as a tunnel may employ an internal cache for handling requests. The effect of a cache is that the request/response chain is shortened if one of the participants along the chain has a cached response applicable to that request. This shortens the response time, especially where several intermediaries are involved.

The HTTP protocol itself is a stateless protocol. This means that one request/response pair occurs per connection, so that neither side needs to keep any information about the state of the connection. This is optimal if we want to make the connection fault tolerant, and flexible for many different situations. This runs over a TCP connection, so that reliability is assured.

HTTP consists mainly of a request command: GET. There are various forms of this request, but it basically looks like

```
GET <url> <protocol version>
```

The Uniform Resource Identifier (the <url>) is in a full pathname form, one where the <protocol> and <host> portions of the original URL are removed. The <protocol version> is the version of HTTP that is assumed. It specifies the name of the protocol and the version number, such as "HTTP/1.1".

The response to this request is either an error specification (including error number and error message) or a stream of data that constitutes a Web page.

The Format of the Web Page Data

If no error results from the request, Web page data is to be returned. This data takes the form of a MIME message. That is, it contains a message header and a message body; the header directs the browser what to do with the body. It is possible that the header is empty; this would be the default case where the body contained only HTML code to be directly displayed by the browser.

The MIME message header is a series of lines in "<key>: <value>" format. The "<key>" can come from a large set of specifiers, but the most useful is the "Content-Type" key. This can dictate the character of the data that is contained in the page body, which in turn can direct the browser on how to display it. For example, the type "text/plain" would be displayed verbatim in the browser's display window, without formatting. The typical type is "text/html", for a typical HTML-based Web page. But many different types are useful, such as "application/ms-word", which might start a Microsoft Word application and feed the page body to it, or "audio/mp3", which might cause an MP3 player to be started using the page data.

5.2.2 Using HTML

Hypertext Markup Language (HTML) is the language used to specify Web pages. That is, HTML is the language recognized by Web browsers, used for formatting and content information. It is a standardized language, with the standard controlled by the World Wide Web Consortium. Symbian OS implements the current version of the standard, which is version 4.0.

HTML is an attempt to specify the properties of a document in a comprehensive, textual form. A document has many properties, including a title, a description, formatting elements, and content. Each property item is specified by a series of *tags*, which are specifications surrounded by angle brackets—that is, the characters "<" and ">". A properly formatted HTML document has a head and a body, and has each property tag paired with the appropriate concluding tag. Therefore, a correct template for starting an HTML document is

```
<HTML>
<HEAD>
    ...header information...
</HEAD>
<BODY>
    ...body information...
</BODY>
</HTML>
```

This is a minimal specification; tags can have parameters specified inside them, which can alter the configuration of the item being described.

Header information includes the title of the document, any keywords that might describe the document, any description of scripts that might be used by the document body, and comments describing the document to human readers. The body information includes formatting information, specification of special HTML content (such as forms or dynamic interaction areas), and textual content itself, which typically forms the heart of the document.

It is important to note here that HTML is textual and, with a few exceptions, rather simple in its formatting specification. The tricks to processing HTML is the parsing of it and its translation to a device's display. These processes require a fairly large amount of processing. Providing a manual on the types of tags possible or even about the many ways Web documents can be specified and used is obviously beyond the scope of this book. However, it should be clear that Web pages download easily and require a fair amount of manipulation and processing when they arrive at their client destination.

The HTML Standard

The World Wide Web Consortium (W3C) is generally considered to be the maintainer of the HTML standard. The W3C maintains many protocols and Web markup specification standards for document layout. They also have browsing tools as well as Web page verifiers. You can access their Web site at *http://www.w3.org*.

HTML is a subset of a larger markup language called Standardized General Markup Language (SGML). A set of resources on SGML can be found on the W3C Web site at *http://www.w3.org/MarkUp/SGML/*. HTML has extensively expanded into a structured data description language called Extensible Markup Language (XML). Information on XML can also be found on the W3C Website at *http://www.w3.org/XML/*.

5.3   Wireless Access Protocol

HTML browsing over the Web has proven to be an extremely popular and flexible method of content delivery. As small devices and wireless communication have developed, it has been very tempting to adapt the model of Web page browsing to a mobile, phone-based platform. However, HTML requires some extensive processing to display, and that processing can take a heavy toll on resources. In addition, downloading the amount of information for HTML pages can tax memory and bandwidth.

Wireless Access Protocol (WAP) was developed to circumvent the problems of "heavyweight" content while retaining the benefits of client-server-based hypertext information. We have seen that WAP requires a new protocol stack, one that streamlines content delivery yet remains layered and secure. The top layer of the WAP stack implements content delivery: the Wireless Session protocol is designed to deliver Wireless Markup Language to the display device.

5.3.1   WSP: Wireless Session Protocol

The constraints of the WAP environment has imposed design restrictions on the entire WAP stack. These restrictions can be seen in the

WSP layer. This layer is meant to emulate the HTTP protocol in a restricted, efficient way.

WSP provides two services to the application layer: connectionless and connection-based services. Connectionless service is a thinner service, providing unreliable delivery with no requirement for acknowledgment from the receiver. In this mode, the WSP layer talks directly to the WDP layer, bypassing the WTP layer and making a short path to the bearer layer. This is a thin transport mode with low overhead. It is the most useful for the delivery of small amounts of data in situations that do not require feedback from the recipient.

Connection-based delivery uses the WTP layer and ensures reliable, secure delivery of data packets. Connection-based delivery demands acknowledgements from receivers and implements retransmissions if the packets are lost. This mode of WSP also adds capability negotiation, header caching, and longer-lived sessions. These last three features emulate features implemented between HTTP browsers and servers. This delivery method is used for the delivery of larger amounts of data or data that is error-sensitive.

Symbian OS supports both connectionless and connection-based sessions by its implementation of the WSP layer.

5.3.2 Using WML

Wireless Markup Language (WML) is a language used to specify formatting of WAP "pages" through a WAP microbrowser application.

WML is based on XML, a markup language superset of HTML used to describe data sets and their semantics. WML uses a metaphor based on decks and cards: instead of pages, WML uses cards, and cards may be collected into decks. WML includes special link directives that navigate quickly between decks.

Like HTML, WML specifies formatting and layout of the document presentation (in this case, the card presentation). WML uses tags to specify formatting directives as well as card and deck configuration. A single WML document can have multiple cards specified so that one download can result in several cards linked and displayed efficiently.

As an example of WML, consider the WML specification below:

```
<wml>
    <card id="index">
        <do type="accept" label="Card 2">
            <go href="#CardTwo"/>
        </do>
```

```
<do type="options" label="WSJ">
    <go href="http://wap.wsj.com"/>
 </do>
<p align="center">
   Welcome!
</p>
<p align="left" mode="nowrap" >
<select>
    <option onpick="http://wap.wsj.com"> Wall Street </option>
    <option onpick="#CardTwo"> Card 2 </option>
</select>
</p>
</card>

<CARD NAME="CardTwo">
  <P>
  This is Card Two!
  </P>
</CARD>
</WML>
```

This WML specification describes two cards, one linked to the other. The specification is minimal, especially when compared to HTML, yet effective. The first screen that this specification describes is shown in Figure 5.3.

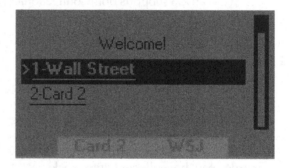

Figure 5.3 Example WML code displayed.

There are several other aspects of WML that extend it beyond displaying information. First, WML includes WMLscript, a scripting language that can be embedded in WML specifications for dynamic card interactions. Second, WML includes a Wireless Telephony Application Interface (WTAI). This interface allows WML to access the telephony functions of the wireless device that it is running on. For instance, using a URL starting with "wtai:" can make a phone call if an option is selected. Finally, access to the WTAI extends WML's functionality beyond just call control; through WTAI, WML can access address book data and phonebook services.

5.4 Other Content Technologies

There are other content technologies that the Symbian platform supports. Among these are the following:

- *FTP:* File Transfer Protocol (FTP) was one of the first methods developed to transfer files between devices over the Internet. Developed to run over TCP/IP networks, FTP actually implements two protocols: (1) a command protocol that is used to direct (2) a data link protocol that exchanges file data. FTP is a simple, robust protocol that is still in wide use today. The Symbian platform supports FTP directly through an application engine in version 6.1.

- *TELNET:* This protocol is less a content provider and more a content access protocol. Telnet is a remote access protocol that allows devices to access TCP/IP service ports on remote devices. The typical use for telnet is to access port 23, which is a remote execution shell service, providing access to command shells on remote machines. Telnet is supported directly on the Symbian platform 6.1 through an application engine.

5.5 Some Perspective on Content

As we leave this chapter, we should stop for a moment to consider the importance of content and the technology each type of content represents.

Messaging is a relatively mature content technology. People have long understood the strategic importance of messaging and implemented many ways to distribute messages to colleagues, coworkers, and customers. Messaging started as fax machine transmissions and local area network email. It used to be that only email between 8:00 AM and 5:00 PM was important because that is when workers could access a computer system to read it. Messaging evolved as global communication became important and timing constraints grew. Now, workers realize that when it is 3:00 AM in the United States (and I am probably asleep), it is 4:00 PM in Korea and someone might need to get me an important message that might even wake me up.

Messaging methods have different impacts on message readers. Email is a less urgent medium. Because messages gather on a mail server before being collected and read, they are subject to the time schedule of the person that reads them. SMS and BIO messages are more urgent and, because of their immediate delivery methods, can be used for time-sensitive and immediate information. Fax messaging lies between these other message media. If it can be delivered to a Symbian OS device, it can be an immediate message. However, many times, a fax transmission is sent to a desktop computer or fax machine and therefore is subject to the same constraints as email—messages are read whenever they are picked up from a delivery location.

Recent studies have shown that messaging systems are a crucial part of businesses today. It has been said that the typical computer user spends about two hours each day, or about 500 hours each year, using functionality provided by the messaging system. Fully 35% percent of critical business information used by computer users is stored in a messaging system, either in individual mailboxes, in folders or within a database. This points out how critical messaging has become.

Browsable content represents opportunities for people to obtain up-to-date information instantly. Both HTML and WML represent many ways for keeping people informed. Companies keep their sales staff up on the information they need; employees can reference company information instantly; anyone can access a weather forecast. Integrating browsable content with databases and dynamic information retrieval has powerful potential.

5.6 Summary

This chapter covered the kinds of communication content that Symbian OS supports. Specifically, we covered three content types: messaging in all its forms, HTML content, and WML content. We covered the four kinds of messages Symbian OS currently supports: email, SMS, fax, and BIO messages.

The next chapter will conclude our look at the basics of the Symbian OS communication architecture by reviewing issues that are connected with data security.

6

Security and Communication

Eavesdropping is a very easy thing to do. It takes very little effort to listen to someone else's conversation, especially in an environment where you might go unnoticed. This is especially hard to resist if you hear your name used in a crowded room. In a social gathering, it is excruciating to not listen to a conversation if you think people are talking about you. It is much easier to walk close to the group, to fake some activity (as if you should be there), and to try to gather as much of the conversation as you can.

In the realm of data communication, eavesdropping is also an easy thing to do. As we reviewed in Chapter 3, when data moves between two devices, an opportunity exists for snooping on that data. In some cases, it is even possible to tamper with the data or to confuse the receiver. Like voices in a room, new voices can be introduced that confuse listeners or drown out speakers.

In this chapter, we review issues that surround the security of communication and the solutions supported by the Symbian platform. We will review ways of snooping on data; we will overview the ways data can be protected; and we will highlight the methods implemented by the Symbian platform.

6.1 An Overview of Security Issues

In general, security is all about *control*. Obtaining and retaining control over both data and access are the keys to security. Naturally, this control is easier to manage when the data remains on a single computer, or when there is no access possible. But when the data leaves a device, or the device is connected to a network, control becomes difficult to manage. There are two areas where we are concerned about data control: *physical issues*, where outside parties can use the physical properties of communication (e.g., cables or light) to eavesdrop on data exchanges and perhaps manipulate those exchanges, and *data issues*, where outside parties can exploit or change the data itself. Access control is also of concern here. In addition to data control, controlling access to devices—both physical and electronic access—is very important, even to small devices.

Along with issues of control, *trust* is also foundational. If we cannot control data completely, then we must be able to trust the entities that can see our data. To avoid gullibility, trust must be granted, not assumed. We grant trust to entities that can prove who they are. So we must be concerned with trust issues like authentication and identification, as well as issues of granting trust.

6.1.1   Physical Issues

The eavesdropping, or snooping, that can be done on data is a major problem in communication. In the brief milliseconds that it takes to transfer data packets from one device to another, many other devices can possibly view and decode those packets. While not all types of transport are susceptible, many transport methods are very open to data snooping.

In general, wired serial communication is extremely difficult to snoop. There is no way to "listen" to a serial cable, unless you splice into that cable. This can indeed happen, especially when cables go for long distances that are not monitored (for example, between buildings or traversing floors). However, without physically altering the environment, eavesdropping on a serial data cable is not feasible.

Wireless serial communication, however, is much easier to snoop. With infrared communication, the light beams cover an area approximately 15 degrees on either side of center from the origin. So if the intended receiver is on one side of the field, a snooping device could be on the other side of the field and still be able to receive a signal. If the sender receives protocol acknowledgements from multiple receivers, it will get confused and stop sending. But a "collector" that simply recorded an IR session and later disassembled it to figure out the data exchange is certainly possible. However, you would think that, with the short range of IR and the need to point directly at the sending device, such a collector would be noticed very quickly.

Network technologies are notoriously easy to snoop. As an example, consider Ethernet. Ethernet is a passive medium, broadcasting its packets across a network. It depends on machines behaving correctly, that only the machine that is the intended destination of a packet will pick up and decode that packet. This is a matter of trust, of course, but this trust is *assumed* to exist. However, nothing stops any connected machine from listening to all packets, collecting all data, and reassembling a conversation between machines. The snooping device simply needs to be wired to the same network and needs to access the network in such a way that all packets are read, not just the ones that are meant for the listening network card. This is a special listening mode, called "promiscuous mode".

Wireless media are even easier to snoop. In a wireless environment, the snooping device does not even need to be wired into the network; it simply needs to be within radio range and have the right receiving equipment. Wireless snooping is easy because it does not look conspicuous. A data collector simply needs to be inconspicuously using his data device, and listening to data traffic at the same time. Wireless Ethernet and Bluetooth can be snooped this way.

Try This Out for Yourself

There are several ways to snoop communication. Try these methods to "listen" to an HTTP client-server conversation browsing Web pages over port 80 on a TCP/IP network.

If you are using a Unix system, you might try the "tcpdump" command:

```
tcpdump tcp port 80
```

then access a Web page through a browser. This command puts the network card of the machine you are using into promiscuous mode and reads all network packets. It reports TCP packets that are sent and received on port 80, the default port used for Web page service. The output can tend to be cryptic, but much information can be assembled, including sites visited and actual HTML of the Web pages browsed.

If you using a Unix workstation that runs Solaris (from Sun Microsystems), the "snoop" command will help you more. Use the command

```
snoop -V port 80
```

This will print the conversation across port 80 in a more readable form.

Note that in Unix systems, putting the network card in promiscuous mode and listening to all packets requires special administrator privileges.

There are not many free software packages for Microsoft Windows installations that will sniff a network. Most software packages are protocol analyzers and cost quite a bit of money.

For Symbian platform devices, there is a package called "Net-Spy" that will sniff network packets. It is written in a combination of Java and C++, and allows users to write "plug-ins" into the application that will analyze network traffic.

Most snooping on communication is not preventable. Because any party can connect and listen to most media, and most of the time can do so undetected, security is typically not concentrated on physical media.

6.1.2 Data Issues

Physical issues deal with access to data; data issues deal with what to do with the data once you have it. Data issues focus on *understanding* data, *using* data, and then *manipulating* data.

Understanding the data obtained through snooping can be harder than you think. Let's say that you have successfully snooped a Web browsing session that includes someone accessing email through a Web server. What you actually have is a large amount of packet data—a direct recording of data frames wrapped in data frames as application layer data moves down a protocol stack to eventually go out over a physical medium. The prize data item you are looking for—say a username and password for the email service that was used—does not stand out for you to read. You must sort through the packet data to find it.

So there is a large sorting job in finding the right data. There are many applications that will help with this. These applications identify the protocol header of each layer in the data frames and can strip away that header to present the real data. Even at this point, however, getting the data you want is not straightforward. You still have to sort through a conversation between computers that may include protocol acknowledgements, raw HTML Web page data, error responses, and the like. There are also applications that will help with this kind of reconstruction, although there are not as many as there are protocol analyzers. This is especially true in younger transport media, like Bluetooth.

At this point, because the conversation between a Web browser and a Web server is not complicated, finding the username and password you seek can be done fairly easily once you understand the way HTTP works. However, other protocol conversations are much more difficult, especially if you do not know the applications involved in the conversations. Again, applications exist that will help you with this, or at least can be written for specific types of data exchanges.

There are two points here: that sifting through protocol exchanges to obtain data is very difficult, and that it is not impossible. On a computer, when a job is "very difficult", it just means that a program needs to be written to do that job, and that the program might take a while to write. When that program is written, however, the job is no longer very difficult. With computers, the fact that something is "not impossible" simply means "it can be done".

Using data once that data has been understood is certainly easy for the snooper and dangerous for the owner of that data. Once you have obtained a username and password from a Web email session, it is easy to engage the same Web service and use the newly acquired information.

The possibility that information could be manipulated presents an even more dangerous scenario for the data owner. Here, data is changed somehow and inserted back into the data stream to be reused. It is possible to affect the original data or to affect the outcome of using the data. Consider a situation where a device was downloading data while moving in a car. As that device roamed between service locations in its service area, its data stream could be interrupted and fed from different points. An intelligent attacker could feed a different data set from different service points, thereby giving the receiver incorrect data.

Protecting against data snooping and manipulation takes some innovation. As we have seen, it is almost impossible to stop snooping from occurring. So, instead, we can scramble the data so that it is unusable to anyone but the intended receiver. *Encryption techniques* encode data using a special key in such a way that only those possessing that key can decode the data and use it. And, since the key now becomes an important data item, we can select the key in ways that only the sender and receiver understand. To prevent manipulation, we can also use methods of verification. The most effective verification methods involve using credentials—special identifying information—that a sender has received from a server, ones that the receiver is expecting (from contacting the same server). Presenting credentials before sending data and forcing the receiver to verify those credentials makes it very tough to receive data from an unexpected source.

6.1.3   Remote Access Control

There are several other ways to lose control of a computing device. Almost by definition, establishing any kind of service gives control away. Servers that open up the serving device to remote access can potentially jeopardize its security.

It is the nature of servers to create this potential problem. Servers expect and invite connections from sources both inside and outside their computing environment. They are usually passive in accepting connections and do little to verify the sender. Once a connection is made, a server will typically accept any data that is sent and process that data immediately to provide a response. By definition, servers do this as quickly and efficiently as possible.

The problem that creates security holes is the level of trust that must be established between the server and the client. There is a certain balancing act that happens here. If the server is going to be fast and efficient, then it will try to trust the client more. If the server does not trust the client, then service will be slower as the server employs encryption, verifies credentials, or examines data before responding to the client. Most servers either ignore trust issues altogether, because their service is too simple to worry about trust issues, or try to strike a compromise between trust and efficiency by assuming a kind of middle level of trust that can be verified easily.

There are more servers on a computing device than you might suspect at first glance. Any time a device is open to receive data, there is a kind of server running that will accept and respond to that data. For example, consider the following situations:

- A *Web server* is always waiting for requests to come in, and collects any data traffic over the port it is listening to. If that data does not make sense, it responds with an error message. However, note that any data can be sent through the listening port.

- A *WAP browser* is open to data between the time it requests pages from a server and the time those pages arrive. Between these two points, it will accept and analyze data.

- As two devices exchange data *using infrared*, each side accepts a data stream for a certain length of time. As we saw in Chapter 4, each side transmits for 500 ms at a time, then stops and listens for data from the other side.

- A *Bluetooth device* in discovery mode makes broadcast requests and waits for responses.

- Any *user program* can use the data ports on a device to send and receive information.

In each of these situations, there was an application of some sort waiting to receive data of a certain form. Notice the level of trust across these situations can vary widely. A Web server will typically accept any request from any source but only process requests that make sense. A WAP browser is conversing with a server through a built-in layer that encrypts the conversation by default. The user program that is sending and receiving data has probably ignored all security issues to concentrate on getting the data exchange right, assuming that security is a feature to be added later.

We can prevent remote access problems by not making assumptions. When we assume that data will be in the right form or that a request cannot come from a malicious source, we expose our naiveté and invite security problems. By assuming that all data is not correct or that all connections might not be error-free, we will increase processing time but are wiser in our approach to outside connections. The penalty here is not so severe; the Symbian platform has several security measures built into it that are efficient and fast to use.

6.1.4 Threats to Symbian OS Devices

We just outlined three areas of security vulnerability: physical issues, data issues, and access issues. Let's consider how these issues impact Symbian OS devices.

Physical issues are important, but device users can do little about them. As we stated previously, snooping on all the various types of media is extremely easy. Mobile telephony signals and wired Ethernet traffic is easy to listen to if you have the right equipment. Since we have no choice as to the medium that is used to transmit data, physical issues are out of most device users' hands.

Data issues are extremely important. Because snooping is so easy, we must assume that any data exchanged between two devices is vulnerable. Considering the kind of data that might be exchanged—anything from personal to electronic commerce information—data encryption is necessary for any transaction.

Because data issues are so important, access issues are important as well. It is unlikely that an attacker will "break into" a Symbian OS device. However, control over which external devices can request information from a local device is important. Control over the exposure of data from your local device is also extremely important. For example, the services offered from a Bluetooth device can expose it to probes and access from other devices without warning.

6.2   Security Measures

6.2.1   Authentication

One way that is often used as verification of identity—most often for remote access—is authentication. Authentication is what happens when a computer or user identifies itself and another computer verifies the identification. Although it is not completely secure, this means of security has the longest history and is still widely used.

There are two types of information needed from the initiator of the authentication process:

- *Identification:* The initiator—computer or human, but most often human—must provide some form of identification. This can be in the form of a username, a real name or even an identification number. The key here is that this piece of information uniquely identifies the initiator.
- *Private information:* This is information known only to the initiator and the computer verifying the authentication attempt. This is typically a password, but it can be one of a number of things. More recently, items like challenge-response information (where the computer prints a random number, and the initiator responds to that number in a unique way) or biometric data (some measure based on the pattern of your fingerprint or blood vessel organization in your retina) have been used.

The idea is that together these data items can uniquely identify the initiator of the authentication. Once these information items are entered correctly, the initiator gains access to the required resource. Typically, authentication is used to gain access to remote shell-based or network services.

There are two large holes when we use authentication as a security scheme. They are (1) that the identification information cannot be verified and (2) that the private information can usually be derived or deduced. The basic problem is that authentication is designed to be used by humans. People cannot easily memorize long strings of random letters for user names or strings of random numbers for passwords. This means that identifying information is usually mnemonic, like a last name ("jipping", for instance) or some mutation of a name of the user ("thejipster", for example). Programs written using rules to guess identification can guess many forms of identifying information. In addition, private information is also easily guessed by using rules that people use to remember such things. A spouse's name or a boyfriend's birthdate are easy to remember but make very poor passwords.

Authentication schemes are used in many places. POP3 and IMAP4 mailboxes are protected with authentication systems; most entry via remote access to execution shell services is "guarded" by authentication systems. Use of PPP to access networks is based on authentication. Typically, the systems "protected" by authentication are legacy systems; newer access methods usually employ encryption or some kind of challenge-response system.

Choosing the Right Password

Choosing the right password is essential for good authentication protection. Unfortunately, the process runs counter to the schemes people use to remember such things. You should not choose passwords that could be feasibly listed in a dictionary. Permutations such as spelling a word or account name backwards, concatenating one or more words together, and prefixing or suffixing dictionary words with letters or digits are also bad choices for passwords. These are among the first permutations a dedicated attacker will check.

Characteristics of good passwords include sufficient length, complexity and obscurity. Use passwords that are at least 8 characters in length, contain random (as near to random as you can remember) combinations of letters and digits, use both upper and lowercase characters, and do not designate something that is real or can be guessed. Choosing a password that can be typed quickly, so somebody cannot follow what you type by looking over your shoulder, is an asset.

Assess yourself on how you have chosen passwords for your accounts. Do you use easily remembered (or guessed) passwords? Do you use the same password on several different accounts?

When one device masquerades as another device, we call this *spoofing*. For example, firewalls on the Internet can be set up to receive data from specific IP addresses. People use this to restrict the computers that can access their data. It is possible for some computers to change their IP addresses to match those the firewalls will allow through, thereby seeing data they would otherwise not have access to. Or again, when you are engaging another person in an instant message session between Bluetooth devices, it is possible for another device to take over the session by masquerading as one of the conversing devices. (Note that I used the word "possible". It can be quite difficult to choose the device identification to accurately spoof another machine, especially when using Bluetooth.)

6.2.2   Security Attacks and Denial of Service

There are different threats to security other than those based on data. These threats typically combine some of the methods discussed above to actively attack computing systems or devices, or to deny some kind of service to devices. While these threats have been designed for larger computer systems in the past, they are being retooled for small devices and can be very insidious.

A device *attacks* another device when it tries to break through its security protection. Because the attacks are typically programmed and are done from one computer to another, they can go on endlessly until security is breached or the user that started the attack gets bored and stops it from happening. There are several types of attacks relevant to small devices:

- *Attacks on authentication:* Often called a "dictionary attack" or "password attack", these assaults make repeated attempts to break through authentication barriers by guessing the identification or private information, interpreting the responses, and trying again with a new guess.

- *Attacks on services:* These types of attacks target known bugs in the implementations of services. The idea is to either crash the service or to put the implementation into some kind of error mode that gives access to other system functions (like shell access). This is usually done by accessing "boundary conditions": overloading internal buffers or using untested commands.

On a small device, a crash can be lethal, bringing the device down to an inoperable state and potentially losing valuable data.

- *Attacks on protocols:* Again, these attacks focus on bugs in protocol implementations. The idea here is to force the device into a state that will accept (and execute) any command or simply freeze the machine.

One dangerous type of attack stands out from the above list: the *denial of service attack* (DoS). A DoS attack is not an attack on security; it does not try to break in to a system. Rather, a DoS attack tries to keep a device so busy that it cannot service requests from or make requests to other devices. There are several ways to keep a processor busy. Logins from nonsensical users that require lookups and responses, repeated rapid queries from networks that require responses and constant requests for the same Web page that require the same page sent over and over again are all good examples of DoS attacks. Not only is the processor on the attacked device kept busy, but the network pathway used to access that processor is kept full of these nonsensical queries, allowing no room for other data packets.

Distributed denial of service attacks (DDoS) are even more malicious. For DDoS attacks, multiple devices throughout a network stage an attack on a device. Usually, this distributed attack is orchestrated by a single attacker that channels network traffic through distributed points over a network, often without them knowing. DDoS attacks have been used over the Internet with a large degree of "success" (if you can call it that); DDoS attacks have brought down service to the Web sites of large companies by literally using thousands of computers to make millions of Web page queries, thereby shutting out actual users with real data requests.

Dissecting a Smurf

A Smurf attack is DDoS attack that combines a knowledge of Internet protocols with spoofing. At the IP layer, a "ping" is a query packet (called an ICMP packet) that asks some simple information of the receiver—normally as simple as "are you there". As a response, the receiver replies to the sender identified in the IP headers. A Smurf attacks puts a different address in the sender field than the real sender, then sends off the ICMP packet.

The result is that the receiver replies to an address that is *not* the sender's address. By using this technique, an attacker can send thousands of packets to the same final destination through many different sources, and the data storm that results looks like

There is very little a computer can do by itself to thwart DoS attacks. The best way to stop these attacks is to stop the attack at the source. Think of the DoS attacks as water through a hose. If you are getting squirted in the face with a steady stream of water from a hose, holding your hands in front of your face will succeed in keeping your face drier, but the rest of your body will still get wet. Finding the spigot and turning off the faucet is the best way to stop the flow. However, finding the source of a DoS attack can be very difficult, especially when that attack is from a distributed set of sources. Often the best you can do is to clamp off the hose at the squirting end—to cut off the data flow as it enters your network. This often requires you to work with your communication service provider to cut off the data flowing into your network.

Note that for a mobile Symbian OS device, DoS and DDoS attacks become less of a threat. The wireless nature of a mobile device means that attackers need to be close to the device to snoop its communication data and discover information they can use to attack it. Also, since such a device is unlikely to be a server, attacking it with a torrent of service requests will do no good. Consider, for example, a phone handset using GSM to download WAP pages. An attacker must be in the vicinity of the GSM conversation to snoop it and must use GSM if it is to jam the device with too much data. About the only thing an attacker could do is call the device many times, which would be quite expensive.

6.3 Securing Transport Technologies

Now that we know the pitfalls, what can be done to secure communication, especially the technologies supported by the Symbian platform? Several steps can be taken at the transport level.

First, we must concentrate efforts where the payoff is greatest. This means *not* working to secure physical transmission. While some level of monitoring will be able to tell if snooping is being done on some level, it is generally not worth the effort spent, because snooping cannot be prevented. As we have stated, the nature of our communication media makes snooping possible and makes preventing it nearly impossible.

Therefore, we should focus on protecting data. Most importantly, we should use encryption wherever possible. For transport technologies, the only protocol stack that has this built-in is the WAP stack. The WTLS layer provides secure encryption and decryption as it moves data between the WTP and WDP layers (see Figure 4.5).

There is little security built into the rest of the transport technologies. There is very little to be done here, since these are standards set up by consortia and committees. One thing we can do is to secure authentication. Authentication is used in several technologies (e.g., PPP) and choosing a good password will help a lot in securing these.

6.4   Securing Content Technologies

Content technologies are implementations more under a user's control, but implementations of standard protocols—such as HTTP or SMTP—are designed by standards committees and computer companies and are outside a user's influence. There is little in the way of security protection in the standard content protocols.

One implementation that stands out as an example of this is Secure HTTP (SHTTP), which is used for certain Web pages with special Web servers. These pages are referenced by a URL with a prefix of shttp:. SHTTP passes all pages through an encryption layer before sending the page's requests to or reading the result from the destination Web server. In addition, the Web server must also implement SHTTP to work with the encryption process used.

SHTTP is a protocol specifically designed for HTTP transport. More generic solutions would help *all* transport and application protocols. A new layer has been proposed for the TCP/IP stack that would implement a generic encryption strategy for transport. The Transport Layer Security (TLS) layer has been proposed to go between TCP and IP in the TCP/IP stack. This would protect all transport data without the need for special protocols. However, TLS is not an adopted standard for TCP/IP. It has been implemented by third parties for the Symbian platform, but does not come as a built-in Symbian platform implementation.

Another example is a system called Pretty Good Privacy (PGP). PGP allows email data to be encrypted before it is sent and allows the decryption of PGP data when it arrives on a device. Because the standard TCP/IP stack provides no encryption in its layers, PGP is positioned as an extra application step between TCP and a POP3 email client.

The Symbian platform does include implementations of encryption standards, built into library interfaces for user applications. As you design your applications, and want to protect application data, you must remember that you need to implement your own methods of protection. We will cover how to apply the Symbian implementations for data in Chapter 10.

6.5 Summary

In this chapter, we have reviewed issues that surround the security of data communication between devices. We reviewed issues about physically snooping on communication media and data issues about dealing with the data picked up when we snoop. We also examined issues that surround remote access to devices. We looked at authentication issues and did a brief overview of spoofing and service attack methods. We wrapped up the chapter by discussing ways to secure both transport and content media.

This chapter concludes the first section of this book, dedicated to examining the basics of communication on Symbian devices. The next chapter, Chapter 7, kicks off the section that serves as the meat of this book—how to write applications that use the communication infrastructure of the Symbian platform.

Section 2

Programming using Symbian OS Communication

7

Getting Started with Communications Programming

This chapter introduces the section that is at the heart of this book: communications software development for Symbian OS. We have covered a lot of conceptual ground to this point. Now it is time to get to work and get your hands dirty.

To develop software you need a set of tools to write, compile, and debug programs—an "environment" for writing software. The software development environment that is used to develop for Symbian OS is a collection of tools: a combination of compilers, libraries, code generators, and emulators from several vendors. This chapter will overview what you need, where to get it, and how to use it. We will start by looking at the software development process and each tool in the Symbian software development toolbox. Then we will focus on the emulators, and how they can be used. We will finish the chapter by looking at how the development environments relate to real hardware—how the emulators use peripherals to target real devices. As we overview the toolsets we need, remember that my intention is not to give a full tutorial in using the Symbian OS development environment; it is, rather, to give an overview with some attention to certain areas that we will be using later.

As we get started, we should establish what environments are available. Symbian releases software development kits (SDKs) in various forms targeted at specific reference designs. Starting with EPOC Release 5, SDKs are distributed free of charge from Symbian's software developer support Web site. As of the writing of this book, the following SDKs are available:

- *EPOC Release 5:* You can get SDKs to develop for EPOC Release 5(ER5). These kits are released for the C++, Java, and OPL languages.

- *EPOC Release 5 Connectivity:* An SDK is also available for those who wish to develop software that uses PLP to communicate with a PC.
- *Symbian OS v6.1 for the Quartz reference design:* The current SDK is for version 6.1 of Symbian OS, using the C++ and Java languages. This SDK is available on the Symbian DevNet site for the Quartz reference design (see below).
- *Symbian OS v6.1 Connectivity:* This SDK assists developers writing software to integrate Symbian devices with PCs via PLP.

Note the representation of reference designs in the SDKs above. EPOC Release 5 did not make distinctions for various reference designs, and therefore there is only one release of the SDK. For the current Symbian platform, only Quartz reference design releases of the SDK are available through Symbian DevNet. SDKs for other reference designs are available from licensees that are manufacturing them. At the time of writing, Nokia has produced two reference design SDKs: one for a Crystal reference design (embodied by the 9210 communicator) and one for its Series 60 reference design (as seen in the 7650 phone).

Where To Get SDKs

The Web site for this book has links to the sites on the Internet where you can obtain the SDKs. You should check out the Symbian DevNet site for SDK patches and updates. In addition, licensees such as Nokia (see *http://forum.nokia.com* for SDKs for Crystal and Series 60 reference designs) have SDKs for their products.

Since the only SDKs available from Symbian are for Quartz, the software examples in this book will be given for Quartz using the SDK available from the Symbian DevNet site. However, since other SDKs we have mentioned are based on Symbian OS version 6.x, most of the functionality will translate to the other SDKs you can get. (N.B. Some will not: Bluetooth support was not complete in the version 6.0 SDK, for example.)

7.1 The Symbian Software Development Environment

Software for Symbian OS is developed using a combination of Symbian tools and libraries, Microsoft development tools, and compilers from the Free Software Foundation. There are essentially two targets for software development: the emulated machines and the real hardware. The Microsoft development tools provide an environment for editing, compiling, and debugging for the emulated devices through its Visual C++ product. Compilation for real hardware is done through the GNU C++ compiler from the Free Software Foundation. Symbian tools and libraries work for both these environments.

The software development process starts with a problem that needs to be solved. Good software design attacks this problem by specifying a solution with good old-fashioned pencil and paper. A written problem statement combined with a written specification of a software design is the best way to end up with a good application. This written design is then used to write algorithms (in some pseudocode language, perhaps English) that will implement the solution statement.

Once all of this design has taken place, a computer program can be developed to implement the algorithms. Figure 7.1 encapsulates the development pathways into a small diagram.

Development begins with the programmer expressing the algorithms in C++. C++ works best when its object-oriented properties are emphasized (over its C origins) and an application's source is expressed as a collection of classes or modules. Each class has a specification and an implementation, usually given in .h and .cpp files. So before we start putting the application together, we can have a large number of source code files.

While the source code is the heart of an application, there are also many specification files involved along the way to a final, released application. They fall into some rough categories:

- *Project files:* Because there can be so many files involved in the construction process, project files are needed to direct the construction. Project files begin with an MMP file: the "makmake" project file. The makmake command takes an MMP file and turns it into a project file for the system that you will be using to construct your application. This might be a Visual C++ project file (a .dsw file) or a "makefile" for a build process using either the Visual C++ (cl.exe) or GNU (gcc) compilers. In version 6.1 of the Quartz SDK, for example, makmake can generate project files for 22 different platforms. Even with this variety, the most common are project files for Visual C++ and makefiles for the GNU compiler to construct ARM binaries.

- *Resource files:* To make applications more modular and adaptable, the Symbian SDKs support the use of resource files. These files contain objects—like test strings and GUI widgets—that

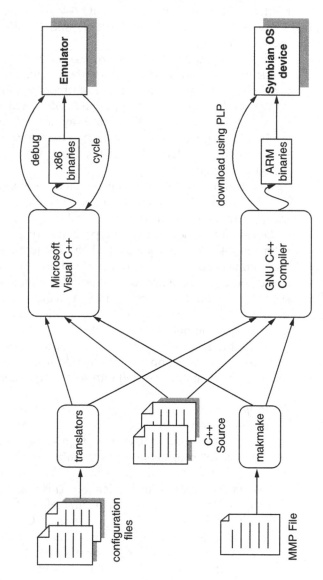

Figure 7.1 The Symbian software development path.

can change while the application's core remains constant. For example, strings used as an application's title could be represented in different languages and contained in separate resource files to localize an application for different countries. This would allow different resource files to accompany one central application executable to customize it. Menus, toolbars, buttons, hot key shortcut combinations are all examples of the type of item that would naturally be placed in a resource file. Resource files (using the .rss suffix) are translated into files used by the compilation process (such as the .rsg files that contain definitions for use in C++ code).

- *Help system files:* Help files used by applications that run under older versions of EPOC have been rather difficult to construct. They are in a database format, which has been specially designed for the help system. In version 6.1 of the SDKs, a new system is available to construct help files. Written in Java, it is a tool where help database files can be constructed, then attached to applications. If an application uses these help files, they must accompany the application for installation.

- *Package construction files:* The final deliverable product will likely be composed of several files—the application itself and libraries or configuration files. To enable easy installation of the files that an application requires, a tool called makesis is used to package them into a SIS file. makesis needs to be told how to create this installation package file, and a .pkg configuration file must be created to enable makesis to construct the package. In version 6.1 of the Symbian SDKs, a new tool called sisar presents a GUI to allow interactive construction of a package file.

At the end of this path is a set of executable binaries that can run on one of many platforms. As an example, the x86 versions that are built for the emulator are constructed either in the Visual C++ IDE or at the command line via the Visual C++ nmake command. As another example, the ARM binaries for target machines use the nmake command to drive the GNU compiler.

7.2 Hello World! A Simple Example

Let's illustrate this process with a simple example. It would be wrong to start off a book on programming without a "Hello World!" example, and the Quartz 6.1 SDK distribution contains several. Let's examine one and see how it is put together.

After installing the Quartz SDK, you will find a collection of files under the directory `Quartz\Epoc32Ex\quartzui\Hello-World`. When they are all put together and the application is running, the emulator will display the simple message shown in Figure 7.2.

Figure 7.2   The Hello World! example.

7.2.1   The C++ Source Code

To start with, this directory contains source code for the `helloworld` example. There are four C++ modules and one `.h` file that specifies the interface specification for all of the C++ classes.

7.2.2   The MMP Project File

The MMP project file is called `helloworld.mmp`. The contents of this file are shown below.

```
// HelloWorld.mmp
//
// Copyright (c) 2000 Symbian Ltd. All rights reserved.
//

// using relative paths for sourcepath and user includes
TARGET          HelloWorld.app
```

```
TARGETTYPE        app
UID               0x100039CE 0x10008ACE
TARGETPATH        \system\apps\HelloWorld
SOURCEPATH        .
SOURCE            HelloWorld_Main.cpp
SOURCE            HelloWorld_Application.cpp
SOURCE            HelloWorld_Document.cpp
SOURCE            HelloWorld_AppUi.cpp
SOURCE            HelloWorld_AppView.cpp
USERINCLUDE       .
SYSTEMINCLUDE     \epoc32\include
RESOURCE          HelloWorld.rss
LIBRARY           euser.lib apparc.lib cone.lib eikcore.lib
```

The information in this file is given in key/value pairs, and is enough
to generate the project files for the compilation systems we need.

- The end result is given by the TARGET and TARGETTYPE
  parameters. We are constructing an application (an app target
  type) and its name will be HelloWorld.app. 16 different target
  types are supported, the most common being for applications,
  DLLs, and console-style executables.

- The UID for this application is given as 0x10008ace in hexadecimal (268470990 in decimal; both representations work).
  A UID is a 32-bit number that uniquely identifies an application to Symbian OS. Three identifiers are needed: the first to
  identify the *type* of the application (DLL, executable, or file
  store; in our example, 0x100039ce represents an executable
  application), the second to identify the application itself (this
  identifier must be unique), and the third to identify components
  that work together within a single application. In this case, we
  have only one executable component and therefore can ignore
  the third UID.

- The paths for the target compiled applications and the source
  code are given by the TARGETPATH and SOURCEPATH specifiers, respectively. (Note for programmers who have used ER5:
  the source path can now be anywhere in the file system. In ER5
  and earlier SDKs, the source path had to be exactly two levels
  deep.)

- The source C++ files are listed with the SOURCE tags. There are
  multiple source files, given with multiple tags.

- The paths to include files are listed, both for system include
  files and user include files (typically .h files). The SYSTEM-
  INCLUDE and USERINCLUDE tags specify these, respectively.
  Note that individual .h files are not listed. These are derived
  from analyzing the source C++ files.

- The resource file used for this application is given by the RESOURCE tag.

- The system libraries that are needed to compile the code in this project are given by the LIBRARY tag.

Obtaining Unique UID Numbers

UID numbers for applications must be unique—that is, unique *across all applications that are written for Symbian OS*. During development, you can use certain development UIDs reserved for software development. These UIDs are in the range 0x01000000 through 0x0fffffff. However, when you prepare software for distribution, it must have a unique non-development UID. To obtain one, send an email to the address uid@symbian.com, and title the message "UID request". State the number of UIDs you require and give your name with your return email address. Symbian will then allocate your UIDs and send them to you via email.

7.2.3 Building Configuration Files

Once we have an MMP project file, the next step is to construct a bld.inf file. This is used by system programs to indicate how many different project files there are. For the helloworld example, this file looks like this:

```
// BLD.INF
//
// Copyright (c) 2000 Symbian Ltd. All rights reserved.
//

PRJ_MMPFILES

HelloWorld.mmp
```

Most bld.inf files can have this simple format. In it, we are specifying that there is a single MMP file, and its name is HelloWorld.mmp. We can now generate the project files and make files using the bldmake command:

```
bldmake bldfiles
```

This will generate some further configuration files and a batch file called abld.bat. This batch file can be used to build a project or create a makefile. The following command line will build an application for the emulator:

```
abld build wins
```

We can also use this batch file to generate construction files. Typing the command

```
abld makefile vc6 wins
```

will generate a project file for Visual C++ and a makefile for GNU C++. These files will be stored as

```
\Symbian\6.1\quartz\epoc32\build\MMP_path\project_name\wins.
```

The `makmake` command can be used to generate the project files in the local directory. It uses Perl to analyze the files specified in the MMP file and generate the individual project files. For our purposes, to use Visual C++, you should invoke the command as follows:

```
makmake helloworld vc6
```

This generates a project file for Visual C++ version 6, dumped into a file called `helloworld.dsw`. (N.B. You must be in the source code directory when executing this command.)

By executing the command

```
makmake helloworld wins
```

you will get a makefile generated in the file `helloworld.wins`. This can be used from the command line to make the example application.

7.2.4 Building the Application using Visual C++

Now let's build the application. We will first do this in Visual C++. Once Visual C++ is started, you should use the **File > Open Workspace...** menu selection and navigate to the `helloworld.dsw` file. Select this file, and the application and configuration files will be read by Visual C++. You should explore the class and file view panes. Notice that we can edit the configuration files we mentioned above right from the IDE.

The build process is started by selecting **Build > Build HELLOWORLD.APP**, or by pressing *F7*. The output from the build sequence will be shown in the build output window, and is not terribly useful, except to scan for errors when they occur. All errors (compile errors and loading/linking errors) will show up in that output. Take a moment to glance over the output and be grateful you do not have to type those commands for each compilation.

Your application can then be executed by choosing either **Build > Execute** or **Build > Start Debug > Go**. Choose the latter if you want to debug the application. Visual C++ must first launch the emulator and will therefore ask you for the "Executable for Debug Session" through a dialog box. You should specify the Quartz emulator executable (a typical location is \Symbian\6.1\epoc32\release\wins\udeb\Epoc.exe), then click OK. The emulator will launch, and you will find the HelloWorld icon on the emulator's display. Click on this icon to launch the HelloWorld application.

7.2.5 Building the Application using the Command Line

Using Visual C++ to build and run applications is convenient when you want to use an IDE. However, there are many times when the command line is quicker and easier to use. As you have already created the command line makefile, building from the command line can be done in one command:

```
nmake -f helloworld.wins
```

Running the above command will produce a series of long command invocations, mostly of the Visual C++ compiler (cl.exe). Perl is used to convert the resource file, and the Visual C++ linker is used to put together the final application for the emulator to run. The end result will be the same as using the Visual C++ environment.

To launch the application from the command line, you need to type the name of the emulator executable (\Symbian\6.1\ epoc32\release\wins\udeb\Epoc.exe). This will launch the emulator and you can select the application within that environment.

7.2.6 Building the Application for a Target Machine

To build the application for a real target machine, you must choose an architecture to compile for, out of the 22 possible. A typical processor is the ARM processor; this can be given to makmake as below:

```
makmake helloworld arm4
```

This creates a makefile called `helloworld.arm4`, which can be used to make the application as follows:

```
nmake -f helloworld.arm4
```

Executing this command at the command line gives a tremendous amount of output, and, if all goes well, generates a compiled application in `\Symbian\6.1\Quartz\Epoc32\Release\urel\ helloworld.app`.

At this point, delivery to a target machine requires the application, any libraries that the application uses, and any configuration files that assist the application. These all need to be placed in various places on the target machine's file system, and the SIS packaging system will help do this. Designing a `.pkg` file that directs where certain files go on the target machine, then packaging everything up with the `makesis` command, will produce a SIS file ready for installation.

7.3 Using the Emulators

7.3.1 Getting Started

The emulator for the Quartz reference design is distributed with the SDK for version 6.1 from Symbian. This emulator is fundamental in developing software for Symbian OS, so getting familiar with it is extremely important. The emulator comes in two variants: a release version and a debug version. The release version is faster and leaner, and suitable for running applications without debugging them. The debug version contains debug information useful to tools such as Visual C++, where it can be used for stepping though code, and testing various functions of the environment to check things like resource usage, memory leaks, and graphics manipulation.

You can start the emulator in two ways:

- Using the Windows "Start" button, you can burrow your way through menus to start it: **Start > Programs > Symbian 6.1 SDKs > Quartz > Emulator (debug)**. This will start the debug version of the emulator.

- You can execute the emulator program directly, either through the Windows Explorer or through command line invocation. The location on a default Symbian OS SDK installation is `\Symbian\6.1\Quartz\Epoc32\Release\wins\udeb\Epoc.exe`.

Figure 7.2 shows an example of the emulator in operation. It works like a generic Symbian OS Quartz device. Symbian OS licensees are allowed to customize the design and to change certain features of the operation to create versions of the SDK which are closer to their product's look and feel.

For design and testing purposes, the function keys have special significance to the emulator. The table below itemizes what they are used for:

Table 7.1   Function keys in the emulator

F1	Works with the application's menu system: starting menus or expanding menu items.
Alt F2	Simulates a "Help" key or function. Can be used for context-sensitive help on applications.
F4	Simulates switching removable media. Removable media are emulated by files in the host PC's directory structure. On the emulator, they can be referenced by the Y: drive designation.
F5	Simulates the opening and closing of the removable media door.
F8	Simulates a "record" button, starting and stopping a record operation.
F9	Simulates a "power on" condition, as if the "On" key were pressed.
F10	Simulates a "power off" condition, as if the "Off" key were pressed.
F11	Simulates the device's case being closed and opened.

Drives and their designations are important on the emulator. The default installation comes with a `C:`drive and a `Z:`drive. On a real Symbian OS device, the `C:` drive designates the memory-based default file system; this drive is emulated as part of the host PC's file system (`\Symbian\6.1\Quartz\Epoc32\wins\c` on a default installation). Likewise, on a Symbian OS device, the `Z:` drive designates the ROM file system, but is emulated as `\Symbian\6.1\Quartz\Epoc32\release\wins\udeb\z` on a default installation. Other device drive emulations may be set up; they are represented on the host PC as files. They can represent regular storage or components like removable media.

7.3.2 Using the Emulator with Communication Devices

The emulator is an extremely useful tool for developing software. However, it is itself software by design—*emulating* hardware while not actually composed of hardware. When we develop communication software, we need to access communication devices. Since these are likely to be external devices not under Symbian's control, they will more than likely be actual hardware devices that need to be connected to the emulator.

So the emulator builds a bridge between software emulation and hardware peripherals. The default installation contains the following hardware connections:

- *Serial ports* for the emulator are connected to the host PC's serial ports. COMM::0 on the emulator is connected to COM1 on the PC; COMM::1 on the emulator is connected to COM2 on the PC.

- The *IR port* on the emulator must be an added device. Infrared port peripheral devices—such as a JetEye 7401 or an Extended Systems 9680B—can be connected to a serial port and can act as an IR port for a PC. Upon startup, the emulator will look for such a device, and will use it as the IR port for the Quartz emulator. The default port the emulator looks at is COM2.

- For *Bluetooth* functionality, the emulator looks for an Ericsson Bluetooth MiniKit (EBMK) connected to a serial port. By default, it looks on COM1 for the EBMK. If it finds a Bluetooth card there, the emulator assumes it has Bluetooth functionality and uses the EBMK to send and receive Bluetooth packets.

- *GSM access* is enabled by the emulator if it detects a GSM phone connected through an infrared port device on a serial port. The phone must be IR enabled (naturally) with the IR port activated. Once this arrangement is detected, the emulator will send and receive SMS messages directly through the phone.

Some of these configurations are customizable through configuration files. Specifically, the port used to detect the devices can be changed. Look in \Symbian\6.1\Quartz\Epoc32\wins\c\system\data for ESK files: irda_wins.esk to configure the IR-to-COM port map and bt.esk to configure the port for the EBMK.

Note that you cannot use a serial port to emulate more than one component. For example, you cannot expect to use the emulator's COMM::0 and a Bluetooth EBMK on the host PC's COM1. You must plan for device usage and specify which ports will be used through the esk files.

7.4   Introducing TodoX: A More Extensive Example

In the next several chapters, we will be using an example called TodoX. This is a simple example of how to exchange to-do list items between two devices. We will begin in the next chapter by using serial communications to exchange to-do list items and will enhance the example to handle new communications technologies as we introduce them from chapter to chapter. This section will include an illustration of how to install and run this software.

7.4.1   Building and Running the Application

As the first step, you must retrieve a copy of the software source from the Web site for this book. Access the URL ***http://www. symbian.com/books/socp/socp-support.html***. Navigate to the section on supporting software and download the file todox.zip. Follow the instructions on the Web site to unzip this archive and get the source files on your computer's disk storage.

Next, find the directory in which you stored the source files. Locate and examine the bld.inf file. This file is just as simple as in the HelloWorld example; it references the todox.mmp file as a project file.

Locate and examine the MMP file, shown below:

```
TARGET          TodoX.app
TARGETTYPE      app
UID             0x100039CE 0x101F3DCF
TARGETPATH      \system\apps\TodoX

SOURCE          TodoX.cpp TodoXdialogs.cpp
SOURCE          TodoXferBase.cpp
SOURCE          TodoXferSerial.cpp TodoXferSerialAO.cpp
SOURCE          TodoXferIRSerial.cpp TodoXferIRSocket.cpp
SOURCE          TodoXferBt.cpp
```

```
SOURCE          TodoXferEmail.cpp
SOURCE          AgendaFileReader.cpp

RESOURCE        TodoX.rss

USERINCLUDE     .
SYSTEMINCLUDE   \epoc32\include
LIBRARY         euser.lib efsrv.lib estor.lib etext.lib
LIBRARY         cone.lib apparc.lib
LIBRARY         eikcore.lib qikctl.lib eikcoctl.lib eikdlg.lib
LIBRARY         bafl.lib c32.lib
LIBRARY         agnmodel.lib agndasvr.lib agnapi.lib agnsynca.lib
LIBRARY         esock.lib irda.lib
LIBRARY         bluetooth.lib btmanclient.lib
LIBRARY         send.lib
```

From this file, we can deduce several things about TodoX:

- It is an application (see the TARGETTYPE line) with a UID of 0x101F3DCF (I obtained this from Symbian for this project).

- The application and its supporting files are stored in the standard location of \system\apps\TodoX (the TARGETPATH line).

- There a large number of source files and quite a few more libraries that are needed (when compared to the HelloWorld example).

- There is a resource file (TodoX.rss) that supports the application.

The easiest way to build this application is to use the bldmake and abld command combination. Start by generating the construction files using the bldmake command in the directory to which you unzipped the source files, as below:

```
bldmake bldfiles
```

This should return to the command prompt with no output. However, the construction files should now be built, and you can build the application by giving the command below:

```
abld build wins
```

You should see much output as the application is compiled and installed.

Now, by running the Quartz emulator, you should see the TodoX icon (a generic one, with a small diamond shape on it). Click on this icon with the mouse and you should start the application. An example of how this might look is in Figure 7.3.

Figure 7.3 Running the TodoX example application.

7.4.2 Exchanging To-do List Items

The application displays a list of to-do list items that you have entered using the "To do" application. To start an exchange of items between computers, you need two PCs running the application. Follow these steps:

- Make sure the computers are connected. For a serial connection, connect the COM1 ports with a null modem cable.

- From the TodoX application on both PCs, click on the Mode menu from the menu bar and select the Serial choice (it is likely to be already selected).

- On the receiving computer, click on the Receive menu choice on the application's menu bar.

- On the sending computer, click on one of the to-do items in the list.

At this point, you should see some messages print on the blue status area on the bottom of the display screen. And you should see a new to-do list item listed on the receiving computer's application. Congratulations!

7.4.3 Editing the Source Files

You should use Visual C++ to work with the source files. To generate a Visual C++ project file, execute the command below:

```
abld makefile vc6
```

After command has run, you should have a file called `TodoX.dsw` in the source directory. Use this file as the workspace file in Visual C++.

7.5 Summary

In this chapter, we have reviewed the tools and procedures used to develop software for Symbian OS, and compiled and executed our first application. We reviewed the emulator environment itself, which provides a solid platform for application testing, and the way that the emulator interfaces with various hardware components connected to the host PC.

The next chapter begins looking at real communications programming by analyzing software development for serial communication. It is perhaps the most familiar for programmers and will serve as a good way to start discussing communications programming.

8

Serial Communications

It is always good when learning new material to start with what you know. It is a safe bet that most computer users have had some exposure to serial communication. For example, if you have ever transferred data between a handheld computer and a PC, then you have probably used serial communication. If you have ever used a modem on a PC, you have used serial communication. Serial communication is perhaps the oldest and the most familiar of data transfer functions. It is a good place to start as we introduce communications programming requirements and interfaces.

We will examine this area in the following way. We will first examine the *patterns* that are involved in communications programming. Across all programming platforms, common patterns emerge and we will analyze them. We will then use these patterns to look at the serial API for Symbian OS. We will also examine active objects as a crucial part of communications programming. Along the way, we will work through some examples and we will begin to look at vCalendar objects.

8.1 Programming Patterns for Communications

There is a set of patterns that emerge from the way that we work with communications programming. There are two sets of patterns that are important for our purposes here: those that develop from a local Symbian device perspective and those that apply to data exchange.

8.1.1 The Local Perspective

On the local Symbian device, there is a pattern to the way that communication is set up and executed. Specifically, communication works through five phases:

- *Initialization:* We start communication on the local Symbian device by initializing the communication system. On a larger, desktop computer, this is not an issue—the drivers and communication components are typically loaded at boot time by the system. However, on a small handheld device, only those servers and drivers that are immediately needed are started. Therefore, the operating system must be prepared before communication starts. This means loading drivers and starting servers as needed.

- *Opening the communication device:* In Symbian OS, the communication device interface is designed much like a file interface. For example, bytes are transferred by read and write operations. Just as the operating system sets up tables and structures when a file is opened, it also sets up its own internal housekeeping when we open a device. In addition, the system checks for access issues and sets up any protection mechanisms that must be in place for the application to use the device.

- *Configuring the communication device:* Once a communication device is open and access is granted, we must configure it. This could be as simple as telling the device to use settings in the communications database or it could involve setting parameters through function calls. There are very few settings for Bluetooth devices, for instance, while there are several for IR ports (e.g., baud rate and parity).

- *Exchanging data:* Now we finally get to the point where real data can be exchanged. To exchange information with another device, we engage that device using a protocol of some sort. All protocols have initialization sequences that must be worked through, with a (possibly lengthy) data exchange sequence, and a termination sequence.

- *Closing the communication device:* As a last step, the device that was used for communication can be closed. This is a signal for the OS to reset the device interface and to free up the resources that were dedicated to maintaining the device's operation.

As a demonstration of these patterns, let's dig into the `TodoX` example that we introduced in Chapter 7. I am going to build this example gradually. Figure 8.1 shows a complete set of the communication classes and their derivation relationships. There are seven example classes and two base classes (`CActive` is a Symbian OS class we will describe later). In the next few chapters, we will demonstrate the exchange of to-do list items over the serial port (in

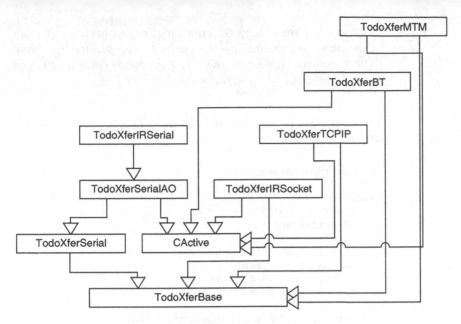

Figure 8.1 Diagram of the TodoX example communication classes.

two different ways), using serial IR, using TinyTP, with Bluetooth, and via email.

Coding for Examples

Beginning here and continuing throughout the rest of the book, you will find many code examples. These examples usually take the form of fragments of code—either real fragments grabbed from the middle of a definition or a complete function definition from a class. In all cases, the complete context of the fragment will be missing and only the minimal amount of code that is necessary is included.

For example, you will notice that class definitions will not include code from private sections or even protected sections. Since we cannot access these definitions, I will not include them.

The problem with this is that I have to make certain assumptions and take liberties with the code. For instance, you will notice that literal strings are expressed with the macro "`_L()`" when I should be using "`_LIT()`". Using the latter form, however, means including more context than I believe is relevant at the time. You will not find "`#include`" statements or macro definitions. I also will eliminate complete sections of irrelevant code by using comments to describe what that code actually did.

The base class header that defines most of this structure is given below:

```
class TodoXferBase
{
public:
  TodoXferBase();
  ~TodoXferBase();

  virtual TInt Init(TDesC&)=0;
  virtual TBool OpenL()=0;
  virtual void Configure()=0;
  virtual void Close()=0;

  virtual void SendItem(CAgnEntry *)=0;
  virtual void ReceiveItem()=0;
  virtual void SendItemVCal(CAgnEntry *)=0;
  virtual CAgnEntry* ReceiveItemVCal()=0;

protected:
  void Send(const TDes8 &aText);
  void Receive(TDes8 &aText);
};
```

Note first that the first four functions implement four of the five phases we discussed for device communication. The next two—SendItem() and ReceiveItem()—implement the data exchange protocol. We have two functions that send and receive vCalendar objects. Finally, the Send() and Receive() functions will be at the heart of the underlying implementation of how to send strings between devices.

The first thing that we have to do is to decide on a protocol for this exchange—but for this introduction, let's assume we have already decided that detail. Further, let's assume that our application has been started. We have selected a serial transfer mode (appropriate for this chapter) and when we tap on a line representing a to-do list item, transfer will begin.

- Initialization will include loading the physical and logical device drivers and starting the communication server, if necessary. In addition, we need to establish a connection with the communication server, and inform the server which communication module to load (recall CSY modules from Chapter 3).

- Opening the device is simple: one system call takes care of this step. We must make sure we field the return codes from the system call properly.

- For a serial port, there are several configuration parameters: baud rate, number of start and stop bits on the data frame, parity, and the handshake protocol. Each of these must be set before the to-do list item can be sent.

- Engaging in the protocol involves some initialization (to discover the remote device and to ensure it is ready), then the exchange of the item, then some signal for termination (basically a flag to announce that there are no more items coming).

- Finally, closing the device also means closing the connection to the communications server.

The remote device—receiver of the to-do list items—must go through a similar sequence of steps. The protocol is a bit different when receiving an item, but the rest of the steps are much the same. Consider the following code:

```
void CTodoXAppUi::SendItem(TInt aIndex)
{
    // Select the chosen entry from the Agenda items
    iReader->ReadEntryL(iEntryIDs[aIndex]);

    // Start comm. phases based on mode of transfer
    switch (iXferMode) {
      case ESerialMode:
          iXferPort->Init(_L("ECUART"));
          iXferPort->OpenL();
          iXferPort->Configure();
          break;

        // ... other cases ...
    }

    // Now we engage the protocol: send the to-do item!
    iXferPort->SendItem(iReader->iEntry);

        // close the device if necessary
        if (iXferMode == ESerialMode) iXferPort->Close();
}
```

We call this function from the AppUi class of the application once a list item has been tapped with the stylus. Notice that the sequence works out in the order we have described it above. The variable `iXferPort` points to different port implementations, but the pattern from initialization through device closing is the same. For example, if `iXferMode` has the value `EBtMode` (indicating Bluetooth data transfer), then iXferPort will still point to a device object (in this case, a `TodoXferBt` object, but subclassed from the same base class). We would use the same sequence of function calls as in the sequence above.

Receiving an item is basically the same:

```
void CTodoXAppUi::ReceiveItem()
{
    CAgnEntry *iEntry;

    // Start comm. phases based on mode of transfer
    switch (iXferMode) {
       case ESerialMode:
          iXferPort->Init(_L("ECUART"));
          iXferPort->OpenL();
          iXferPort->Configure();
          break;

       //... other cases ...
    }

    // Now we engage the protocol: receive the to-do item!
    iXferPort->ReceiveItem();

    // Close the port if necessary
    if (iXferMode == ESerialMode) iXferPort->Close();
}
```

8.1.2 Between Symbian Devices

Between two Symbian devices, there is also a pattern that develops in the protocol that controls the data exchange. There is always a protocol that is used, even when the function used to exchange data is made up by the programmer. Protocols are, by definition, the arrangements that both sides go through to get the data across. Whether it is a standard protocol or one that a programmer invents, a protocol is always used nonetheless.

Protocols typically have three phases:

- *Establishment:* The two sides must establish and initialize a connection before any data is exchanged. Each side will initialize data, allocate resources, and otherwise prepare for the exchange. In addition, each side works with the other to get to the right state with respect to the data exchange.

- *Data exchange:* This is the core of a protocol, the phase where real data flows between the two sides. Issues such as flow control and error checking are important here, as well as the format of the data and the methods used for exchange.

- *Termination:* In this phase, the protocol shuts down. In the best case, it does so gracefully, informing each side of the impending shutdown and allowing for error checking and the releasing of resources. In the worst case, timeout occurs and the protocol is aborted in whatever state it was in.

The protocol sequence in Figure 8.2 depicts the protocol for our to-do list item exchange example. It is admittedly simplistic, but it serves our purpose. The top tier is the establishment phase, where each side announces it is ready and the sender informs the receiver how many items are coming. The middle tier is the data exchange phase, where each item is sent in three parts: priority, due date, and item text. The bottom tier is the termination phase, where each side announces it is done, and they terminate the conversation. We will discuss this protocol later in more detail.

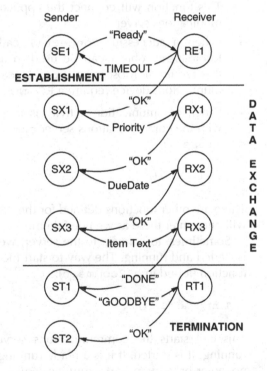

Figure 8.2 The protocol sequence for the to-do list item example.

It might not be easy to see the worth of these patterns now. They appear quite simple. As we progress through the Symbian OS communications architecture, we will see how these patterns appear again and again. Understanding them will greatly help in understanding how the communications architecture works.

8.2 The Communications Server

Using communications in Symbian OS begins with the communications server. The communications server functionality is implemented by the `RCommServ` class. The typical procedure to use a communication device is as follows:

1. Create an instance of the `RCommServ` class.

2. Connect to the communications server. Instances of the `RComm-Serv` class can access the connector function:

   ```
   TInt Connect();
   ```

   This function will connect the application to a running communications server.

3. When a successful `Connect()` call has been made, the `RCommServ` object can be used in all subsequent API calls that require it. Most initial `Open()` calls to start using a communications device require a `RCommServ` object.

4. When communication activity is completed, the connection with the communications server must be severed with a call to `Close()`:

   ```
   TInt Close();
   ```

There are other functions defined for the `RCommServ` class, but we will encounter these as we need them.

Sometimes, to connect to the server, we must make sure that it is started and running. The way to start the server is to use a utility function (found in `c32comms.h`):

```
TInt StartC32();
```

This call starts the communications server. If the server is not running, it is started. If it is already running, nothing happens. It is not an error to try to start a running server.

8.3 The Serial API

So, let's dig in and take a look at the serial communication API. As a guide, we will use the patterns we outlined in the previous section.

As an aside, note that there will be two versions of the serial code developed for the TodoX example. The one shown in this section demonstrates how to use the serial port without active objects. Later in this chapter, we will reexamine the example and rewrite the code to use active objects.

8.3.1 Initializing the System

Step 1: Load the drivers

There are several steps to initializing the serial interface. As a first step in the process, the drivers must be loaded. This means both the physical and the logical drivers. Two functions from the User class library apply here:

```
static TInt LoadPhysicalDevice(const TDesC& aFileName);
```

This call causes the OS to load the device driver for the physical device given as the argument to the function. Notice the parameter is a string, the name of the file containing the driver. The call returns a code to reflect the success or failure of the device loading.

```
static TInt LoadLogicalDevice(const TDesC &aFileName);
```

This call causes the OS to load the device driver for the logical device given as the argument to the function. Again, the parameter is a filename, and the call returns a code to reflect success or failure.

The name given for the driver file is assigned by Symbian and must be present in defined places in the file system. The code fragment below explains the name assignments

```
#if defined (__WINS__)
_LIT(PDD_NAME, "ECDRV");
_LIT(LDD_NAME, "ECOMM");
#else
_LIT(PDD_NAME, "EUART1");
_LIT(LDD_NAME, "ECOMM");
#endif
```

The definitions are different, depending on your environment. The symbol __WINS__ is automatically defined if you are compiling code for the emulator environment.

Note here that the filenames have no suffix; the OS automatically adds the suffix when needed (.PDD or .LDD). Also, the filenames are not specified with an absolute pathname; the system will search for the proper driver files (usually in \System\Libs on all drives present).

Step 2: Connect to the communication server

The next step is to connect to the communications server. We should start the server and connect to it as described in Section 8.2.

Step 3: Load the serial CSY module

To interface the communications server with the hardware, we must load the appropriate CSY module. In the serial case, this is the ECUART module, and loading is straightforward. Again, we use an RCommServ instance to call

```
TInt LoadCommModule(const TDesC &aFileName);
```

This call again uses a string filename and causes the communications server to load the CSY module specified. As with loading drivers, the system will automatically append the suffix (.CSY) and will commence a system-wide search for the drivers specified, so no absolute pathname is needed.

Step 4: Initializing in the to-do list example

Before we can initialize the serial port, we must have an RComm-Serv object. In the TodoX example, the TodoXferSerial class declares this object, as well as other objects and functions we will need.

```
class TodoXferSerial: public TodoXferBase
{
public:
    TodoXferSerial(CTodoXAppUi*);
    ~TodoXferSerial();

    TBool OpenL();
    TBool OpenL(TDesC&);
    TInt Init(TDesC&);
    void Configure();
    void Configure(TBps baudrate, TDataBits databits,
        TParity parity, TStopBits stopbits);
    void Close();
```

```
            void SendItem(CAgnEntry *);
            void ReceiveItem();
            void SendItemVCal(CAgnEntry *);
            CAgnEntry* ReceiveItemVCal();

        private:
            void Send(const TDes8 &aText);
            void Receive(TDes8 &aText);

        protected:
            RCommServ server;
            RComm commPort;
            CTodoXAppUi* iAppUi;

        };
```

Initializing the serial port in the TodoX example is done through the Init function of the TodoXferSerial class:

```
    TInt TodoXferSerial::Init(TDesC &aModuleName)
    {
        TInt result;

        // Load the physical device driver
        result = User::LoadPhysicalDevice(PDD_NAME);
        if (result != KErrNone && result != KErrAlreadyExists)
           User::Leave(result);

        // Similarly for the Logical device driver
        result = User::LoadLogicalDevice(LDD_NAME);
        if (result != KErrNone && result != KErrAlreadyExists)
           User::Leave(result);

        // Start comm server if necessary
        result = StartC32();
        if (result != KErrNone && result != KErrAlreadyExists)
           User::Leave(result);

        // Connect to the comm server
        result = server.Connect();
        if (result != KErrNone) User::Leave(result);

        // Load the comm module
        result = server.LoadCommModule(aModuleName);
        User::LeaveIfError(result);

        return ETrue;
    }
```

Note that the calls to load device drivers will return two accept-able result codes. These are either KErrNone, for no error, or KErrAlreadyExists, for the case that the drivers are already loaded. All other result codes cause the code to abort through User::Leave(). This is also the case with starting the communications server: acceptable result codes indicate no error or an existing running server.

8.3.2 Opening the Serial Port

Opening the serial port is straightforward, but requires an instance of the RComm class. An RComm class object represents a hardware port and lies at the base of the protocol stacks. Opening a port uses one of the following RComm::Open functions:

```
TInt Open(RCommServ &aServer, const TDesC &aName,
    TCommAccess aMode);
TInt Open(RCommServ &aServer, const TDesC &aName,
    TCommAccess aMode,TCommRole aRole);
```

Both functions require a communications server object, the name of the port to open, and the mode used to access that port. The name of the port is a string, chosen from the names assigned to ports by the port drivers. In version 6.1 of Symbian OS, there are two serial ports, called COMM::0 and COMM::1. The access mode is chosen from the enumeration type TCommAccess:

```
enum TCommAccess {ECommExclusive,ECommShared,ECommPreemptable};
```

The port may be opened for exclusive use by the current application, may be shared with other applications, or may be "pre-emptable", that is, given up upon request by another application.

The second version of the call allows the caller to configure the role of the port either as a DCE (the communication initiator) or a DTE (the communication receiver):

```
enum TCommRole {ECommRoleDTE, ECommRoleDCE};
```

The result code from the Open call will indicate the status of the open operation. A result code of KErrLocked indicates that the port is in use and opened by another application.

Back to our TodoX example, we can use the RComm object declared for the TodoXferSerial class to open the serial port:

```
TBool TodoXferSerial::OpenL()
{
    TBuf16<25> portname;

    portname.Copy(_L("COMM::0"));
    return OpenL(portname);
}
```

```
TBool TodoXferSerial::OpenL(TDesC &aPortName)
{
    TInt result;

    result = commPort.Open(server,aPortName,ECommExclusive);
    User::LeaveIfError(result);

    return ETrue;
}
```

Note that we want exclusive use of the port for the duration of the to-do item exchange.

There is another way to open the port that an RComm object represents. Specifically, this uses the OpenWhenAvailable call and is designed more for active objects. We will elaborate further when we discuss active objects later in the chapter.

8.3.3 Configuring the Serial Port

Once the port is open, we must configure it. The more abstractly we view the hardware, the easier that hardware is to configure. Unfortunately, we do not have a very abstract view of the serial port; we are, in fact, dealing directly with the port through the communications server as we defined before. So we have several details to work with.

For serial ports, we use two calls from the RComm class to get and set their configuration:

```
void Config(TDes8 &aConfig) const;
TInt SetConfig(const TDesC8 &aConfig);
```

The argument to both calls is a TDesC8 string declaration, which in this case is more accurately viewed as an array of 8-bit quantities. Each of those bytes contains a configuration parameter. Through the magic of C++ typing, we can view this byte array as a structure through the TCommConfigV01 class:

```
class TCommConfigV01
{
public:
  TBps iRate;
  TDataBits iDataBits;
  TStopBits iStopBits;
  TParity iParity;
  TUint iHandshake;
  TUint iParityError;
  TUint iFifo;
  TInt iSpecialRate;
```

```
    TInt iTerminatorCount;
    TText8 iTerminator[KConfigMaxTerminators];
    TText8 iXonChar;
    TText8 iXoffChar;
    TText8 iParityErrorChar;
    TSir iSIREnable;
    TUint iSIRSettings;
};
```

Each of these variables represents a configuration parameter for an RComm object. Rather than fill these pages with the definitions of each one, you should review them in d32comm.h. When an RComm object is constructed, each of these is given a default value.

A good example of how to configure the port is given in the TodoX example. Consider the Configure function from the TodoXferSerial class:

```
void TodoXferSerial::Configure(TBps baudrate,
                               TDataBits databits,
                               TParity parity,
                               TStopBits stopbits)
{
  TCommConfig cBuf;
  TCommConfigV01 &c=cBuf();

  // Get the current configuration
  commPort.Config(cBuf);

  // Set new settings
  c.iFifo = EFifoEnable;
  c.iRate = baudrate;
  c.iHandshake = KConfigObeyCTS;
  c.iTerminatorCount = 0;
  c.iDataBits = databits;
  c.iParity = parity;
  c.iStopBits = stopbits;

  // Write the settings out
  commPort.SetConfig(cBuf);
}
```

First, notice that we use the TCommConfig structure to get and set the configuration. The TCommConfig structure is the byte array; the TCommConfigV01 structure is the class we use to manipulate each element in the byte array by name. Again, by taking advantage of C++ type casting rules, we can align the memory areas of these two structures and make them work together as one.

In the above example, we first get the configuration, then adjust it and set it again. This saves code, because many of the settings are correct already and we only want to change a few of them. We could start with an uninitialized TCommConfig structure, especially if there were many parameters to change. But when we only need to alter a few settings, copying the old configuration works well.

8.3.4 Exchanging Data

We are now (finally!) ready to exchange data with the other computer. At this point, we will assume that the other side has gone through the same steps that we have and is waiting for data from the sender.

Data is received and sent through the Read() and Write() functions and their variations from the RComm class. We will look at these operations separately. As we look at the functions that implement reading and writing, it is important to remember that reading and writing data are *asynchronous* operations. This means that these operations might have to wait for data to arrive, and this waiting will cause blocking in the execution of the application.

Reading data

Reading data from the serial port is done through various forms of the Read() function from the RComm class. There are five forms of Read() we will consider:

```
void Read(TRequestStatus &aStatus, TDes8 &aDes);
void Read(TRequestStatus &aStatus, TDes8 &aDes,
    TInt aLength);
void Read(TRequestStatus &aStatus,
    TTimeIntervalMicroSeconds32 aTimeOut,TDes8 &aDes);
void Read(TRequestStatus &aStatus,
    TTimeIntervalMicroSeconds32 aTimeOut,TDes8 &aDes,
    TInt aLength);
void ReadOneOrMore(TRequestStatus &aStatus,TDes8 &aDes);
```

Each form reads data through the RComm object and places that data in the aDes buffer given as the argument. This buffer is of type TDes8, which means it is an array of bytes. All communication—whether through the emulator or from real hardware—is done in 8-bit quantities.

Each form also contains an argument of the type TRequest-Status. The operations attempt to read through their RComm object until they complete, at which point the TRequestStatus object changes its value to reflect the status of the operation. This is the way asynchronous operations create result codes; they cannot return codes immediately as synchronous functions do.

The first two variations reflect differences in the amount of the input data stream and the length of the input buffer. The first form will read data until the buffer given as the second argument is full. The second form will read aLength bytes and return whether the buffer is full or not. The third and fourth forms add a timeout feature to the first and second implementations. In addition to filling the buffer, they will timeout after aTimeOut microseconds, and return a buffer filled with whatever data was obtained in that time interval. Should the buffer fill up during those aTimeOut microseconds, the functions will cancel the timer and return.

The last form is a special one in that it examines the port hardware and returns whatever it can. If the serial driver's buffer contains data, this function will retrieve that data up to the length of the input buffer. If there is no data waiting, then the function blocks until the first byte is delivered. It then returns this byte.

Because reading is an asynchronous operation, we must be able to wait until it is done. We can use one of several functions from the User class to accomplish this:

```
static void WaitForRequest(TRequestStatus &aStatus);
static void WaitForRequest(TRequestStatus &aStatus1,
                           TRequestStatus &aStatus2);
static void WaitForAnyRequest();
```

Each function blocks execution, waiting for the status variable to change its value. When the value changes, the function returns and execution resumes. The first version waits for one status variable; the second version waits for two; the third will return on a change to any status variable.

Writing data

Writing data follows much the same pattern as reading. The write operation is also asynchronous; it blocks until it can complete its operation and works in conjunction with a TRequestStatus variable.

There are four forms of the write operation:

```
void Write(TRequestStatus &aStatus,const TDesC8 &aDes);
void Write(TRequestStatus &aStatus,const TDesC8 &aDes,
    TInt aLength);
void Write(TRequestStatus &aStatus,
    TTimeIntervalMicroSeconds32 aTimeOut,
    const TDesC8 &aDes);
void Write(TRequestStatus &aStatus,
    TTimeIntervalMicroSeconds32 aTimeOut,
    const TDesC8 &aDes, TInt aLength);
```

Each form sends data out through an RComm object; each sends an eight-bit buffer that was given as a parameter; each sets its status variable according to the status of the write operation. Two forms (the second and fourth) send a specific amount of data from the buffer. Two forms (the third and fourth) use a timer to wait aTimeOut microseconds for the write operation to succeed.

More on waiting for operations

The asynchronous nature of I/O has positive and negative facets. While it makes reading and writing more complicated, it also provides an opportunity for the processor to use the waiting time for other things (it may even power down the Symbian device during this time).

The behavior of the I/O operations is as follows: each function will return immediately, regardless of the completed status of the operation. Only when the TRequestStatus variable has an integer value of zero (KErrNone) is the data in the operation's buffer valid. Until that point, you are free to execute other code. The WaitForRequest function calls simply save you the execution cycles of spinning in a loop constantly checking the value of the status variable.

Because the I/O operation is executed in parallel, it can be cancelled. Given that the code is not blocked in a WaitForRequest function, one of the RComm functions below can be called:

```
void ReadCancel();
void WriteCancel();
```

These cancel Read and Write operations, respectively.

Reading and writing in the to-do item example

Reading and writing serial data in the TodoX example is accomplished through two low-level calls:

```
void Send(const TDes8 &aText);
TBool Receive(TDes8 &aText);
```

These functions operate directly on the serial interface and are called by SendItem() and ReceiveItem(), which implement the item exchange protocol.

The Send() function illustrates an issue we have looked at before: data frame format. Even sending a string—a sequence of bytes—over a simple serial port interface requires a minimal data frame. The issue is string length: how do you indicate the length of the string that is to be sent? Our data frame shown in Figure 8.3 includes the length of the string with the bytes that compose the string's value as the first byte of the frame.

length	character bytes

Figure 8.3   A simple data frame format.

This is a simple data frame. It informs the remote receiver of the number of bytes the sender is sending. Since the receiver does not get this information any other way, sending it this way is important.

The code of the `Send()` function is below:

```
void TodoXferSerial::Send(const TDes8 &aText)
{
  TInt len;
  TRequestStatus status;
  TBuf8<2> buffer;

  len = aText.Length();

  // Send the length
  buffer.SetLength(0);
  buffer.Append((TChar)len);
  commPort.Write(status, buffer, 1);
  User::WaitForRequest(status);
  User::LeaveIfError(status.Int());

  // Send the text
  commPort.Write(status, aText);
  User::WaitForRequest(status);
  User::LeaveIfError(status.Int());
}
```

Note that even when we are sending an integer, it is captured as a byte and sent—the easiest way to do this is as appended to an eight-bit buffer of characters. Further, note that even though we can send any size of string this way (up to the bounds of the TInt type), Agenda application to-do entries can only be up to 255 characters long.

The `Receive()` function is the counterpart of the above sending code. It receives an integer as a character, decodes the value, then pulls in that many bytes:

```
TBool TodoXferSerial::Receive(TDes8 &aText)
{
    TInt len;
    TRequestStatus status;
    TBuf8<2> buffer;

    // Read the length
    commPort.Read(status, buffer, 1);
    User::WaitForRequest(status);
    User::LeaveIfError(status.Int());

    // Read the text character by character
    len = (TInt)buffer[0];
    if (len <= 80) {
        commPort.Read(status, aText, len);
        User::WaitForRequest(status);
        User::LeaveIfError(status.Int());
    } else {
        len = 0;
    }
    return ETrue;
}
```

Extend TodoX with Expect

A useful function for the TodoX example would be one called
Expect. This function would take a string (a const TDesC8
argument) and would read from the commPort until that string
was found, or until a specific time has elapsed.

Write this function for the TodoX example. You should be able
to implement the timing without needing any kind of timer if you
do not use ReadOneOrMore(). However, you might want to use
ReadOneOrMore() for this function, and then implementing a
timeout would not be possible. Check the CTimer class for this.
This will make you appreciate using active objects (see a later
section).

8.3.5 Closing the Port

When all is done, the termination of communication occurs in two
steps. First, we close the port. Second, we close our connection to
the communication server. Each operation is handled by a call to

```
void Close();
```

from the RHandleBase class, since both RCommServer and
RComm are descendants of this class.

In the to-do list item example, closing the port is handled by the `Close()` function from the `TodoXferSerial` class:

```
void TodoXferSerial::Close()
{
    commPort.Close();
    server.Close();
}
```

8.4 Other Interface Calls

There are many other calls associated with the `RCommServ` and `RComm` classes. We will get to many of them eventually, but we will highlight a few more of them here.

8.4.1 RCommServ

There are several calls of interest here, highlighted below:

```
TInt UnloadCommModule(const TDesC &aName);
```

This call is the reverse of the `LoadCommModule()` call we used above in the initialization of the communication server. While `LoadCommModule()` will load a CSY module, `UnloadComm-Module()` will remove the CSY module from the kernel's tables. Unloading may be desirable if kernel resources are scarce.

```
TInt NumPorts(TInt &aNum);
```

This call returns the number of ports served by the communication server. These will usually include at least the serial port and the IR port.

```
TInt GetPortInfo(const TDesC &aName, TSerialInfo &aInfo);
TInt GetPortInfo(TInt aIndex, TDes &aModuleName,
    TSerialInfo &aInfo);
```

These calls retrieve information from the communication server about the ports that it serves. Information may be retrieved by port name (the first call) or port number/module (the second call). In either case, the call returns the information in the form of the last parameter—a `TSerialInfo` object, defined as below:

```
class TSerialInfo
{
public:
  TPortDescription iDescription;
  TPortName iName
```

```
    TUint iLowUnit;
    TUint iHighUnit;
};
```

This class contains a description of the serial port (in terms of CSY modules), the name of the port, and the device number range.

8.4.2   RComm

The RComm class has many functions defined for it. There are a few more of interest for us at this stage.

```
void OpenWhenAvailable(TRequestStatus &aStatus,
    RCommServ &aServer, const TDesC &aName)
void OpenWhenAvailable(TRequestStatus &aStatus,
    RCommServ &aServer, const TDesC &aName, TCommRole aRole)
```

These calls are a variant of the Open() call, and work differently from the Open() call when the port requested is not available. Instead of returning an error code, these calls block and wait for the port to become unused. When the port becomes available, these calls will open the port, setting the status variable, and return.

```
void OpenWhenAvailableCancel();
```

This call will cancel the operation that is begun when the Open-WhenAvailable() functions block and wait for a port. Because of their heavily asynchronous nature, these calls are more suited for active objects than for straight usage. We will discuss active objects in the next section.

```
TInt QueryReceiveBuffer() const;
```

This call checks how much data is waiting in the receive buffer to be consumed by the next Read call.

There are also several functions that are used to notify an application when an I/O condition exists. The system can notify an application when a port's configuration changes, for example, or when data arrives. These calls are asynchronous and must be waited for. The status variable setting indicates the notification condition. These functions are accompanied by a companion function which cancels the notification condition. We will encounter these later on.

8.5 Active Objects

If "the ends justifies the means", as it is said, then the TodoX example works just fine. The end result is that a to-do list item is transferred between devices. However, the means by which this is carried out is not desirable. In the current implementation of the example, the application is essentially suspended while each data communication is executed. This could get quite annoying if you were to transfer many items between devices. You can see this if you run the TodoX example on the emulator and watch closely: the status messages appear *out of sync* with the operation they report on (they should appear before that operation takes place but they actually appear afterwards).

A solution to this would be to use a threaded application. One thread would handle the communication I/O and another would handle the user interface interaction. In fact, the best solution here would be one implemented by the OS—even in the kernel—because of the notification issues and thread suspension that must go on.

Active objects represent Symbian OS's solution to this issue. An active object is a thread that handles event notifications from the kernel. We are specifically interested in device-oriented events, e.g., the arrival of data in a buffer or the completion of an I/O operation. There are also other events that are meaningful to communications, e.g., an alarm event when a timer counts down to zero, indicating timeout.

Active objects are derived from the CActive class, which provides access to a CActiveScheduler object. An active object must implement at least two functions:

```
void RunL();
void DoCancel();
```

The RunL() function is the heart of an active object implementation. Upon construction, the active object will create and initialize anything it needs to. When a function is called that performs an asynchronous operation that might involve waiting, instead of calling User::WaitForAnyRequest(), the active object needs to call SetActive(), inherited from the CActive class. This suspends the active object thread, turning over control of the asynchronous operation to a scheduler. When this operation completes and generates an event the active object has registered for, the scheduler calls the RunL() function for the active object.

The DoCancel() function must be implemented to cancel the actions implemented by the active object. On receiving a request to cancel the operations for an active object, the system will first check whether there is an outstanding request to this object, then will call DoCancel().

8.5.1   State Diagrams

To effectively use an active object, especially with communications, we need to develop a *state diagram*. A state diagram is a depiction of the states that an application can be in and how it moves between those states. These states are usually defined—for our communications purposes, that is—by the times that our application is waiting for a communication event.

Consider Figure 8.2 again. The circles can represent states; the "S" states are ones a sender can be in and the "R" states are ones that a receiver can be in. We can express a state diagram by looking at just the sender or just the receiver side.

The states of communication are determined by the actions of waiting for a communication event. So, each Read or Write, for instance, should instigate a new state. This means we have to split up the states from Figure 8.2 into those that wait for Read operations to complete (the "S" states) and those that wait for Write operations to complete (the "R" states).

Figure 8.4 contains the new state diagram for a to-do item sender. It depicts all the states a sender can be in, and the ways we move between the states. A SError state has been added, and a special designation is given to the last state—ST2. That state is a "final state", that is, if we are in that state when input is complete, we have correctly traversed the state diagram. Otherwise, we have to flag an error.

8.5.2   Translating State Diagrams to Active Object Code

Once we have a state diagram, we can produce the code for the active object.

We must first have a way to start the active object. This is a function that initializes the active object and executes the first I/O operation. This function passes control to the thread scheduler by using the function call below:

```
void SetActive();
```

A call to this function relinquishes control of the thread to the scheduler and allows the system to wake up the thread when the I/O operation is complete.

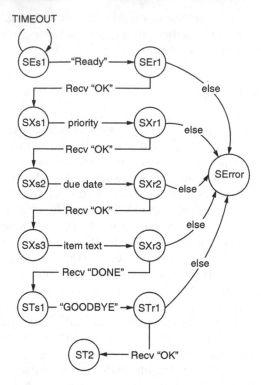

Figure 8.4 State diagram for the sending side of the Todox example.

In the TodoX example, this is the implementation of SendItem for a new class, TodoSerialXferAO. This function is shown below:

```
void TodoXferSerialAO::SendItem(CAgnEntry *aEntry)
{
    iEntry = aEntry;

    CParaFormatLayer *iParaFormatLayer = CParaFormatLayer::NewL();
    CCharFormatLayer *iCharFormatLayer = CCharFormatLayer::NewL();

    // Set up to-do item data
    iTodoItem = CAgnTodo::NewL(iParaFormatLayer, iCharFormatLayer);
    iTodoItem = (CAgnTodo *)(aEntry->CastToTodo());
    priority = iTodoItem->Priority();
    duedate = iTodoItem->DueDate();

    // Start the protocol
    iAppUi->SetProgress(_L("Starting the protocol"));
    buffer.Copy(KReady);
    Send(buffer);

    iSendingState = ESEs1;
}
```

Notice the differences between this implementation and the one for `TodoXferSerial`. First, many of the variables are now global to the class. This is because the operation extends over the whole class now, not just one function. Second, we use a new variable—`iSendingState`—to remember the state we are in. Finally, notice the lack of `User::WaitForAnyRequest()` calls. The system is doing the waiting for us. This is more obvious by the new implementation of Send():

```
void TodoXferSerialAO::Send(const TDes8 &aText)
{
  TInt len;
  TBuf8<100> buffer;

  len = aText.Length();

  // Send the length
  buffer.SetLength(0);
  buffer.Append((TChar)(48+len));
  buffer.Append(aText);
  commPort.Write(status, buffer, len+1);

  SetActive();
}
```

There are no `User::WaitForAnyRequest()` calls and there is a call to `SetActive()` at the end of the function.

Once we have started the active object and turned over control to the scheduler, we need a way to continue its execution whenever I/O operations complete. This is found in the implementation of the `RunL()` function. This function is essentially one big `switch` statement, based on the value of the state variable. Each case in the `switch` statement looks something like this (from `TodoXferSerialAO`):

```
case ESEr1:
  if (status == KErrNone) {
      if (buffer != KOk) {
          iSendingState = ESError; // indicate an error
      } else {
          iAppUi->SetProgress(_L("Sending the priority"));
          buffer.Format(KPriorityFormat, priority);
          Send(buffer);
          iSendingState = ESXs1;
      }
  } else {
      iSendingState = ESError; // indicate an error
      iAppUi->SetProgress(KRcvErrMessage);
  }
  break;
```

At the beginning of each case, we can assume that the previous I/O operation has completed with a value status variable. We check the status variable to determine if the operation completed successfully. If it was successful, we process the results, engage another I/O operation, and change the state variable for the next invocation of RunL(). If it has not completed successfully, we must deal with it somehow—perhaps aborting the active object or resetting the communication stream. At the end of the case, if we want to continue, we must call SetActive() again.

8.5.3 Using an Active Object

Using an active object is not much different from using a sequential communication object. However, there are a few subtle differences:

- Active objects are typically initialized in addition to being instantiated. This means that we need a new operator to get an active object, then use initialization code to set the object up. In the TodoX example, this is accomplished by TodoXferSerialAO::NewLC():

```
TodoXferSerialAO* TodoXferSerialAO::NewLC(CTodoXAppUi*
aAppUi)
{
    TodoXferSerialAO* self=new (ELeave) TodoXferSerialAO(aAppUi);

    CleanupStack::PushL(self);
    self->ConstructL();

    return self;
}
```

This code calls the ConstructL() function in addition to instantiating a TodoXferSerialAO object. The main thing ConstructL() does is to add the current active object to the scheduler:

```
void TodoXferSerialAO::ConstructL()
{
    CActiveScheduler::Add(this);
}
```

This code could have done other operations. This is much like an object's constructor, but it must be run after object instantiation.

- When the active object returns, nothing can be assumed about the completion of the I/O operation. In the TodoXferSerial class, we could assume that, when SendItem() returned, the item was sent to a receiver. However, in the `TodoXferSeri-alAO` class, we can only assume that the transfer was *started*, not completed. This is why we close the communication port only if we are using the `ESerialMode` mode to transfer items and allow all others to close the port themselves when they are done.

- There must be a way for the active object to signal to the calling class that it is done performing an operation. As we discussed before, the active object is asynchronous, and therefore cannot simply return a value to a calling object. It requires a callback function from the calling object. In the `TodoX` example, this is handled by the `ProcessReceivedItem()` function, which deletes the active object and enters the to-do item on the display.

> **Further Reading on Active Objects**
>
> For more information on active objects, there are two references that are extremely valuable. *Professional Symbian Programming*, by Martin Tasker, *et al.*, gives a good introduction to active object programming. Also, the Active Object sections in the Symbian OS version 6.1 system documentation is very good. You can find this by using the **Programs > Symbian 6.1 SDKs > Quartz > C++ SDK Documentation** menu sequence from the Windows Start button.

8.6   A Note About vCalendar Objects

Before leaving this chapter, note that the `TodoX` example is a bit contrived. I arbitrarily chose three properties of a to-do list item and worked them into a simple transfer protocol. There are, in fact, many other properties—like alarm settings, for instance—that need to be included in a complete to-do list item transfer implementation.

In fact, we can completely represent a to-do item by using a vCalendar. As we stated back in Chapter 5, vCalendar objects are designed as objects with a standard format, so that different platforms and operating systems can share them. Consider Figure 8.5, which contains a representation of a to-do item from the list shown in Figure 7.3.

The Symbian OS implementation of vCalendar objects includes the functionality needed to transfer them between devices. I will cover this in later chapters.

```
BEGIN:VCALENDAR
VERSION:1.0
BEGIN:VTODO
UID:2
DESCRIPTION:Eat lunch with Bob
DUE:20010706T000000Z
PRIORITY:2
X-EPOCTODOLIST:To-do list
X-EPOCAGENDAENTRYTYPE:TODO
CLASS:PUBLIC
DCREATED:20010706T000000Z
LAST-MODIFIED:20010831T091100Z
CATEGORIES:X-65536
END:VTODO
END:VCALENDAR
```

Figure 8.5   An example vCalendar representation of a to-do list item.

8.7   Summary

This chapter has initiated the section on communications programming by addressing serial communications. We covered several
important topics:

- We started by examining the patterns that are found in communications programming. There are five stages to programming
  the local device, and three stages to engaging the remote device
  in a data exchange protocol. Along the way we introduced an
  example: TodoX, which exchanges to-do list items between
  devices via the serial port.

- We then took a look at the API for communication using the
  serial port. Instead of an exhaustive itemization, we looked at the
  API functionally, itemizing what was needed for programming.

- We defined active objects as a way to implement threaded communications using the kernel. Active objects make applications
  more responsive by parallelizing them, establishing a thread
  for the I/O operations that might cause an application to halt
  temporarily while waiting.

- Finally, we mentioned vCalendar objects as a way to upgrade from the TodoX example.

The next chapter will tackle IR communications. At first, IR looks like serial communications through a new port. However, we will introduce sockets that will enable us to reach into higher level protocols.

9

Communicating via Infrared: Serial Communication

Sir William Herschel is credited for discovering the infrared region of the electromagnetic spectrum. His son, Sir John Herschel, demonstrated in 1840 that infrared light existed by showing that different light had different rates of absorption and transmission. Early uses for IR were from astronomy (examining infrared light sources) to the military (lasers). It took until 1916 for infrared light to be used to transmit data, and then it was used to transmit secret messages during war. Infrared capabilities of one form or another have shown up on communication devices since the 1980s.

The infrared port on a Symbian device represents a transition of sorts between the serial communication of the last chapter and the more complex protocol structures we will tackle in future chapters. It can be programmed at the raw data level of a serial port and at the higher level of an upper layer protocol. We will let this transitory nature guide the way we discuss IR: this chapter will deal with serial IR programming, and we will wait to discuss upper level programming until Chapter 11.

This chapter will be relatively short. We will first pause to review how serial IR programming fits into the Symbian OS communications architecture. We will then dig into how to program the IR port as a serial device. We will complete this chapter with a look at sending vCalendar objects across a serial IR interface.

9.1   Admiring the Landscape

Serial IR programming gives us a great opportunity to pause for a moment and admire the way the Symbian OS communications infrastructure is designed. Converting an application from serial port communication to serial IR communication is simple and requires little code alteration, because of the modularity built into the architecture.

Consider the module/driver structure that develops when using serial port communication. By the time we are able to correctly call `Read()` and `Write()` functions from the RComm class, we have a structure much like the one in Figure 9.1. Because of the low level of serial communication, we only have three module layers represented here. We can think of the application—the TodoX example, for instance—as the protocol module. Applications at this level communicate with the device through these three layers (recall them from Chapter 4):

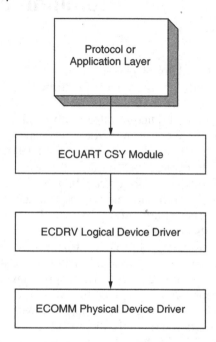

Figure 9.1 Module/driver structure for serial communication.

- The CSY module handles low-level, device independent software protocol issues. For example, data framing and buffering are issues handled here.
- The LDD module handles device-dependent hardware protocol issues, a hardware level counterpart to the CSY module. Any issues that have to do with data packets or formats are implemented again here for hardware.
- The PDD module is concerned only with moving bits from the LDD module to the hardware device. All issues other than managing the bit stream are ignored.

So if we want to change the device we use for communication, while maintaining the same method of communication, we only have to make some small changes to this structure. First, if the method of communication is the same—serial communication in each case—then the protocol module or application remains the same. We might change buffering or data frame formats or error control functions, so the CSY module will likely change. If our hardware is designed correctly—with the same interfaces—then the LDD and PDD modules can remain the same. We will use different device drivers when we open a different device.

It is this modular design that makes Symbian OS easy to extend and program (once we learn the basics). It means that extensions to the operating system only require installing new modules and loading them at the correct times. It also means that programming interfaces will remain consistent and applications will change little, if at all.

9.2 Serial Communication via the IR Port

Treating the IR port as a serial port is a great example of this operating system modularity. Writing an application that uses the IR port in a serial mode *is no different* in terms of the API than writing an application for the serial port. The patterns we developed in the last chapter apply directly; the API function calls work the same; the same concepts of asynchronous calls and active objects apply as well.

The major change from using the serial port is that different modules and drivers are to be used. Specifically, we need IRCOMM.CSY instead of ECUART.CSY and we need to open the IRCOMM device instead of COMM::0. At the risk of repetition, nothing else changes. The stack uses the same logical device driver and the same physical device driver.

Let's consider the TodoX example. We can subclass the TodoXferIRSerial class from TodoXferSerialAO, the serial example's active object class. The definition is below:

```
class TodoXferIRSerial : public TodoXferSerialAO
{
public:
    TodoXferIRSerial(CTodoXAppUi* aAppUi);
    ~TodoXferIRSerial();

public:
    static TodoXferIRSerial* NewLC(CTodoXAppUi* iAppUi);
    static TodoXferIRSerial* NewL(CTodoXAppUi* iAppUi);
```

```
public:
    TBool OpenL();
    TBool OpenL(TDesC&);
}
```

We need a class constructor (if only to call the superclass's constructor) and I have included the other functions only for completeness (so that one can use `OpenL()` with no arguments, for instance). We use all the other functions from the `TodoXferSerialAO` class, including `Read()`, `Write()`, `ReadItem()`, and `WriteItem()`.

We initialize the protocol differently as we load a different communication module to initialize the port, as this fragment from the `SendItem()` function of the `TodoX` example show:

```
void CTodoXAppUi::SendItem(TInt aIndex)
{
    iReader->ReadEntryL(iEntryIDs[aIndex]);

    switch (iXferMode) {

      ...
        case EIRSerialMode:
        case EIRSocketMode:
            iXferPort->Init(_L("IRCOMM"));
            iXferPort->OpenL();
            iXferPort->Configure();
            break;
      ...
}
```

So that you can see the similarity, I have included the `OpenL()` code below.

```
TBool TodoXferIRSerial::OpenL()
{
    return OpenL(_L("IRCOMM::0"));
}


TBool TodoXferIRSerial::OpenL(TDesC &aPortName)
{
    TInt result;

    result = commPort.Open(server,aPortName,
        ECommExclusive);
    User::LeaveIfError(result);

    return ETrue;
}
```

To convert our serial port `TodoX` example, that is all that is required. We have targeted the code at a new device and, since that device uses the same communication method as our serial example, this is all we have to do.

9.3 vCalendar Objects

In Chapter 8, I said I would deal with vCalendar objects in this chapter. However, this section is simply a teaser. The real meat of handling vCalendar objects appears in Chapter 13, where we discuss messaging. Here, I will overview some issues.

To send vCalendar objects over serial I/O, we need to handle them as text. Handling vCalendar objects in a textual form is a little difficult in Symbian OS. These objects are designed as BIO message content, not really as objects with textual content read by humans. Because of this, there are few function calls that will generate textual vCalendar representations.

One such function comes from the `CAgnModel` class, the class that lies at the center of Agenda item handling. Its definition is below:

```
void ExportVCalL(RWriteStream &aWriteStream,
    CAgnEntry* aEntry,
    const CVersitParser::TVersitCharSet aCharSet =
    CVersitParser::EUTF8CharSet);

void ExportVCalL(RWriteStream &aWriteStream,
    CArrayFixFlat<TAgnEntryId>* aEntryIdList,
    const CVersitParser::TVersitCharSet aCharSet =
    CVersitParser::EUTF8CharSet);
```

The `ExportVCalL()` function takes an entry or an array of entries and writes the textual representation to the `aWriteStream` object. Objects that derive from the `RWriteStream` class include both file and memory streams, so Agenda entries can be exported to files or memory as vCalendar objects.

Extend `TodoX` with Textual vCalendar Objects

One way to test how well you understand the concepts to this point is to extend the `TodoX` example to use textual vCalendar objects. You should call the (now empty) function call `SendItemVCal(CAgnEntry *aEntry)`, which should convert the vCalendar entry to text and use the established protocol to send it. You also need to implement the `ReceiveItemVCal()` function that returns a pointer to a `CAgnEntry` object.

To do this, you will need to use the

```
WriteVCalObject(CAgnEntry* aEntry, RWriteStream aStream)
```

function from the `AgendaFileReader` class. This will convert the vCalendar object to text and write it to the `RWriteStream` object. If you examine the implementation of the `WriteVCalObject()` function, you will see it is implemented in terms of `CAgnModel::ExportVCalL()`.

9.4   Summary

This chapter detailed the techniques needed to use IR serial communications. The details, however, were not complicated; IR serial communications is based heavily on serial port communications, and very few changes need to be implemented. The chapter concluded with a brief discussion of the textual representation of vCalendar objects.

The next chapter is on sockets, a concept that is vital to programming the rest of the protocols in Symbian OS communications architecture. We revisit IR communications using sockets in Chapter 11.

10

Using Sockets

I enjoy the American television show *Star Trek*. Since its debut in 1967, it has gone through many changes, through five franchises, with a constant stream of new technology popping up in the show. Of all the innovations in the show, one of the most incredible inventions is the use of a "language translation matrix". Somehow, every person on the show speaks the same language—people from every country on earth and every alien species. While this is never explained on the show, it is implied that this is due to a computer (usually a starship's computer) using a translation matrix to translate one language to another in real time. It is amazing to me that each person hears only this translated speech—not the original source—and with no apparent artificial implants! I speak English and you hear Klingon! That's amazing technology!

Sockets are a bit like this language translation matrix. On one side, we might have an application that simply wants to send data—correctly, efficiently, rapidly—over an IR port. On the other side, another application wants to receive this data as it was sent—text, bytes, whatever. In between the two endpoints, there is much transformation that goes on—using a protocol stack as a translation matrix. Sockets allow the applications to ignore the translation matrix/protocol stack.

We will overview sockets in this chapter. Since sockets feature prominently in most of the communication methods for the rest of this book, a close look is warranted. We will first introduce the idea behind sockets, then examine three central implementations: the socket server, socket objects themselves, and name/address resolution.

10.1 Introduction to Sockets

Serial communication, good as it is, is still the raw exchange of data between two points. It can be considered, at best, a data link layer protocol. It is an effective—but limited—means of communication that allows data transfer over a physical medium. Its limitations are many, including a restricted transfer rate and very little error detection. To implement services like flow control and error correction, and to take advantage of more sophisticated communication techniques like multipoint communication, we must gain access to higher level communication protocols and use hardware devices through those protocols. We use sockets to gain this protocol access.

Sockets were invented by the designers of Berkeley Unix and were first used as a way to access TCP/IP protocols. In the Berkeley terminology, a socket is an "endpoint for communication". By itself, as an endpoint, a socket is not very useful. But when connected to another socket on another computer, the pair becomes a communication channel that uses a protocol to transfer data. You can think of sockets as two ends of a conversation and the protocol as the translator.

In fact, to write code that uses upper layer protocols—say TinyTP for IrDA—you can no longer deal with the device directly. This would be counterproductive; it would involve implementing protocol concepts that have already been implemented. Sockets allow us to take advantage of the protocol implementations already built for us by Symbian.

Sockets depend on four things: protocol modules, a socket server, a socket object, and a name resolution service.

10.2 Protocol Modules

To implement each of the many protocols it uses, Symbian OS uses protocol modules. We introduced protocol modules back in Chapter 3. You can think of them in the same way you do device drivers: there is a common programming interface that is implemented differently by the various protocol modules. In fact the analogy to device drivers works further: protocol modules are loaded and unloaded; they can be supplied by third party vendors implementing new protocols; and they are used by a server as loadable libraries to implement protocol stacks. For example, the various protocols in the TCP/IP suite are implemented by the TCP.PRT module and Bluetooth protocols are implemented by the BT.PRT module.

Loading a protocol module is usually automatic. The first time a socket that uses a particular protocol is opened, that protocol module is loaded. You can also load protocol modules programmatically through an RSocketServ object. Unloading a protocol module is also automatic, usually at the discretion of the operating system. However, an API exists that can be used to unload a protocol module as well.

Look for Yourself

Symbian OS uses a configuration file to specify which protocol modules are available and what they are used for. When it is needed—it is only used for additional third party protocol modules and not for built-in ones—it lists the protocol and the modules used for it.

Look on your emulator or on your hardware Symbian OS device. Look it up as C:\System\data\esock.ini. I have included a snippet of such a file from a Psion netBook:

```
[sockman]
protocols= plp,irmux,tinytp,tcp,udp,icmp,ip

[tcp]
filename= TCPIP.PRT
index= 4
bindto- ip,icmp

[udp]
filename= TCPIP.PRT
index= 3
bindto= ip,icmp

...
[nifman]
default= netdial

[agents]
ethernet= ethagt.agt
netdial= netdial.agt

[interfaces]
ethernet= ethint.nif
irlan= ethint.nif

[drivers]
ethernet= ethcard.drv
irlan= irlan.drv
```

10.3   RSocketServ: The Socket Server

Just as applications use a communications server to talk through CSY modules to hardware devices, they must also use a socket server to implement access through protocol modules to use protocols. The RSocketServ class is the class that implements the socket server.

In order to create a session with the socket server, an application must first connect to it. Connections are made by the following RSocketServ class function

```
TInt Connect(TUint aMessageSlots =
    KESockDefaultMessageSlots);
```

Calling the Connect() function will establish a connection with the socket server (making sure that it is running) and allocate a number of message slots for that connection. A message slot is used by a read or write operation. Since a socket can perform a read and a write asynchronously, a socket will usually require two message slots. The number of sockets you will use through the socket server will determine the number of message slots in the connection. The default number (if one is not given in the Connect() call) is eight.

While it is not necessary, protocol modules can be loaded and unloaded programmatically. This may be desirable if rapid response to all socket operations is extremely important. Without preloading, a socket server will load a protocol module with the first socket creation that uses the protocol that module implements. By loading modules at the start of an application, this load time can be redistributed to the beginning of the application. The function below loads a protocol module:

```
void StartProtocol(TUint anAddrFamily, TUint aSockType,
    TUint aProtocol,TRequestStatus &aStatus);
```

A call to StartProtocol() must give four parameters: the *family* of protocols that the caller wants (such as KAfInet for Internet protocols or KAfPlp for PLP protocols), the type of socket that will be used (such as a stream-based or datagram-based socket), the specific protocol selected from the protocol family (e.g, KProtocolInetICMP or KProtocolPlpLink), and a status variable we can use to monitor the operation (it is an asynchronous operation).

A socket server can be forced to unload a protocol module by the following function:

```
void StopProtocol(TUint anAddrFamily,TUint aSockType,
    TUint aProtocol,TRequestStatus &aStatus);
```

The parameters have the same meaning as with `StartProtocol()`.

Once we are finished with a socket server, we close the connection to it via its `Close()` function:

```
void Close();
```

10.4   `RSocket`: Using Sockets

Sockets are implemented via the `RSocket` class. Sockets have certain properties that must be chosen as they are created and have certain patterns to their use. They work differently if a server is using them than if a client is using them.

10.4.1   Socket Properties

Sockets have certain properties, chosen based on how they are used. A socket is either *connected* or *connectionless*. A connected socket maintains a *virtual connection* between the two endpoints. This means that address information for the remote endpoint needs to be given only once, and that each access to the connection can be done without respecifying this information. A connectionless socket forces the application to specify the remote endpoint information each time it is used and has no virtual connection. A connected socket is easier to use and is more reliable yet requires higher overhead in its implementation. Connected sockets use mechanisms to ensure that data arrives at the remote endpoint in the exact order they were sent, and that they arrive error-free or do not arrive at all. Connectionless sockets make no such guarantees about data arrival or reliability.

Connected sockets are implemented with *streams*. A stream is a logical connection between two endpoints that implements the properties of a connected socket. Specifically, streams implement the following properties:

- *Reliability:* With a stream, data are delivered accurately (as they were sent) without error or are not delivered at all. If there is no data delivery, this is detected, and the socket owner is notified.

- *Error control:* Errors are detected automatically, and the remote endpoint is usually asked to retransmit the data packet that had the error. Maintaining error control usually involves using checksums on data packets and forcing remote endpoints to acknowledge when they receive packets.

- *Ordered delivery:* As we have discussed before, data that flows between two endpoints is typically broken up and sent as fragments. Streams make sure those fragments arrive at their destination in the order they were sent and that the larger data packets are reassembled correctly.

Connectionless sockets are implemented with *datagrams*. Recall that a datagram is another name for a single data packet. A connectionless socket sends individual datagrams between endpoints rather than using a logical connection. No acknowledgement is required; no extensive error control or ordering mechanisms are used.

The reliability of connected sockets comes at a price. There are more protocol layers involved and hence more protocol overhead. There is more communication between endpoints and hence more data traffic. Connected sockets are implemented with streams; they are more complex than connectionless sockets.

10.4.2 Patterns in Socket Usage

There are patterns in how applications use sockets. In fact, these emulate the patterns we discussed back in Chapter 8 on how to use the serial port.

Initialization

With sockets, initializing "the system" means conversing with the socket server. We must start the server (if we need to) and establish a connection to it. To do this, we need to create an RSocketServ object and call its Connect() function:

```
RSocketServ socksvr;

err = socksvr.Connect();
User::LeaveIfError(err);
```

If the return code is anything other than KErrNone, something has gone wrong, and we must handle the error. Once the current active object has connected to the socket server, that server can be used in further calls that need to obtain sockets.

Opening the socket

Instead of opening a communication port, as we did in Chapters 8 and 9, we now must open (and converse with) a socket. Sockets are designed to have an API that closely reflects the API of a communications port, so the following functions should look familiar:

```
TInt Open(RSocketServ &aServer,TUint addrFamily,
    TUint sockType,TUint protocol);
TInt Open(RSocketServ &aServer,const TDesC &aName);
TInt Open(RSocketServ &aServer);
```

Each of these calls opens a socket for use by an application. The first form is the most specific and allows you to completely specify a socket. There are four parameters: a reference to a connected socket server, the address family of the socket (we discussed this previously for protocol loading in socket servers; an example is KAfInet for Internet protocols), the type of socket that will be used (such as a stream-based or datagram-based socket), and the specific protocol selected from the protocol family (e.g, KProtocolInet-ICMP or KprotocolPlpLink). The socket type is chosen from the following choices (from es_sock.h):

```
const TUint KSockStream=1;
const TUint KSockDatagram=2;
const TUint KSockSeqPacket=3;
const TUint KSockRaw=4;
```

The first two implement stream-based and datagram-based sockets, respectively. The third choice represents a middle ground between streams and datagrams, enforcing sequential packet delivery without all the other trappings of connected sockets. Finally, the last choice allows a socket connection with just a raw datastream—a situation where you would "build your own" packets. We will demonstrate this type of socket in Chapter 12.

The second form of the Open() function opens a socket and configures it by the name of the protocol given in the second parameter. This is the name of the protocol as given to it by Symbian OS and comes from the configuration file esock.ini in the emulator.

The third form of the Open() function creates a blank socket for use by application servers. The actual configuration for the socket is set when a connection is received from a client. This is covered in the next section.

Configuring and connecting sockets

Once a socket is open, it still needs to be connected to another "communication endpoint"—another socket. This is handled differently depending on the type of socket: connectionless/datagram-based or connected/stream-based.

Configuring connectionless sockets   Connectionless sockets have a very brief, one-time connection with the remote socket. We configure connectionless sockets by giving them a *local* address and using special versions of I/O calls that include the remote socket's address. This is the minimal configuration that we can have.

We assign a local address to a socket through the following function from the RSocket class:

```
TInt Bind(TSockAddr &anAddr);
```

A call to Bind() will give the socket local information about the address and protocol it is supposed to represent, derived from the anAddr parameter. This information is built into the TSockAddr class and will be different for different protocols (addresses for TCP/IP, for example, are different than for Bluetooth).

Once a connectionless socket is bound to a local address, it is ready to send or receive data. These sockets can now be used with calls that specify the remote address, like SendTo() or RecvFrom().

Configuring connected sockets   Connected sockets are configured with the address of the remote socket, so that they remain tied together for the duration of the connection. The way this is done will be different based on whether the socket will be used for a server or a client application.

Client sockets are the easiest to use. A client socket makes a call to one of the functions below:

```
void Connect(TSockAddr &anAddr,TRequestStatus &aStatus);
void Connect(TSockAddr &anAddr,
   const TDesC8 &aConnectDataOut,TDes8 &aConnectDataIn,
   TRequestStatus &aStatus);
```

Both calls require an address to connect the socket to and a status variable to monitor the progress of the connection. Connecting is an asynchronous operation, and there may be some waiting involved for the remote side to make its connection. The effect of both calls, upon return, is to connect the socket to a server and to create a channel, accessible through the socket. The second form of the Connect() function sends (through aConnectDataOut) and receives (through aConnectDataIn) some initial data upon connection.

Servers must go through some additional steps. A server must listen for a connection from a client, accept the connection, and then "shape" a socket to fit the incoming connection so that

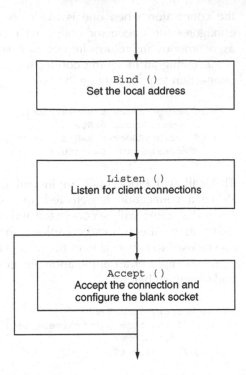

Figure 10.1 Configuration of an application server socket.

communication is possible. A server uses blank sockets, crafting them to fit the client's needs.

A server's sequence is depicted in Figure 10.1. A blank socket is bound to a local address (using the RSocket::Bind() function). Then the application must listen for incoming connections that specify the address bound to this socket. Once an incoming connection has been detected, the application must accept the incoming connection and configure a blank socket to service that connection. Once a connection is accepted, the socket channel is created, and data may flow between the two endpoints.

Listening is done through the Listen() function:

```
TInt Listen(TUint qSize);
TInt Listen(TUint qSize,const TDesC8 &aConnectData);
```

Listening for multiple connections is handled concurrently from a queue of size qSize. This queue will contain qSize number of open connections waiting to be connected to sockets. Connection requests from remote devices that occur when the queue is full are rejected. The second form will receive some data through the connection when one is made. Notice that this call simply configures the queue for collecting incoming requests. It is not asynchronous and returns immediately with a result code.

Accepting an incoming connection joins a blank socket to the connection request through the following functions:

```
void Accept(RSocket &aBlankSocket,
    TRequestStatus &aStatus);
void Accept(RSocket &aBlankSocket,TDes8 &aConnectData,
    TRequestStatus &aStatus);
```

This call will block until an incoming connection is detected. When a connection is detected, the blank socket specified by aBlankSocket will be connected and configured with addressing information. After this call completes, the newly configured socket can be used to converse with the remote device.

An example of an application server's use of sockets is in the code fragment below:

```
RSocketServ iSockSvr;
RSocket iListener, iServiceSocket;
TInetAddr iAddress;
TRequestStatus iStat;

//... code to create sockets and connect to the server

// Open the listener socket
err = iListener.Open(iSockSvr, KAfInet, KSockStream,
    KundefinedProtocol);
User::LeaveIfError(err);

// Open the blank socket
err = iServiceSocket.Open(iSockSvr);
User::LeaveIfError(err);

// Bind the listener socket to ANY address from port 3100
iAddress = new TInetAddr(KInetAddrAny, 3100);
iListener.Bind(iAddress);

// Set up a queue of 5 possible connections at a time
iListener.Listen(5);
// And wait for a connection, joining the blank socket to
// to the incoming request
iListener.Accept(iServiceSocket, iStat);
SetActive();
```

Note that we are assuming an active object here, hence the use of SetActive(). In this example, the code waits for devices using TCP/IP through port 3100.

It bears repeating that two sockets are involved in an application server. One socket is the listener socket and accepts incoming connection requests. The second socket is a blank socket that is joined to the incoming request once it has been accepted. It is through this second socket that active data exchange takes place.

Finally, note that the `Accept()` function implements an asynchronous operation and that it can be cancelled with the following function:

```
void CancelAccept();
```

Exchanging data over sockets

Reading and writing data using sockets is designed to closely resemble what we did with direct communication with hardware ports. The API is very similar but adds a few convenience functions.

Connectionless sockets Reading and writing with datagrams means that the address (host and port) of the remote side of the connection must be specified with the I/O request. This takes special functions that are based on `Read()` and `Write()` but also use address information.

Reading from a connectionless socket uses the `RecvFrom()` function:

```
void RecvFrom(TDes8 &aDesc,TSockAddr &anAddr,TUint flags,
    TRequestStatus &aStatus);
void RecvFrom(TDes8 &aDesc,TSockAddr &anAddr,TUint flags,
    TRequestStatus &aStatus,TSockXfrLength &aLen);
```

Both calls give a buffer, an address of the device to receive the data from, some flags that configure the read, and a status variable to monitor the receipt of data. As usual, the first form will try to fill its buffer, and the second form will only read aLen bytes. The behavior of this function is to block until a datagram from the sender specified in the anAddr parameter is received.

Writing to a connectionless socket is done through the `SendTo()` function:

```
void SendTo(const TDesC8 &aDesc,TSockAddr &anAddr,
    TUint flags,TRequestStatus &aStatus);
void SendTo(const TDesC8 &aDesc,TSockAddr &anAddr,
    TUint flags,TRequestStatus &aStatus,
    TSockXfrLength &aLen);
```

Again, we have a buffer containing the data to send, an address to send the datagram to, some flags to control the transfer, and a status variable for monitoring. The first form sends the entire buffer; the second form only sends aLen bytes. The blocking behavior here is controlled by the flags in the call; the default behavior is to send without waiting for receipt.

Connected sockets Because we do not need to include address information with connected socket I/O, we have a bit more flexibility in the functions we can use.

At the lowest level, Read() and Write() functions work as we have defined them before. However, they have parameters in a different order:

```
void Read(TDes8 &aDesc,TRequestStatus &aStatus);
void CancelRead();
void Write(const TDesC8 &aDesc,TRequestStatus &aStatus);
void CancelWrite();
```

Notice that each comes with a canceling function, because each is asynchronous. In addition, notice that each comes in only one version—lacking a version with the buffer length specification.

The more flexible way to do socket I/O is to use Recv() and Send() functions. These functions include buffer length specifiers and flags to control the I/O, along with the other required parameters:

```
void Recv(TDes8 &aDesc,TUint flags,
    TRequestStatus &aStatus);
void Recv(TDes8 &aDesc,TUint flags,
    TRequestStatus &aStatus,TSockXfrLength &aLen);
void CancelRecv()
void Send(const TDesC8 &aDesc,TUint someFlags,
    TRequestStatus &aStatus);
void Send(const TDesC8 &aDesc,TUint someFlags,
    TRequestStatus &aStatus,TSockXfrLength &aLen);
void CancelSend();
```

Each function really looks like (and is implemented by) lower level Read() and Write() functions. Each function is complemented by its own canceling function.

There is one more function that can be used to receive data on a connected port. As with reading from a hardware port, we can also be flexible with the amount of data we receive and process. The function below allows us to do this:

```
void RecvOneOrMore(TDes8 &aDesc,TUint flags,
    TRequestStatus &aStatus,TSockXfrLength &aLen);
```

This call will cause a read of as much data as is available in the input buffer. The number of bytes read is returned in the aLen variable.

Closing sockets

Sockets are terminated using a few more steps than raw devices. This is so that the protocol layers involved in the socket connection may also shutdown.

First, the socket may have pending connection requests or buffers with data ready to be retrieved. To close a socket gracefully, we should use the CancelAll() function:

```
void CancelAll();
```

This will cancel any asynchronous operations that may be waiting for data or connections.

The next step is to close the socket. There are two ways to do this, depending on whether synchronous or asynchronous operations are desired. The synchronous way to do this is to use Close():

```
void Close();
```

This will terminate the socket and cause the operating system to release any resources dedicated to it. The asynchronous way to do it is to use the Shutdown() function:

```
void Shutdown(TShutdown aHow,TRequestStatus &aStatus);
void Shutdown(TShutdown aHow,const TDesC8
    &aDisconnectDataOut,TDes8 &aDisconnectDataIn,
    TRequestStatus &aStatus);
```

The first form informs the system how to shut the socket down and gives a status variable for monitoring. The "how" of the shutdown process is given by the definition of TShutdown:

```
enum TShutdown {ENormal,EStopInput,EStopOutput,EImmediate}
```

The "normal" way is to drain the socket, waiting for both input and output buffers to empty. The other functions will stop the input but drain the output, drain the input but stop the output, or just stop both. The second form of Shutdown() allows disconnect messages to be sent and received.

The typical way to close a socket is to use the synchronous Close() function. This works best when there are no pending operations or buffered data waiting (using `Close()` in these situations will stop the operations and lose the data). The asynchronous functions should be used when some waiting for operations or buffers is necessary.

10.4.3 Some Odds and Ends

There are a few socket maintenance functions and some convenience functions that bear mention:

- Socket options are configuration parameters that control the behavior of sockets. There are generic options that apply to all sockets (such as a debug mode) and there are specific options that apply to specific protocols (such as raw mode for TCP/IP sockets). There are four functions that work with options:

```
TInt GetOpt(TUint anOptionName,TUint anOptionLevel,
    TDes8 &anOption);
TInt GetOpt(TUint anOptionName,TUint anOptionLevel,
    TInt &anOption);
TInt SetOpt(TUint anOptionName,TUint anOptionLevel,
    TInt &anOption);
TInt SetOpt(TUint anOptionName, TUint anOptionLevel,
    const TDesC8 &anOption=TPtrC8(NULL,0));
```

These functions will get an option value—in either string or integer form (hence the two versions)—or will set an option. We can also set options asynchronously. The `Ioctl()` function does this for us, along with its canceling function:

```
void Ioctl(TUint aCommand,TRequestStatus &aStatus,
    TDes8* aDesc=NULL, TUint aLevel=KLevelUnspecified);
void CancelIoctl();
```

- The local address and port of a socket can be retrieved through the following function calls:

```
void LocalName(TSockAddr &anAddr);
TUint LocalPort();
```

The hostname can be retrieved using the `RHostResolver` class, but the you must use the functions above for the address and port.

- You can retrieve the address of the remote endpoint of a socket using

```
void RemoteName(TSockAddr &anAddr);
```

- You can obtain information about the protocol a socket is using by calling the following function:

```
TInt Info(TProtocolDesc &aProtocol);
```

This call returns an instance of the `TProtocolDesc` class, listed below, which contains valuable information about a protocol:

```
struct TProtocolDesc
{
public:
  TProtocolName iName;
  TUint iAddrFamily;
  TUint iSockType;
  TUint iProtocol;
  TVersion iVersion;
  TByteOrder iByteOrder;
  TUint iServiceInfo;
  TUint iNamingServices;
  TUint iSecurity;
  TInt iMessageSize;
};
```

10.5   Resolving Host Names and Addresses

Computers that communicate with one another must be able to tell each other apart. They must know, for example, if data is coming for them or for some other device. For identification reasons, communication devices are given an *address*, some identifying data sequence that uniquely identifies a device for the protocol it is using. Addresses are protocol-dependent and can look convoluted. TCP/IP addresses, for example, are currently four sets of numbers, tied together with dots: e.g., 192.168.3.76. To complicate matters, services on computers are typically identified by port number, adding to the complexity of addressing the SMTP port as 192.168.3.76:25.

These can be hard for humans to remember, however. So names are given to devices. It is easier, for instance, to remember *http://www.symbian.com* than to remember 195.224.64.203. Names are also given to services, allowing port 23 to be addressed as the Telnet port and port 80 as the HTTP port and so on.

Tying host and service names to their address counterparts is the job of the *resolver*. The resolver provides access to lookup services that can look up addresses when given names and vice versa. There are resolution services for many protocols; perhaps the most familiar is the Domain Name Service (DNS) for TCP/IP.

Symbian OS provides a name resolution interface through the
RHostResolver class. Like the RSocket class, the RHostResolver class depends on a connection with a socket server. Once
you have connected to a socket server, using the name resolution
interface looks much like using a socket: you must open a connection to the host resolver, interact with it, and then close the
connection.

The function call for opening a connection to the host resolution
service should look familiar:

```
TInt Open(RSocketServ &aSocketServer,TUint anAddrFamily,
    TUint aProtocol);
```

You must specify a connected socket server, an address family and
a protocol as parameters. The function returns a code that indicates
success or failure. As an example, the fragment of code below opens
a connection to the resolution service:

```
err = socksvr.Connect();
User::LeaveIfError(err);
err = resolver.Open(socksvr, KAfInet, KProtocolInetTcp);
User::LeaveIfError(err);
```

This fragment opens a connection to the name resolver for TCP/IP
using the Internet address family.

With an open resolver, we can make queries through several
functions:

```
void GetByName(const TDesC &aName,
    TNameEntry &aResult,TRequestStatus &aStatus);
TInt GetByName(const TDesC &aName,TNameEntry &aResult);
void GetByAddress(const TSockAddr &anAddr,
    TNameEntry &aResult,TRequestStatus &aStatus);
TInt GetByAddress(const TSockAddr &anAddr,
    TNameEntry &aResult);
```

Each of these functions comes in synchronous and asynchronous
versions; a status variable is included in the asynchronous versions.

GetByName() takes a name and returns addressing information
by way of a TNameEntry structure, which itself is an array of
TNameRecord structures. TNameRecord looks like this:

```
class TNameRecord
{
public:
  inline TNameRecord();
  enum {EAlias =0x00000001};
  THostName iName;
```

```
        TSockAddr iAddr;
        TInt iFlags;
    };
```

Basically, this is a hostname/address pair. It is put into an array because there may be several pairs associated with a single device.

GetByAddress() goes the opposite direction from GetBy-Name(): it takes an address and returns the name of the device in the given TNameEntry class.

If there are multiple names or addresses for a device, the Next() function will bring up the next value:

```
    void Next(TNameEntry &aResult,TRequestStatus &aStatus);
    TInt Next(TNameEntry &aResult);
```

Sometimes a device will support multiple addresses for an interface, have multiple interfaces, or simply have aliases by which it is known. Next() must return a status code of KErrNone for the next name/address pair to be valid.

Multiple Hostnames and DNS

In the TCP/IP network area, it is common for a computer to have multiple hostnames with one IP address. Some examples are

- A computer that has one name to computers on an internal network and another name to those on an external network—like a firewall.
- A Web server that has a name to match local computers (e.g., *http://frodo.middleearth.biz*) and a service name to match services it offers (e.g. *http://www.middleearth.biz* or *http://mail.middleearth.biz*)

Find computers on your local network with multiple names.

There is another use for name resolution that goes beyond the standard use for resolving names and addresses. Device discovery in IrDA communications uses host resolution functions, as we will see in the next chapter.

```
    void GetHostName(TDes &aName,TRequestStatus &aStatus)
    TInt GetHostName(TDes &aName)
```

Finally, GetHostName() focuses on the local device. It will return the name of the local host if there is a name for it.

10.6   Summary

Sockets are the means by which we take advantage of protocols designed for higher level communications access. In this chapter, we overviewed sockets and protocol modules, then focused on three elements used in the socket system:

- The *socket server*, which handles the mechanics of allocating socket resources and loading protocol modules
- The *socket* itself and all the ways of using it provided by Symbian OS
- The *host resolver*, which handles the mapping between names and addresses for protocols

The next chapter takes a new look at IrDA communications by accessing different protocols through sockets. IrDA provides a great example that illustrates the ideas we discussed here.

11

Communicating via Infrared: Using Sockets

Chapter 10 introduced sockets as a way to access upper layer protocols through a consistent, modular programming interface. Programming the IR port is a great place to start using sockets. To program the IR port at a level different from IRCOMM, we need to access IrDA protocols implemented by Symbian OS. This is done using sockets, and this chapter will demonstrate the concepts we developed in Chapter 10 via this kind of IR port communication.

We will start by reviewing the IrDA protocols that are available for use and their properties. We will then overview definitions Symbian OS has constructed for these protocols. Then we will look at socket programming through the IR port: we will see the stages we saw in Chapter 10 from two sides—the sender side, which will look like a client, and the receiver side, which will look like a server.

11.1   A Quick Protocol Review

Back in Chapter 4, we discussed the protocols that have been developed for using the IR port. Along with the IRCOMM protocols, there are three protocols that are useful for user applications:

- *IrMUX:* This protocol implements a datagram-based communication channel between devices. IrMUX connections reflect the properties of datagram-based connections: unreliable data communication that does not rely on acknowledgement. Multiple IrMUX connections can coexist over a single IR port.

- *TinyTP:* This protocol implements a reliable connected channel between devices. It uses error control to detect problems and maintains a connection between endpoints until data exchange is completed. Multiple TinyTP connections can coexist over the same IR port.

- *IrTranP:* This protocol implements a TinyTP connection for the exchange of digital images, for example, with digital cameras.

In addition to these protocols, we mentioned the IAS—the Information Access Service—that acts as a service database for the IR-based device.

Before we embark on this tour of IrDA sockets, I think it is appropriate to ask the question "why?". Why complicate communications when IRCOMM is relatively simple, has relatively low overhead, and mimics other, well-understood protocols? The answer is that these upper level protocols provide functionality that IRCOMM does not: error control, flow control, and the multiplexing of IR services by multiple applications through the same port. By using datagrams to implement data transfer, these protocols can be faster, more error free, and can share the IR port in ways IRCOMM was not designed to implement.

11.2 System Definitions for IrDA

11.2.1 Addressing Definitions

To use IrDA sockets, we need a set of system definitions. These definitions clarify the general system concept of a socket and focus specification on IrDA.

The sockets we will be using will be created using addresses from the KIrdaAddrFamily group and have the properties specified by the TIrdaSockAddr class. IrDA addresses are integers, but there are other characteristics that are associated with IrDA devices that identify them. These are grouped in the SIrdaAddr structure:

```
struct SIrdaAddr
{
  TUint iHostDevAddr;
  TUint iRemoteDevAddr;
  TBool iSniff;
  TBool iSolicited;
  TUint8 iIrlapVersion;
  TUint8 iFirstServiceHintByte;
  TUint8 iSecondServiceHintByte;
  TUint8 iCharacterSet;
  TUint8 iServiceHintByteCount;
  TUint8 iHomePort;
```

```
    TUint8 iRemotePort;
    TUint8 iSpare;
};
```

From this structure, we can see the two integer device addresses: local and remote. The `iSniff` variable tells whether the device is capable of "sniffing" or discovering other devices. The `iSolicited` variable tells whether the device at this address initiated the connection or was solicited by another for the connection. Of the other variables, the service hint bytes in `iFirstServiceHintByte` and `iSecondServiceHintByte` are of interest. These bytes depict the level of IrLMP support we can expect from the device at this address. Together, these bytes form 16 bits whose value specifies what services are available. Finally, there are two integers denoting the ports on which the services are identified. These allow multiplexing of data streams over the same connection by tying an identifying integer (the port number) onto each data stream.

Service Hints

The service hint bytes contain IrLMP support information. There are twelve different services supported in version 6.1 of Symbian OS. These are detailed in the file `\Epoc32\include\ir_sock.h`. Examine this file, and look for the service definitions in the section labeled "EXPORTED CONSTANTS". Service support definitions in this file are masks (such as `KIrPnPMask`) that are ORed together (for example, `KIrPnPMask | KIrFaxMask | KIrModemMask`) to represent the set of services provided by a device's IR support.

11.2.2   IrDA Socket Options

There are several options that can be read or set for IrDA sockets. Of immediate interest are two of these:

```
const TUint KUnexpeditedDataOpt        = 0;
const TUint KExpeditedDataOpt          = 1;
```

These values determine the urgency of data written to a socket. Unexpedited sending is the default; expedited sending must be specifically set on the socket if it is to be used. Expedited sending of data implies the data is important, and the data packets are given priority over others that go out over the IR connection (see section 11.11).

11.3   Initializing the Socket Server Connection

The first step in connecting two devices over IR is system initialization. For IrDA, this means connecting to the socket server.

Connecting to the socket server is a simple operation. We need
to have an instance of the RSocketServ class, and we need to
call its Connect() function. We also need to nudge it to load the
protocol we will be using.

The TodoX example uses TinyTP to transport data. From the
TodoX code, socket server connection looks like

```
// Load the physical and logical device drivers
result = User::LoadPhysicalDevice(PDD_NAME);
if (result != KErrNone && result != KErrAlreadyExists)
    User::Leave(result);
result = User::LoadLogicalDevice(LDD_NAME);
if (result != KErrNone && result != KErrAlreadyExists)
    User::Leave(result);

// Start comm server if necessary
result = StartC32();
if (result != KErrNone && result != KErrAlreadyExists)
    User::Leave(result);

// Connect to the socket server
result = socksvr.Connect();
User::LeaveIfError(result);

// Load the protocol: TinyTP
result = socksvr.NumProtocols(nProtocols);
User::LeaveIfError(result);
result = socksvr.FindProtocol(_L("IrTinyTP"),protocolInfo);
User::LeaveIfError(result);
```

First, note that we still had to load the physical and logical device
drivers. Even though we are not directly interfacing with them, they
will be used by the IrDA protocol stack. Second, note the way we
load the IrTinyTP protocol module. We tell the socket server to

find the protocol, which forces it to load the right module if it is not present. This function call also fills in the information about the protocol we were looking for in the variable `protocolInfo`, which we will use later in socket calls. We could have looked for "`IrMUX`", which would have given us a socket that used IrMUX.

11.4 Opening the Socket

Opening the socket is straightforward—a call to `OpenL()` in the `RSocket` class. We must specify what kind of protocol we want, but this was derived for us when we looked up the protocol module and loaded it.

In the `TodoX` example, we define a new `OpenL()` function as follows:

```
TBool TodoXferIRSocket::OpenL()
{
    TInt result;

    result = sock.Open(socksvr, protocolInfo.iAddrFamily,
        protocolInfo.iSockType, protocolInfo.iProtocol);
    User::LeaveIfError(result);

    return true;
}
```

We use information stored in `protocolInfo` that we derived previously to give us information about address family, socket type, and protocol. These parameters are all derived from the fact that we chose the TinyTP protocol as the method for socket communication.

11.5 Configuring the Socket: Device Discovery

Configuring a socket is different than configuring a device. With serial communications, we had a real hardware device with which to work. With socket programming, we have a software socket abstraction and layers of protocol with which to work.

With IrDA sockets, configuration means *device discovery*. We need to force the device we are working with to look for other IR devices that can be sending or receiving the data we expect. We did not need to do this for serial communication, because there was only one device on the other side, and we did not care what its "address" was. Symbian OS implements device discovery through the name resolution interface, using an instance of the RHostResolver class and its GetName() function.

In the TodoX example, device discovery is implemented in the Configure() function:

```
void TodoXferIRSocket::Configure()
{
    TInt result;
    THostName hostname;

    TPckgBuf<TUint> buf(1);
    sock.SetOpt(KDiscoverySlotsOpt,KLevelIrlap,buf);

    result = resolver.GetByName(hostname,iHostEnt);
    resolver.Close();
    User::LeaveIfError(result);

    addr = TIrdaSockAddr(iHostEnt().iAddr);
}
```

Notice that we had to set up the socket to do device discovery using the IrLAP protocol through the SetOpt() function call. Using a one-element array, we set up discovery to have a single slot, i.e., we will be looking for one device. Further, note that the GetByName() function I chose to use is the synchronous form. Using the asynchronous form would mean that this should be part of the active object implementation (in RunL()).

After the call to Configure() completes successfully, device discovery has been performed and we have a compatible device that might be willing to connect. Note that at the end of the Configure() function, the address of the remote device is derived from the TNameEntry object using iHostEnt(). We can derive a bit more information from this address, as seen from the functions below taken from the TIrdaSockAddr class:

```
TUint GetRemoteDevAddr() const;
TUint GetHostDevAddr() const;
TBool GetSniffStatus() const;
TBool GetSolicitedStatus() const;
TUint8 GetIrlapVersion() const;
TUint8 GetCharacterSet() const;
TUint8 GetFirstServiceHintByte() const;
TUint8 GetSecondServiceHintByte() const;
TUint8 GetServiceHintByteCount() const;
TUint8 GetHomePort() const;
TUint8 GetRemotePort() const;
```

These are self-explanatory and correspond to the SIrdaAddr structure we discussed earlier. Since that structure is private in the

`TIrdaSockAddr` class, these functions are the only way to get at this information.

A data receiver will not do device discovery. It is not the discoverer; it must be discovered. In Chapter 10, we discussed this type of situation. The data receiver is a server and must configure itself to listen for a connection from a data sender. The server will configure the socket by binding the socket locally, setting up a listening queue on the socket, and opening a second socket to connect to the incoming connection. In the `TodoX` example, this looks like

```
void TodoXferIRSocket::ConfigureReceiver()
{
    TInt result;
    THostName hostname;

    // Create the listener socket
    iListener.Open(socksvr, protocolInfo.iAddrFamily,
        protocolInfo.iSockType, protocolInfo.iProtocol);
    addr.SetPort(KIRPortNumber);
    iListener.Bind(addr);
    iListener.Listen(5);

    // Create a blank socket for later
    iServiceSocket.Open(socksvr, protocolInfo.iAddrFamily,
        protocolInfo.iSockType, protocolInfo.iProtocol);
}
```

11.6 Exchanging Data

Now we have created a socket and either discovered a device that is waiting for a connection or fielded a connection request and responded. We must engage in the protocol phases we have outlined in previous chapters: initiate the protocol, exchange data, and terminate the protocol.

We should use active objects to exploit the asynchronous nature of the I/O functions we will be using. For these active objects, the fact that we are using sockets will add some states to the state diagrams that we constructed for serial communication. For sockets, we added some new steps to the connection process: we added an asynchronous call to a `Connect()` function for senders/clients and a call to `Accept()` for receivers/servers. This changes our state diagram; we need an initial connect or accept state. For the `TodoX` example, Figure 11.1 shows the new state diagram for senders, adding a new `SEC` state.

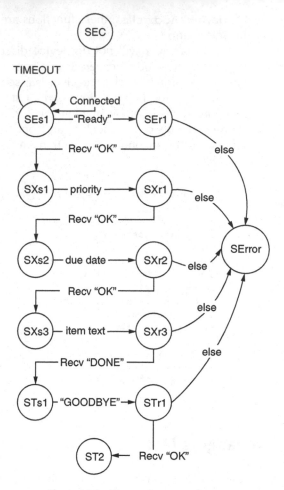

Figure 11.1   New TodoX state diagram.

11.6.1   Initiating the Protocol

For socket-based communication, initiating the data exchange protocol means connecting the socket to the remote device in addition to sending initial protocol synchronization data. For the TodoX example, we must connect a channel, then send our "Ready" string. We start by connecting to a port on the remote device. Recall that a port number is used to identify the data stream that is being serviced by a specific remote process. We identify which port we are binding to, assuming the receiver is binding to the same port on its side.

The SendItem() function from the TodoXferIRSocket class in the TodoX example illustrates the sender sequence nicely:

```
void TodoXferIRSocket::SendItem(CAgnEntry *aEntry)
{
    iEntry = aEntry;

    CParaFormatLayer *iParaFormatLayer =
        CParaFormatLayer::NewL();
    CCharFormatLayer *iCharFormatLayer =
        CCharFormatLayer::NewL();

    // Get to-do item information
    iTodoItem = CAgnTodo::NewL(iParaFormatLayer,
        iCharFormatLayer);
    iTodoItem = (CAgnTodo *)(aEntry->CastToTodo());
    priority = iTodoItem->Priority();
    duedate = iTodoItem->DueDate();

    // Set up the address and connect
    addr.SetPort(KIRPortNumber);
    sock.Connect(addr,status);

    iSendingState = SEC;
    SetActive();
}
```

This looks a lot like the code from the active objects we used
to implement serial communication. The difference is that now
we engage an initial connection step prior to diving into the data
exchange.

On the receiver side, we must start with a call to
Accept() and wait for a sender. The ReceiveItem() function
in the TodoXferIRSocket class from the TodoX example
implements this:

```
void TodoXferIRSocket::ReceiveItem()
{
    CParaFormatLayer *iParaFormatLayer =
        CParaFormatLayer::NewL();
    CCharFormatLayer *iCharFormatLayer =
        CCharFormatLayer::NewL();

    iTodoItem = CAgnTodo::NewL(iParaFormatLayer,
        iCharFormatLayer);
    iListener.Accept(sock,status);

    iReceivingState = REA;
    SetActive();
}
```

Once we have connected and completed the Accept() call, the
active object's RunL() function is called, and we can enter into the

data exchange as we did with the serial active object implementation. For the TodoX sender, this fragment of code implements this:

```
switch (iSendingState) {
  case SEC:
    if (status == KErrNone) {
      iAppUi->SetProgress(_L("Establishing protocol"));
      buffer.Copy(_L8("Ready"));
      Send(buffer);
      iSendingState = ESEs1;
    } else {
      User::Leave(status.Int());
    }
    break;
```

This should look familiar from the way the serial versions started the data exchange. The receiver side is analogous, moving the protocol initialization code to the RunL() function.

11.6.2 Exchanging Data

Once we have connected the sockets end-to-end and started the protocol, the interface and data sequence for socket I/O is very much the same as for serial I/O. While you can use Read() and Write() functions in the same way as with serial solutions, using Send() and Recv() functions are recommended because they are more flexible.

As an example, consider the Send() function from the TodoX example:

```
void TodoXferIRSocket::Send(const TDes8 &aText)
{
  TInt len;
  TBuf8<100> buffer;

  len = aText.Length();

  // Send the length of the buffer
  buffer.SetLength(0);
  buffer.Append((TChar)(48+len));
  buffer.Append(aText);
  sock.Send(buffer, len+1, status);

  // Get active!
  SetActive();
}
```

This code is very close to the serial version but uses Send() rather than Write(). There may be occasions when we need to use the flags in the `Send()` or `Recv()` functions. These flags differ depending on the context in which they are used.

11.6.3 Shutting Down the Protocol

For IrDA sockets, shutting down the protocol requires no special socket operations. While initiating the protocol required connecting the socket, there is no special "disconnect" operation. Shutting down the socket automatically disconnects it from the remote endpoint.

11.7 Terminating the Socket Connection

As we discussed in Chapter 10, the socket might need to be "drained" of requests before we close it. Also, the connection to the socket server needs to be shut down.

The `Close()` function from the `TodoX` example illustrates this:

```
void TodoXferIRSocket::Close()
{
    sock.CancelAll();
    socksvr.Close();
    sock.Close();
}
```

We could have used the asynchronous version of `Close()`, i.e., `Shutdown()`. This would have done the same thing, but we would have had to weave it into the `RunL()` function definition to respond to its completion.

11.8 Using IAS

The Information Access Service (IAS) provides a database that holds information about IrDA connections and their properties. You can query this database, even on the remote device, to find out more information about the IrDA connection. Queries can be made after device discovery has been successfully completed.

IAS queries use two classes we have not yet mentioned. The first is `RNetDatabase`, a class that is used to generically access socket connection information, and `TIASQuery`, a class that specifically constructs IAS database queries.

Queries are made up of two components: an IAS class and an IAS attribute. The IAS class is not a C++ class; it is a configuration specifier. (I would like to rename this unfortunate definition, but it is a standard.) Classes have attributes, and there can be multiple attributes per class. A table of some of these is given below:

Table 11.1 IAS Classes

IAS Class Name	IAS Attribute Name	Response
Device	DeviceName	Remote device hostname
	IrLMPSupport	Level of support by remote device for IrMUX
IrDA:IrCOMM	Parameters	Collection of parameters detailing IrCOMM support
	IrDA:IrLMP:LsapSel	Range of remote port numbers for IrCOMM service
	IrDA:TinyTP:LsapSel	Range of remote port numbers for TinyTP service
	IrDA:InstanceName	Name of IAS instances on remote device
IrDA:IrOBEX	IrDA:TinyTP:LsapSel	Range of remote port numbers for IrOBEX service

To make an IAS query, we need to construct `RNetDatabase` and `TIASQuery` objects, build the query using the `TIASQuery` object, and call the `Query()` function of the `RNetDatabase` object. The query will include both the IAS class and attribute names. Consider the code below:

```
TIASResponse TodoXferIRSocket::IAS(TDesC8& aClassName,
    TDesC8& aAttributeName)
{
    TInt result;
    RNetDatabase rnd;
    TIASQuery query;
    TIASResponse response;

    result = rnd.Open(socksvr,  protocolInfo.iAddrFamily,
        protocolInfo.iProtocol);
    User::LeaveIfError(result);

    query.Set(aClassName, aAttributeName,
        addr.GetRemoteDevAddr());
    rnd.Query(query, response, status);
    User::WaitForRequest(status);

    return response;
}
```

Notice the call to `Query()` is provided a status variable to monitor and a `TIASResponse` response variable to fill with the query response. By now you can figure out that `Query()` is an asynchronous function.

The status variable will give `KErrNone` for successful completion of a query. However, two other values are significant here: `KErrBadName` will be returned if there is no remote class with the name given, and `KErrUnknown` will be returned if the class name is present but the attribute is not there.

The return value stored in the `TIASResponse` object is one of four types.

- Type 3 results are strings.

- Type 2 results are sequences of bytes.

- Type 1 results are integers.

- Type 0 results are "missing" results—they are not given because of errors.

IAS queries are meant to provide information from the remote device as to how it is providing service and how it will support protocols. This information is useful especially in heterogeneous environments where the level of support from the (unknown) remote device cannot be assumed.

11.9   Using IrMUX

In the `TodoX` example from the previous sections, we used TinyTP as the protocol of choice for IrDA communications. We chose this because it is easier to use—it is more reliable and fewer errors result from transmission. However, IrMUX is also a protocol available to you when programming IrDA communications.

IrMUX is a datagram-based protocol. It implements an unreliable, connectionless data transfer between two sockets. While sockets using IrMUX are programmed using the same general functions we have discussed, there are a few differences.

- *Loading protocol modules:* The IrMUX protocol module is loaded with the name "IrMUX" to the `RSocket-Serv::FindProtocol()` function.

- *Sending data through the socket:* As we stated in Chapter 10, the most appropriate way to send data through connectionless sockets is to use the `SendTo()` and `RecvFrom()` functions. These functions can be used with the address of the discovered device as an argument.

- *Socket shutdown:* While an IrMUX socket is terminated the same way a TinyTP socket is, the implementation is different. While Symbian OS will cause a connected TinyTP socket to finish any remaining data requests, it will simply cut off and discard any data I/O pending for connectionless IrMUX sockets.

IrMUX—and connectionless sockets in general—are typically used in situations where the higher overhead per packet is not necessary. This includes situations where there is a lot of data traffic or the data is comprised of single, simple datagram messages.

Using `Connect()` with Connectionless Sockets

If you read the system documentation for Symbian OS version 6.1, you will find references to using connected socket methods with connectionless sockets. The documentation implies, for instance, that `Read()` and `Write()` may be used with IrMUX sockets.

Do you believe this implication? To check this out for yourself, you need to answer some questions:

- If you use `Read()` and `Write()` with IrMUX sockets, how do you specify the device address that will receive the datagrams?

- One answer to the previous question is to use `Connect()` as you do with connected sockets to "preregister" the device address. Can you use `Connect()` with connectionless sockets?

The way to verify your answers to the above questions is to (a) inspect the `ir_sock.h` file and documentation for clues and (b) code up some experiments and see for yourself. What would you expect to see if `Read()` and `Write()` would *not* work with connectionless sockets? What would you expect to see if they did?

11.10 Using IrTranP

We have covered both TinyTP and IrMUX protocols. A third protocol that we have defined for IrDA is IrTranP, a protocol for the exchange of digital pictures. This protocol is not implemented via a socket interface. Rather, the implementation uses a class object—the `CTranpSession` class—and implements the entire protocol from within this object. This class uses a special

`MTranpNotification` class, which contains a set of callback functions that are called at various stages in the picture exchange process. This `MTranpNotification` class is an abstract class; you must provide a class derived from it, implementing the callback functions, to the `CTranpSession` class object when you instantiate it. Once the `CTranpSession` class is set up, a call to its `Get()` function will get the exchange session rolling. As the exchange progresses, the following callback sequence is used:

- When a successful connection is made to a remote device, the `Connect()` callback function is called in the `MTranpNotification` object.

- After connection, the remote device will start sending the picture data, and the `CTranpSession` class object will make repeated calls to the `ProgressIndication()` callback function of the `MTranpNotification` object to relay progress information.

- When the data exchange is complete, the `CTranpSession` class object will call the `MTranpNotification::GetComplete()` callback function.

- When the connection to the remote device is broken, a call to the `Disconnected()` callback function of the `MTranpNotification` object is made.

11.11 A Word About Expedited Socket Output

At the beginning of this chapter, we mentioned that IR output through sockets could be done in one of two modes: unexpedited or expedited. The former mode is the default; to use expedited sending of data, an option must be specifically set on the socket. To do this, we have two choices. The first would use the `SetOpt()` function from the `RSocket` class and specify the `KExpeditedDataOpt` option value, as follows:

```
sock.SetOpt(KExpeditedDataOpt,&buffer,KLevelIrMUXSAP);
```

This, however, is not the recommended way. The recommended way gives more control to the programmer to make both expedited and unexpedited sends over the same socket. To use this technique, we would use the `Send()` function from the `RSocket` class, using the flags in the call to specify expedited I/O:

```
Sock.Send(buffer, KsockWriteUrgent, status);
```

11.12 Summary

In this chapter, we have discussed the methods we need to use to implement non-serial communication across the IR port. We accessed these upper layer IrDA protocols through the use of sockets, thereby providing a great illustration of the concepts developed in Chapter 10. We examined each stage in socket usage and applied each stage to IrDA communications, using both TinyTP and IrMUX protocols. We concluded by briefly reviewing IrTranP and expedited IR output.

In the next chapter, we move from point-to-point communication into the world of multipoint communication. We examine TCP/IP protocols and how we use them in Symbian OS.

12

Communicating with TCP/IP

In 1973, a research project was initiated that investigated and developed technology to interlink networks of various kinds together into one "internetwork". This internetwork was held together by protocols that came to be known as the Transmission Control Protocol/Internet Protocol, or TCP/IP, suite, and these protocols stand today as the *de facto* standard for internetworking. Through the 1980s into the 1990s, the roughly 100 protocols in the TCP/IP suite saw many commercial and public domain implementations.

As we saw in Chapters 3 and 5, Symbian OS supports much of the TCP/IP protocol suite. In this chapter, we will look at what it takes to program using TCP/IP on Symbian OS. This is our first look at multipoint connections. Serial and IrDA communications are both point-to-point; TCP/IP protocols address networks that are multipoint in nature. Some of our concepts will adapt to accommodate this new way of communicating.

We will start by discussing some new concepts that arise when we communicate over a network. We will discuss how we connect to a network. The core of this chapter will have a familiar outline: system initialization, opening and configuring TCP/IP sockets, exchanging data, and closing connections. We will also discuss the differences between stream sockets and datagram sockets in TCP/IP. And we will actually get to see more examples than just to-do list item exchanges!

12.1 Considerations for Network Communication

As we have seen, a new medium brings new issues to consider. This section will discuss several new issues with respect to networks.

12.1.1   Connecting to the Network

The network protocol layers we deal with in this chapter all exist above the data link layer. So as we use these protocols, we assume that network connections exist at the data link layer already and that these protocols will interface with whatever exists to connect us to a network.

Figure 12.1 depicts this situation. We are focusing on the top two layers above the horizontal line: IP protocols that make up the network layer and TCP protocols that make up the transport layer. The other layers are not our concern in this chapter but are important for the protocols we *are* concerned about to function. As we covered in Chapter 4, Ethernet, PPP, and IrLAN are protocols that we can use to transport TCP/IP data. These are generically referred to as *network interfaces*.

Symbian OS implements control over these network interfaces through the *network interface manager* or NifMan. While it may sound like some odd superhero, NifMan is actually a server that is used by Symbian OS when a transport is needed, but a network interface has not been started. The server uses a plug-in method for modules to implement such interfaces. We will work with NifMan in the next section.

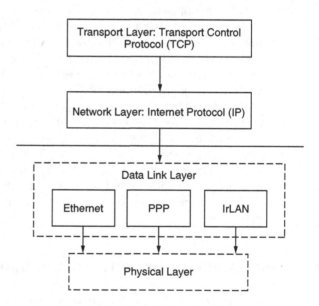

Figure 12.1   Protocol layers in this chapter.

12.1.2 TCP/IP Protocol Review

There are three types of protocols we are concerned with when we program with TCP/IP layers.

- TCP protocols implement a reliable, connected link between two communication endpoints. Any application protocol that desires a reliable connection will probably use TCP as its transport method. For example, HTTP and Telnet are two protocols that typically manage *sessions* of connectivity—long periods of data exchange for which connected links are designed.

- UDP protocols implement a connectionless link between a device and one or more endpoints. By definition, this is an unreliable connection that uses datagrams. Protocols that implement short messages or information queries typically use UDP as their transport method, as do name services such as DNS.

- IP protocols provide the network connections that support TCP and UDP communication. Addressing and routing are major concerns at this layer to identify machines and get data packets from point to point. IP layers on different devices exchange control and routing information with each other (through protocols like Internet Control Message Protocol (ICMP) and Routing Information Protocol (RIP)).

Most TCP protocols are client/server oriented. The HTTP service is a good example of this. Most request-based protocols that fall into the UDP category are also client/server oriented, where the requestor is the client and the information provider is the server. Network Time Protocol (NTP) is a UDP protocol that requests time updates; most average network devices are NTP clients that request time synchronization from time servers across the Internet.

As you might expect, Symbian OS implements TCP/IP protocols through the socket interface. There are standard definitions for TCP sockets and UDP sockets. IP sockets require a bit more ingenuity to use: there are a few standard definitions (e.g., for ICMP implementations), but we need to do some special programming to have complete access to a datagram's format.

12.1.3 System Definitions for TCP/IP

As with IrDA sockets, Symbian OS has set up certain parameters and definitions that we must use for TCP/IP programming.

IP addresses are characterized by the KAfInet address family. Specific protocols are given their own constant values (in \Epoc32\include\in_sock.h):

```
const TUint KProtocolInetIcmp = 1;
const TUint KProtocolInetTcp = 6;
const TUint KProtocolInetUdp = 17;
const TUint KProtocolInetIp = 0x100;
```

The properties of IP addresses are defined by the TInetAddr class, which has many functions to construct, compare, and analyze addresses. Many definitions are based on a single convenience macro:

```
#define INET_ADDR(a,b,c,d) \
    (TUint32)(((a)<<24)|((b)<<16)|((c)<<8)|(d))
```

Since an IP address is really just a 32-bit integer (at least at IP version 4), this macro allows specifying them in the popularized "dotted" notation. We can give 192.168.100.5 as INET_ADDR(192,168,100,5), which will produce the real integer address: 3232261125.

> ## IP Address Classes
>
> A good way to familiarize yourself with the IP address macro definitions is to try working through an example or two with them.
>
> IP addresses are broken up into address classes, based on which part of the address is the network portion and which is the host portion. A class A address uses the first octet as the network portion, class B uses the first two octets, and class C uses the first three. Go through the macro definitions, and figure out how to extract the network and host parts of an IP address for each of the three address classes.

A look through \Epoc32\include\in_sock.h will reveal many options and protocol setting values. We will be discussing these throughout this chapter.

12.2 The Network Interface Manager: NifMan

Because of the modularity of the socket concept, TCP/IP layer socket connections assume a layer that implements network connectivity lies beneath them. Since there are many ways to connect up a network, Symbian OS uses a NifMan server to coordinate and manage network interfaces. The key aspects of NifMan that we are concerned with here are its pluggable interface and the ability to monitor its progress.

The interface to the NifMan server is used by plug-in modules or *agents*. Agents are implementations of the data link layer for a particular connection method. Agents implement a network interface and give the NifMan server a way to check the progress of the connecting of that interface to the network. The plugin portion of the interface is found in a `.agt` file; the implementation of the network interface itself is found in a `.nif` file.

A good example of an interface agent is the NetDial agent. The NetDial agent allows the NifMan server to check on the progress of a dial-up network connection. The network interface itself is PPP, but the agent interfaces the NifMan server with the kernel so that progress can be checked.

Look for Agents

Look for agents and network interface implementations on your Symbian device or on your emulator.

The emulator has one agent that actual devices do not: `ntras.agt`. This interface implements an agent to monitor the connection between an emulator and the Remote Access Service of a PC running Windows NT. What interface do you think can be used with this agent?

There are also agents on hardware devices that you might not find on emulators. Psion netBooks, for example, might have an agent and a network interface that implement Ethernet support through the PC card slot. Look for agents and network interfaces specifically designed for your device.

The progress indicators from the NifMan server are accessed through an `RNif` class object. Once an `RNif` object is instantiated, you have two choices as to how to get progress reports: synchronously or asynchronously. The functions below access the progress indicators:

```
TInt Progress(TNifProgress &aProgress);
void ProgressNotification(TNifProgressBuf &aProgress,
   TRequestStatus &aStatus);
void CancelProgressNotification();
```

The first function is the synchronous function. The TNifProgress object parameter must be filled in by the function. The TNif-Progress class is used for accessing information only:

```
class TNifProgress
{
public:
  inline TNifProgress();
  TInt iStage;
  TInt iError;
};
```

Upon successful function completion, the iStage variable in the structure will have information pertaining to the connection progress. There are five states a connection can be in; the TAgent-ConnectType enumeration in \Epoc32\include\nifman.h details the values.

The other two functions are for the asynchronous call—one makes the request and the other cancels the request. The ProgressNotification() call includes a buffer that holds a progress object and a status variable for monitoring.

There are some other functions in the RNif class that are of interest:

- TInt LastProgressError(
    TNifProgress &aProgress)
  This reports the most recent error to have occurred in the progress of the network interface connection.
- TInt NetworkActive(TBool &aIsActive)
  This call will return the status of the network in the included parameter.

The NifMan is useful in a number of ways, typically to manipulate the network interface. Section 12.7 has an example of how to use a NifMan object to check the status of network interface and to shut it down.

12.3 Initializing the System for TCP/IP

Initialization for TCP/IP is much the same as it was for IrDA: connect to the socket server and load the device drivers. This fragment connects the current object to the socket server:

```
result = socksvr.Connect();
User::LeaveIfError(result);
```

This code should look fairly mundane by now.

Because TCP/IP protocols make up a large part of what the socket server does, the protocol modules are loaded by default. You can, of course, load them manually by using the `LoadCommModule()` functions in the `RSocketServ` class, but it is usually unnecessary. The name of the protocol module is "Tcpip".

12.4 Opening and Configuring a TCP/IP Socket

With TCP/IP sockets, opening a socket and configuring a socket are usually done at the same time. Once the initial open (with its configuration parameters) has been completed, the socket requires different configuration options to be applied, depending on the service status of the device as a client or server.

12.4.1 Choosing a Socket Configuration

There are several choices to make about socket configuration; these choices determine what type of socket will be opened. We have discussed these choices before:

- *Stream- vs. datagram-based:* Stream-based sockets are connected sockets, implementing reliable data transfer. Datagram-based sockets are connectionless sockets, implementing unreliable data transfer. For TCP/IP, Symbian OS also supports two other modes: sequential packet transport, which ensures ordered packet arrival but no error checking, and raw transport, which essentially bypasses the protocol layers to send raw data packets through the data link layer, with no guarantees of anything.

- *Type of TCP/IP protocol:* Here, we have the three choices we outlined above: TCP, UDP, or IP. TCP sockets are stream-based, connected sockets. UDP and IP sockets are datagram-based, connectionless sockets.

Opening a TCP/IP socket is done in the standard way—calling `Open()` from the `RSocket` class. The address family is `KAfInet`. The socket type is chosen from the list below:

```
const TUint KsockStream = 1;
const TUint KsockDatagram = 2;
const TUint KSockSeqPacket = 3;
const TUint KSockRaw = 4;
```

Each of these constants corresponds to a transport mode. The socket protocol is chosen from the following list:

```
const TUint KProtocolInetIcmp = 1;
const TUint KProtocolInetTcp = 6;
```

```
const TUint KProtocolInetUdp = 17;
const TUint KProtocolInetIp = 0x100;
```

Note that ICMP is a special protocol supported directly by Symbian OS.

Let's take some examples. If we were to open a socket to a Web server, it would be a TCP-level, connected socket. We could open one with the statement below:

```
result = WebServerSocket.Open(socksvr, KAfInet,
    KSockStream, KProtocolInetTcp);
```

If we wanted to open a socket to a Domain Name Service (DNS) server, we would want a datagram-based socket that worked with UDP protocols. We could open one with the statement below:

```
result = DNSServerSocket.Open(socksvr, KAfInet,
    KSockDatagram, KProtocolInetUdp);
```

If we wanted to open a socket to use ICMP to ping another computer, that would use IP-level protocols, but we would have to assemble our own packets. Hence, we would want to specify raw packets in this way:

```
result = ICMPSocket.Open(socksvr, KAfInet, KSockRaw,
    KProtocolInetIcmp);
```

Other TCP/IP Socket Configurations

The configuration you choose for a socket is really dependent on the type of service you intend on accessing with that socket. As with the three examples above, how the service is offered from a server determines how the socket should be configured. Most standard TCP/IP services have standard configuration requirements.

Consider the services below. For each of these, think about how you would have to configure a socket to access the service.

- POP3 mail servicey
- IMAP mail servicey
- NNTP news reading service
- Telnet remote connection servicey
- FTP file transfer service (FTP is actually two services: a command connection and a data connection)y
- Daytime time update service (not necessarily NTP: try port 13)

12.4.2 Finishing Configuration: Connecting Client Sockets

Client sockets must connect to servers via the `Connect()` function from the `Rsocket` class. Before a socket is connected, however, it must have an address to which it will connect. This is done by constructing a `TInetAddr` object.

Two components make up a `TInetAddr` object: an IP address and a port number. Recall that port numbers are the way specific applications or services are identified on a device and that they are used to tag a datastream so that data connections can be multiplexed on a server. To connect sockets, then, we need to set up both address and port specifications in the `TInetAddr` object, as below:

```
address.SetPort(INET_ADDR(192,168,100,10), 80);
```

This would set the IP address to `192.168.100.10` and the port to `80` (the HTTP service port).

Once the `TInetAddr` object is set, the `Connect()` function can be called, and the socket can attempt to connect to the device and port specified by its arguments:

```
WebServerSocket.Connect(address, status);
```

Remember that `Connect()` is an asynchronous function and requires a status variable to monitor its progress.

12.4.3 Finishing Configuration: Binding Server Sockets

Configuring sockets used by servers means that we must bind the opened socket to a local address, set up a listening queue on the socket, and open a second socket to connect to the incoming connection.

For TCP/IP servers, we must bind the socket to the address and port for which we want to listen. Special settings exist for *any* address or *any* port, but these must be set explicitly in a `TInetAddr` object. For example, the code below will create an address that will match any IP address with its port set to 1100:

```
TInetAddr ServerAddress = new TInetAddr(
    KInetAddrAny, 1100);
```

The constant `KInetPortAny` will match any port. (In reality, these constants are simply a specification of `0.0.0.0` as the IP address and `0` as the port number, respectively.)

Once we have constructed a `TInetAddr` object, binding the server socket is straightforward—it is the same as for IrDA sockets.

Setting up the listening queue is also simple. Consider the following code (where iListeningSocket is a RSocket object that has already been created):

```
TInetAddr iListeningAddress =
    new TInetAddr(KinetAddrAny, 2000);
iListeningSocket.Bind(iListeningAddress);
iListeningSocket.Listen(5);
```

This code sets up a socket to listen for incoming connections on any IP address looking for port 2000. The listening queue is set up for five simultaneous connections.

Before a server can accept connections, it must open up a second blank socket to use for an incoming connection.

```
result = iServiceSocket.Open(iSockSvr);
User::LeaveIFError(result);
```

Finally the server can wait for connections by calling the Accept() function on the original listener socket:

```
iListener.Accept(iServiceSocket, status);
```

12.4.4   Using the Host Resolver

It is often the case that we have a hostname to connect to or listen for rather than an address. In this case, we must convert this hostname to a TInetAddr object prior to using it for a Connect() or a Bind() call.

The sequence we use looks very much like what we did for IrDA sockets, except there is no real discovery of devices. Instead, the host resolver takes advantage of Domain Name Service (DNS) to do the name-to-address conversion. Consider the following code:

```
RHostResolver resolver;
TNameEntry iHostEntry;
TPtrC AddressName;
TInetAddr Address;
result = resolver.Open(socksvr, KAfInet, KProtocolInetTcp);
User::LeaveIfError(result);
AddressName.Set(_L("http://www.symbian.com"));
resolver.GetByName(AddressName, iHostEntry, status);
User::WaitForRequest(status);
Address = iHostEntry().iAddr;
Address.SetPort(80);

WebServer.Connect(Address, status);
```

Here, `WebServer` is an instantiated `RSocket` object. This code will resolve the host name ***http://www.symbian.com*** to its actual IP address, then combine that address with a specification of port 80 and connect to it on behalf of a client.

12.4.5 Getting Information from a Socket

After a socket has been opened and configured, and the `Connect()` or `Bind()` and `Accept()` functions have completed, it may be necessary to extract some information from the socket. For example, you may want figure out the address of the remote side of the socket. The `LocalName()` and `RemoteName()` functions handle extracting this information.

```
void LocalName(TSockAddr &anAddr);
void RemoteName(TSockAddr &anAddr);
```

These functions are similar in the way you call them. `Local-Name()` returns a `TSockAddr` object that—when converted to a `TInetAddr` object—will give the address and port number of the socket as it is bound in the current application. `RemoteName()` will do the same for the remote endpoint. `LocalName()` is especially useful in situations where you do not know the local address of the device—for example, if it was set up by someone else or by a network service (e.g., a server using Dynamic Host Configuration Protocol (DHCP)). The values of these calls are valid after `Bind()` has been used on servers and `Connect()` has been used on clients.

If just the port information is needed, you can use the functions below:

```
TUint LocalPort();
TUint RemotePort();
```

12.4.6 TCP/IP Socket Options

There are many options available for TCP/IP sockets, much more than I can cover here without putting you to sleep. Most are meant for specific situations, for example, getting routing information from an ICMP packet, rather than general TCP/IP packet settings. All are set using `Ioctl()` calls. Remember that `Ioctl()` varies its format depending on the option and whether that option is being set or simply queried for its value. The options are given in `\Epoc32\include\in_sock.h`.

12.5   Exchanging Data

Once we have opened and configured a socket and have either connected or accepted a connection, we have a socket with applications on both ends looking to exchange data. At this point, we will use the same API as for other socket connections. There is very little that changes from IrDA socket data exchange to TCP/IP socket data exchange.

We do, however, have access to more flexibility with TCP/IP sockets. We can access raw sockets, for example, that allow the formation of any type of data packet. If we do not want to exchange byte streams, for example, but want to send specific types of data, we need to use raw sockets. An NTP client request, for example, has a specific packet format that must be sent from an IP layer. We can construct this using raw sockets.

Because the API is the same, protocol issues do not change. We still have protocol initialization and termination concerns and must adjust our access to the type of socket connection (streams or datagrams) that we are using.

12.6   Closing a Socket

Closing a TCP/IP socket is no different than closing other sockets: we should drain stream sockets of data requests (if we need to) and then close down the socket. Draining can happen synchronously with the `Cancel()` function or asynchronously with the `Shutdown()` function. Then we call the `Close()` function on the socket to close it down and free up its resources.

12.7   Closing and Checking Network Interfaces

As we stated in Section 12.2, we can access the status of a network interface with an `RNif` object. In addition to simply checking connection progress, we can check the condition of the network interface and can shut it down through objects of this class.

Consider the function below:

```
TBool CPullerAppUi::IsNetworkOpen()
{
    TInt result;
    TBool res;
    RNif iNif;

    // Open the network interface
    result = iNif.Open();
    if (result != KErrNone) return EFalse;

    // Now test it
    res = ETrue;
    result = iNif.NetworkActive(res);
    if (result != KErrNone) res = EFalse;
    iNif.Close();

    return res;
}
```

This function uses an RNif object to open a network interface and check the active status through that object.

We can also shutdown an interface using an RNif object. The function below demonstrates this:

```
void CPullerAppUi::DisconnectFromNetwork()
{
    RNif iNif;
    TInt result;

    result = iNif.Open();
    if (result != KErrNone) return EFalse;
    result = iNif.Stop();
    iNif.Close();
}
```

The Stop() function will close down a network interface that has been successfully opened.

12.8   Another Example: Fetching a Web Page

Let's consider a new example. Let's say we want an application that will fetch and store a Web page. We will develop a class, PageGrabber, whose specification looks something like this:

```
class PageGrabber : public CActive
{
    enum TState {ENotConnected, ENameResolved,
                 ESocketOpened, EGrabbingPage,
                 EShuttingDownConnection};
```

```
public:
    PageGrabber(CPullerAppUi* aAppUi);
    ~PageGrabber();

public:
    static PageGrabber* NewLC(CPullerAppUi* iAppUi);
    static PageGrabber* NewL(CPullerAppUi* iAppUi);

public:
    void ConstructL();
    void IssueRequest(URL aURL, TDes* DestDir,
        RFs afsSession);

    void DoCancel();
    void RunL();

private:
    CPullerAppUi* iAppUi;
    URL webpage;
    RSocketServ socksvr;
    RSocket sock;
    RHostResolver resolver;
    RFile outstream, logstream;
    RFs fsSession;
    TState iConnectState;
    TNameEntry iHostEnt;
    TRequestStatus iStatus;
    TSockXfrLength reslen;
    TInt count;
};
```

An object of this class is to be created with an `AppUi` class (i.e., an application interface) as an argument. The purpose of this class is to retrieve a Web page and store it in a file. This class is implemented as an active object and is thus derived from the `CActive` class.

12.8.1   Constructors and Deconstructors

We start here with the class constructor.

```
PageGrabber::PageGrabber(CPullerAppUi* aAppUi)
    : CActive()
{
    iAppUi = aAppUi;
    iConnectState = ENotConnected;
    count = 0;
};
```

Notice here that in addition to setting up some variables, we are initializing a state variable `iConnectState` that will be used to control the action of the active object. The initial value reflects the fact that no socket is connected to a remote Web server.

We define a few functions that will allow for the safe creation of `PageGrabber` objects. These call the class contructor and use a clean up stack to safely manipulate memory.

```
PageGrabber* PageGrabber::NewLC(CPullerAppUi* aAppUi)
{
    PageGrabber* self=new (ELeave) PageGrabber(aAppUi);
    CleanupStack::PushL(self);
    self->ConstructL();

    return self;
}

PageGrabber* PageGrabber::NewL(CPullerAppUi* aAppUi)
{
    PageGrabber* self = NewLC(aAppUi);
    CleanupStack::Pop();

    return self;
}
```

The second phase constructor `ConstructL()` will simply add this active object to the scheduling queue.

```
void PageGrabber::ConstructL()
{
    CActiveScheduler::Add(this);
}
```

There is not much to deconstruct. We make sure that the active object is cancelled.

```
PageGrabber::~PageGrabber()
{
    CActive::Cancel();
}
```

12.8.2 Cancelling the Page Grabber

Recall that an active object must have two functions implemented by subclasses: `DoCancel()` and `RunL()`. We will implement `RunL()` in a later section; the implementation of `DoCancel()` is below:

```
void PageGrabber::DoCancel()
{
    sock.CancelAll();
    sock.Close();
    outstream.Close();
}
```

It consists of several `Close()` calls with a synchronous canceling of I/O requests on the socket.

12.8.3 The PageGrabber State Diagram

To understand how pages are grabbed, we must first look at the state diagram for the `PageGrabber` active object. The set of states the active object can be in is given by the following enumeration:

```
enum TState {ENotConnected, ENameResolved, ESocketOpened,
             EGrabbingPage,
             EShuttingDownConnection};
```

There are six possible states, and Figure 12.2 shows how we transition between them. The transitions are labeled with the calls that each state transition is waiting for or the condition that causes the transition. The diagram is a bit simplistic in that transitions to the error state have been left out.

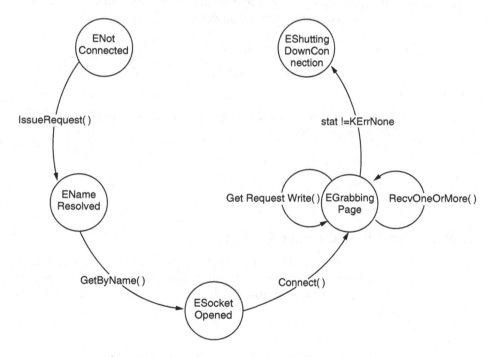

Figure 12.2   State diagram for the PageGrabber active object.

12.8.4 Starting the Page Grab

The grabbing of a page is started by calling the `IssueRequest()` function of the `PageGrabber` class. The calling application will use something like this:

```
iGrabber = PageGrabber::NewL(this);
iGrabber->IssueRequest(webpage, &fname, fsSession);
```

where `iGrabber` is an object of the `PageGrabber` class, webpage is defined to be of type `URL`, fname (a filename) is a string (`TBuf<256>` is easy), and `fsSession` (a file server session) is of type `RFs`. This call will return right away and will set a page grab in motion.

N.B. The `URL` class is one written for this application. The functions are self-explanatory; please look them up in the source code.

The definition of `IssueRequest()` is below. The code does two things: it generates a random filename if the filename given is formed incorrectly, and it starts the active object sequence.

```
void PageGrabber::IssueRequest(URL aURL, TDes *aFilename,
    RFs afsSession)
{
    TBuf<256> str;
    TBuf<25> nfname;
    TInt err,pos;
    TPtrC iAddressDesc;
    TParse filestorename;

    // Copy the arguments for later use
    fsSession = afsSession;
    webpage.Copy(aURL);

    // Run some tests on the filename given
    fsSession.Parse(*aFilename,filestorename);
    ConeUtils::EnsurePathExistsL(
        filestorename.DriveAndPath());
    err = outstream.Replace(fsSession,
        filestorename.FullName(),
        EFileWrite|EFileStreamText);

    // The filename was a bad name (empty or something else)
    // We generate a random name here
    if (err == KErrBadName) {
        TTime now;
        TInt64 seed = now.Int64();
        now.HomeTime();
        nfname.Format(_L("fn%d"), (TInt)Math::Rand(seed));
```

```
            pos = aFilename->LocateReverse('\\');
            str.Copy(aFilename->Left(pos+1));
            str.Append(nfname);
            str.Append(_L(".htm"));
            fsSession.Parse(str,filestorename);
            err = outstream.Replace(fsSession,
                filestorename.FullName(),
                EFileWrite|EFileStreamText);
        }

        // Abandon ship if there is still a problem
        User::LeaveIfError(err);

        // Announce our intentions
        str.Copy(_L("Opening Network Connection"));
        iAppUi->SetProgressText(&str);

        // Connect to the socket server
        err = socksvr.Connect();
        User::LeaveIfError(err);

        // Now resolve the name given in the URL
        err = resolver.Open(socksvr, KAfInet, KProtocolInetTcp);
        User::LeaveIfError(err);
        iAddressDesc.Set(aURL.host);
        resolver.GetByName(iAddressDesc, iHostEnt, iStatus);

        // This is the first step in the process. Set the
        // connection state and kick the active object
        iConnectState = ENameResolved;
        SetActive();
    }
```

This code checks the filename, opens it, and starts the resolver resolving the hostname of the URL given. Note that the host resolver can resolve numeric IP addresses as well as names, which means that a name like 192.168.100.10 will resolve just as well as *http://www.symbian.com*, and both are legal.

12.8.5 Implementing RunL()

We implement RunL() as a large switch statement. This function will run when pending I/O functions return, and how these returns are handled is based on the value of the iConnectState variable, run through the switch statement. Let's look at this function, walking through the switch statement one case at a time.

The first case is used when name resolution has completed.

```
void PageGrabber::RunL()
{
    TInt pos,err;
```

```
            TBuf8<800> line;
            TInt portno;

            switch (iConnectState) {
                case ENameResolved:
                    if (iStatus == KErrNone) {
                        // set up the address
                        portno = webpage.port;
                        address = iHostEnt().iAddr;
                        address.SetPort(portno);

                        // open the socket
                        err = sock.Open(socksvr, KAfInet,
                                KSockStream, KProtocolInetTcp);
                        User::LeaveIfError(err);

                        // start the connection process
                        Sock.Connect(address, iStatus);

                        // change the state and start the wait
                        iConnectState = ESocketOpened;
                        SetActive();
                    } else {
                        // handle an error in name resolution
                    }

                    break;
```

If name resolution has completed successfully, we should have an address value in the `address` variable. The next step is to retrieve the IP address from the resolution results and the port number from the URL and to build a `TInetAddr` object from them. We then use this object to open a socket and start the connection to the remote Web server.

When the case below is invoked, we have a connection, and the remote Web server is waiting for a command from this process.

```
            case ESocketOpened:
                if (iStatus == KErrNone) {
                    // Set up the command string for the Web page
                    // fetch
                    line.Copy(_L("GET "));
                    line.Append(webpage.protocol);
                    line.Append(_L("://"));
                    line.Append(webpage.host);
                    line.Append(webpage.file);
                    for (pos=0; pos<line.Length(); pos++)
                        if (line[pos] == '\\') line[pos] = '/';
                    line.Append(_L("\xD\xA"));

                    // Send this command to the Web server
                    sock->Write(line, iStatus);
                    // Move a new state and return to the scheduler
```

```
        iConnectState = EGrabbingPage;
        SetActive();
    } else {
        // handle a connection error
    }

    break;
```

The code constructs a simple GET command and sends it to the Web server (we discussed the GET command in Section 5.2.1). Note the Append() call that puts the string "\xD\xA" at the end of the command string. This is necessary for the Web server to find the end of the string.

The third case is the response from the Web server with the Web page we asked for or a set of HTML lines stating an error. Either way we store it to a file.

```
case EGrabbingPage:
    if (iStatus == KErrNone) {
        // Set up the receive
        reslen = 250;
        sock->RecvOneOrMore(aDesc,0, iStatus,reslen);
        outstream.Write(*aDesc);

        // Record and wait!
        iConnectState = EGrabbingPage;
        iProcessingState = ENormal;
        SetActive();
    } else {
        iConnectState = EShuttingDownConnection;
        // signal connection shutdown
    }

    break;
```

Here, we use RecvOneOrMore() to pick up data from the socket and write whatever we have to the file. We use RecvOneOrMore() to buffer the effects of network delay or disconnection from the network. When an error occurs, either the stream is closed by the remote side or some connection error has occurred. Either way, we shut down the connection.

Finally, this last Boolean condition finds the case where we are shutting down our socket connection.

```
if (iConnectState == EShuttingDownConnection) {
    iAppUi->ShutDownGrab(); // signal shutdown to app
    sock.CancelAll();
    sock.Close();
    outstream.Close();
    delete this;
}
```

In this code, we signal to the application that the connection is down, and we go through the standard socket shutdown routine. Notice that at the end of the code, the active object deletes itself. This is an easy way to make sure the object is deleted only after all the socket I/O has been completed.

> ### Deleting the Socket
>
> In the code above, the active object deletes itself. It is slightly odd behavior for an object to delete itself. How could you structure it so that the object that created this active object correctly deleted it? What would you have to check in order to make sure all resources were correctly handled? What issues are involved?
>
> Further, can you tell why we allocated a socket as a pointer in the first place? Why did we not just use a declared socket object?

12.9 Sending Datagrams

Protocols such as HTTP, FTP, Telnet, and WAP work with connected sockets with data streams. However, many UDP and IP connections need data sent in different ways. By their nature, these protocols are designed in request-response pairs, and the request must have a specific format.

Consider, as an example, Network Time Protocol (NTP). NTP servers are supposed to have access to accurate time sources and to respond with a sample of the accurate time when an NTP client makes a request. This request comes in on port 123 and takes the form of an NTP packet, shown in Figure 12.3. NTP socket communication is a UDP connection using datagrams.

At first glance, sending NTP packets may appear straightforward. One simple way to do this would be to use multiple `Write()` or `SendTo()` statements, one per field in the NTP packet. This involves several mistakes, but the biggest is that each statement causes data to be sent out as a datagram, resulting in the NTP case as 15 datagrams, each in the wrong format, rather than a single, correct datagram.

A correct way to send datagrams with specific formats is to send a single buffer containing all the data in the datagram. It can be a bit challenging to configure a buffer full of bytes in the correct format, but C++ helps us out through the ability to overlay memory.

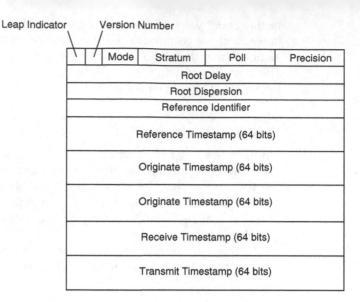

Figure 12.3 NTP datagram format.

Let's consider a C++ structure that depicts an NTP datagram:

```
struct pkt {
    u_char li_vn_mode;   /* contains leap indicator, version
                            and mode */
    u_char stratum;      /* peer's stratum */
    u_char ppoll;  /* the peer polling interval */
    s_char precision;    /* peer clock precision */
    s_fp rootdelay;      /* distance to primary clock */
    u_fp rootdispersion;/* clock dispersion */
    u_int32 refid;       /* reference clock ID */
    l_fp reftime;  /* time peer clock was last updated */
    l_fp org;  /* originate time stamp */
    l_fp rec;  /* receive time stamp */
    l_fp xmt;  /* transmit time stamp */
};
```

The data types referenced above are not standard Symbian types. This code is used from public domain source code for NTP services. Symbian OS design adapts well to this code as well as its own. The types are as follows:

- `u_char`: unsigned char, 8 bits

- `s_char`: signed char, 8 bits

- `u_int32`: unsigned integer, 32 bits

- `u_fp`: unsigned floating point, 32 bits

- `s_fp`: signed floating point, 32 bits
- `l_fp`: long, signed floating point: 64 bits

To build a buffer that holds this packet, we declare the following:

```
u_char outpack[64];
struct pkt *xpkt = (struct pkt *)outpack;
TBuf8<64> icpbuffer;
```

Here, we have declared a buffer of 8-bit bytes, 64 bytes long. Through the magic of C++, we have made the memory space of this buffer occupy the same memory space as the `pkt` structure. So any changes we make to the memory referenced by the `xpkt` pointer will be made in the `outpack` buffer. When we are finished constructing the NTP packet, we copy the `outpack` buffer to the `icpbuffer` and send the `icpbuffer` to NTP server.

We can see this in the portion of the `RunL()` function shown below. In this code, we have already connected a socket to the remote NTP server and must now construct the packet and send it. There is a fair amount of the NTP client code I am not showing you—so that we can illustrate sending a datagram packet—so bear with some of the macro definitions.

```
case ESocketOpened:
    if (iStatus == KErrNone) {
    // assemble the NTP packet
        xpkt->li_vn_mode = PKT_LI_VN_MODE(LEAP_NOTINSYNC,
                            sys_version, MODE_CLIENT);
    xpkt->stratum = STRATUM_TO_PKT(STRATUM_UNSPEC);
    xpkt->ppoll = NTP_MINPOLL;
    xpkt->precision = NTPDATE_PRECISION;
    xpkt->rootdelay = htonl(NTPDATE_DISTANCE);
    xpkt->rootdispersion = htonl(NTPDATE_DISP);
    xpkt->refid = htonl(NTPDATE_REFID);
    // Clear the time fields
    L_CLR(&xpkt->reftime);
    L_CLR(&xpkt->org);
    L_CLR(&xpkt->rec);

        // get the local time and put it into the
        // time fields
        l_fp xmt;
        (void) gettimeofday(&tv, (struct timezone *)0);
        xmt.l_i = tv.tv_sec + JAN_1970;
        dtemp = tv.tv_usec * FRAC / 1e6;
        if (dtemp >= FRAC) xmt.l_i++;
        xmt.l_uf = (u_int32)dtemp;
        xpkt->xmt.l_ui = htonl(xmt.l_ui);
        xpkt->xmt.l_uf = htonl(xmt.l_uf);
```

```
                    // Send the packet
                    icpbuffer.SetLength(0);
                    icpbuffer.Append(outpack, MAXPACKET);
                    sock.Write(icpbuffer, stat);

                    iConnectState = ESendingNTPRequest;
                    SetActive();
                } else {
                    // signal a connection failure
                }

        break;
```

Notice how the code treats the structure pointed to by the `xpkt` variable as a C++ struct, then copies the same memory space by using the `outpack` buffer as an array.

Other datagram protocols can be worked with in a similar way. These include lookup services like DNS and LDAP, information protocols like RIP (for routing) and WHO (logged in users on a time-sharing system), and miscellaneous protocols like daytime and echo protocols. ICMP would also be accessed the same way, although you need to open a socket of the protocol `KProtocolInetIcmp` and a type of `KSockRaw`.

12.10   Summary

This chapter has surveyed what it takes to communicate using Symbian devices over TCP/IP networks. We looked at several different ways sockets are used to send packets over the different TCP/IP protocol layers. Specifically, we looked at the following topics:

- We briefly reviewed the relationship between TCP/IP and Symbian devices. We reviewed how connections to a network are made, what TCP/IP protocols are supported, and what constructs Symbian OS provides for us to talk about TCP/IP.

- We looked at the NifMan—the network interface manager—and how network interfaces are manipulated.

- We then went through the stages of using sockets and how TCP/IP fits into these stages.

- We reviewed two examples: retrieving a Web page from a server as an example of TCP level protocols and implementing an NTP client as an example of using datagram packets.

The next chapter takes sockets and tackles Bluetooth protocols with them. We will be introducing new examples as well as revisiting our old friend, `TodoX`.

13

Bluetooth Communications

In 908, Thyre, the wife of Denmark's King Gorm the Old, gave birth to a son. The boy was named Harald Blatant—or, translated, Harald Bluetooth—and he became king of Denmark from 940 to 981. He possessed great skills of communication and could make people talk to each other; during his rule, Denmark and Norway were Christianized and united. It is these skills in communication and unification that Bluetooth designers tried to capture as they chose his name to identify the wireless technology that we will examine in this chapter.

Bluetooth identifies a suite of protocols and a model for radio transmission that focuses on short range wireless communication. As with other protocol stacks, the Symbian OS provides support for the Bluetooth protocol suite by extending the socket model to include Bluetooth protocol modules. In addition to Bluetooth sockets, the Symbian OS has a solid implementation of Bluetooth device and service discovery and of the Bluetooth security model.

We will look at this Bluetooth support in this chapter. We will start, as we have with previous chapters, by reviewing the Bluetooth model and the way the Symbian OS addresses it. We will then take a close look at device and service discovery, which features prominently in the way Bluetooth works. We will follow this by relating sockets to the Bluetooth model, through all the socket phases we have discussed in other chapters. We will close the chapter by looking at an example of instant messaging using Bluetooth protocols.

13.1   Considerations for Bluetooth Communication

13.1.1   Reviewing the Bluetooth Model

The Bluetooth model for communications is built from a specification for radio transmission, a driver for this radio module, and a stack of protocols built on top of the driver that implements various forms of data transmission. Back in Section 4.5, we overviewed the Bluetooth protocols and, in Figure 4.6, we displayed a diagram of these protocols and how they relate to one another.

For our purposes—i.e., transferring data over Bluetooth—we can group the protocols into software and hardware groups and focus on the software. Figure 13.1 holds a redrawing of Figure 4.6, with a separation of protocols into hardware and software groups. LMP, Baseband, and Audio protocols are typically handled by Bluetooth hardware; L2CAP, SDP, and RFCOMM are typically implemented in software.

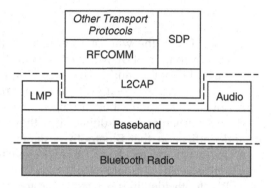

Figure 13.1 Protocol layers in this chapter.

We will focus on the software protocols. We will use sockets that work through the L2CAP layer or the RFCOMM layer. L2CAP sockets allow finer-grained control of the connection, implementing properties much like TCP in the internetwork world. RFCOMM sockets have properties like serial communication. The typical choice of applications is to use L2CAP sockets. SDP will be used to discover remote devices and the services they offer. In the Bluetooth world, discovery is important. As Bluetooth devices are generally mobile, and a Bluetooth radio signal has a short range, it is likely that Bluetooth devices will frequently move in and out of range of other Bluetooth devices. This movement means that discovery may have to be ongoing, an asynchronous activity that proceeds in parallel with an application's functionality.

13.1.2   Spotlight on Bluetooth Device Services

In the other socket-based communications we have covered—IrDA and TCP/IP—we have encountered a two-part addressing of socket connections. In these previous two contexts, addresses were made up of hardware addresses and service ports. For IrDA, the assignment of service port numbers is arbitrary; for TCP/IP, service port numbers are assigned for some services and arbitrary for others. For IrDA, there were no attributes attached to the port; for TCP/IP, there was a small set of attributes (e.g., protocol and socket type).

The Bluetooth model extends this device/service address pairing for socket connections, taking service address and attribute assignment to a higher level of formality and complexity. Bluetooth services are identified by a unique ID number, and are characterized by a list of service attributes. In turn, each attribute is characterized by an ID number, an attribute type and a value. The set of triples (ID, type, value) that describe a service are stored in a database maintained on each Bluetooth device, with a single record for each service and its attributes. So each Bluetooth device must maintain a database of services, composed of service records, where each record is a list of service attributes.

For example, let's say we have a digital camera that provides an "image" service. We want it to be the source for images for wireless devices. Simply allowing incoming connections to know that it is providing an image service is not enough; devices that might use this service would want to know more information. For example, useful information here might be image format, image height, image width, and color depth. In addition, a remote device might want to determine if the camera also provides a "shutter" service—that is, the ability to take a picture. We might visualize these services like the diagram in Figure 13.2. The database is

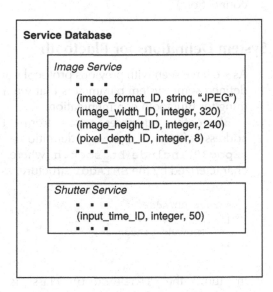

Figure 13.2 Example service database contents.

composed of a set of services, which in turn is a set of attribute triples. In our example, we might have at least four attribute triples for the "image" service.

Bluetooth device discovery, then, can also include service discovery. With Bluetooth, a device not only looks for another Bluetooth device, it might also look for a Bluetooth device that provides a specific service. In the camera example, a handheld Bluetooth device might want to be able to snap pictures that are in JPEG format, of any size, with 8-bit color depth. The camera we described above would match that device search.

It is worth noting here that this type of service discovery is a marked improvement from IrDA and TCP/IP discovery methods. Using IrDA sockets, we are able to find a device and to query its IAS about service attributes. However, this service attribute information is very spare; we can only find port number information or the level of support for various protocols. Using TCP/IP sockets, we are not even able to collect this much information. We must know ahead of time which IP address and which port number we want to connect to; there is no way to ask a machine what ports are open. (In all fairness, there are certainly methods of using TCP/IP to find devices that provide services listening on ports. We could broadcast for devices, for example, or perform a scan on a particular device for open ports. However, this is not part of the socket connection process; this would be a separate, time-consuming operation performed before attempting socket connection.)

13.1.3   System Definitions for Bluetooth

As we have seen with previous protocol stacks, the Symbian OS has defined some system parameters that we must use when programming for Bluetooth communication.

Bluetooth addresses are from the KBTAddrFamily address family. System definitions can be found in \Epoc32\include\bt_sock.h, where Bluetooth addresses are characterized by the SBTAddr structure, as below:

```
struct SBTAddr
{
  TBTDevAddr iAddress;
};
```

In turn, the TBTDevAddr class is defined in the file \Epoc32\include\bttypes.h as follows:

```
static const TInt KSdpUUIDMaxLength = 16;
const TInt KBTDevAddrSize=0x06;
const TInt KBTMaxDevAddrSize = KBTDevAddrSize;

class TBTDevAddr
{
public:
    IMPORT_C TBTDevAddr();
    IMPORT_C TBTDevAddr(const TInt64 &aInt);
    IMPORT_C TBTDevAddr(const TDesC8 &aDes);
    inline TBool operator==(const TBTDevAddr &aAddr) const;
    inline TBool operator!=(const TBTDevAddr &aAddr) const;
    inline const TUint8 &operator[](TInt aIndex) const;
    inline TUint8 &operator[](TInt aIndex);
    inline void Reset();
    inline TPtr8 Des();
    inline const TPtrC8 Des() const;
private:
    TFixedArray<TUint8, KBTDevAddrSize> iAddr;
};
```

From these definitions, you can see that a Bluetooth address is represented by an array of size KBTDevAddrSize (currently six) that contains 8-bit bytes. This makes sense, since Bluetooth addresses are 48-bit quantities.

In the bt_sock.h file, there are four protocol definitions:

```
const TUint KBTLinkManager = 0x0099;
const TUint KL2CAP = 0x0100;
const TUint KRFCOMM = 0x0003;
const TUint KSDP = 0x0001;
```

These are for the link manager protocol, L2CAP, RFCOMM, and service discovery protocol, respectively.

Read On

There are many definitions in the bt_sock.h and bttypes.h files. You should read through these simply to familiarize yourself with the various socket options and error constants. We will address some of these later in this chapter.

13.2 Discovering Bluetooth Devices and Services

As we mentioned in the above discussion about services, device and service discovery are a very important part of using Bluetooth protocols. In typical Bluetooth use scenarios, devices go in and out of range easily and quickly. Discovery happens regularly and is the best way to monitor this movement and to stay connected to services.

13.2.1 Explicitly Setting the Device and Service

It should be stated first that, while it can be very useful, the discovery of devices and services is not always necessary. A device could have a specific remote device for which it is waiting to exchange data, or the user could specifically request a particular Bluetooth device and service. In these cases, we can set the device address or the service ID explicitly and not bother to do device discovery at all.

Bluetooth device addresses are 48-bit quantities. We need a 64 bit integer to hold them, or a `TInt64`. We use this `TInt64` quantity to set the device address. As an example, if we are exchanging data with a device whose hardware address is `65097113885`, or `0xf2817211d`, we can create a device address explicitly using the following declaration:

```
TBTDevAddr deviceAddress(TInt64(0xf2, 0x817211d));
```

This would construct the device address `deviceAddress` to have the correct predefined setting.

The service can be explicitly set as well. Services in Bluetooth are specified by service ID numbers. If, for example, you choose ID number 100 as the service to exchange data across, you can set this just as you would with IrDA or TCP/IP:

```
TBTSockAddr addr;

addr.SetBTAddr(deviceAddress);
addr.SetPort(100);
```

We could now use the `addr` variable in a `Connect()` method call to use Bluetooth sockets.

13.2.2 Discovering a Device

The sequence used in the Symbian OS for discovering devices looks very much like the one we used for IrDA device discovery: we will use the host resolver to find the devices we need. We can discover devices by a device *address* or by a device *name*.

To discover a device by address, we need to execute code such as the following:

```
TInquirySockAddr inqaddr;
TNameEntry tnentry;

inqaddr.SetIAC(KGIAC);
inqaddr.SetAction(KHostResInquiry);
resolver.GetByAddress(inqaddr, tnentry, status);
User::WaitForRequest(status);
```

The inquiry proceeds as follows. First, we must set the *inquiry access code*; it can be one of the following constants:

```
const TUint KGIAC = 0x9e8b33;
const TUint KLIAC = 0x9e8b00;
```

In the first case, the code signifies a general unlimited query; in the second case, the query is a limited one. A general query requires that all discoverable devices must respond to the discovery query (a broadcast). A limited query forces remote devices to respond only to certain messages (a multicast). In a dense environment like a conference, airport terminal, or classroom, there may be many devices that are discoverable. Regulating the query mechanism is a way to fine-tune the discovery process and reduce discovery time.

For the next step, we set the type of inquiry we are trying to make. The constants are defined as below, for both by-address and by-name discovery:

```
const static TUint KHostResInquiry = 1;
const static TUint KHostResName = 2;
```

Finally, we make the call to the GetByAddress() method and wait for a response. This call is asynchronous. Both by-address and by-name discovery are implemented through the GetByAddress() method; the GetByName() method is invalid for Bluetooth. If the call to GetByAddress() succeeds, the response is much like the response for IrDA: the discovered device information will be returned in the TNameEntry object that was sent as a parameter. If more than one device is discovered, the information on other devices can be retrieved by use of the RHostResolver::Next() method.

13.2.3 Discovering Services

Service discovery is needed when an application does not know ahead of time that a particular remote device has the service it requires. Service discovery is done in two steps: first we search for the service ID, then we search for the service attributes of the discovered service.

The service discovery agent

Service discovery is done using the Service Discovery Agent (SDA). The agent uses the Bluetooth Service Discovery Protocol (SDP) to search for and match a service on the remote device. SDP is implemented as an asynchronous activity, and the application that started the service search must set up notification callback methods to be notified about the success or failure of the search.

The agent is represented in the Symbian OS by an object of the CSdpAgent class. An object of this class encapsulates the use of SDP between remote devices. The CSdpAgent class has the following definition:

```
class CSdpAgent : public CBase
{
public:
  IMPORT_C static CSdpAgent* NewL(
     MSdpAgentNotifier &aNotifier,
     const TBTDevAddr &aDevAddr);
  IMPORT_C static CSdpAgent* NewLC(
     MSdpAgentNotifier &aNotifier,
     const TBTDevAddr &aDevAddr);
  IMPORT_C ~CSdpAgent();
  IMPORT_C void SetRecordFilterL(
     const CSdpSearchPattern &aUUIDFilter);
  IMPORT_C void SetAttributePredictorListL(
     const CSdpAttrIdMatchList &aMatchList);
  IMPORT_C void NextRecordRequestL();

  IMPORT_C void AttributeRequestL(
                 TSdpServRecordHandle aHandle,
                 TSdpAttributeID aAttrID);
  IMPORT_C void AttributeRequestL(
                 TSdpServRecordHandle aHandle,
                 const CSdpAttrIdMatchList &aMatchList);
  IMPORT_C void AttributeRequestL(
                 MSdpElementBuilder* aBuilder,
                 TSdpServRecordHandle aHandle,
                 TSdpAttributeID aAttrID);
  IMPORT_C void AttributeRequestL(
                 MSdpElementBuilder* aBuilder,
                 TSdpServRecordHandle aHandle,
                 const CSdpAttrIdMatchList &aMatchList);
     ...
};
```

To start with, an agent needs an MSdpAgentNotifier to notify of its progress. This is an object that is defined with specific callbacks:

```
class MSdpAgentNotifier
{
public:
    virtual void NextRecordRequestComplete(TInt aError,
        TSdpServRecordHandle aHandle,
        TInt aTotalRecordsCount) = 0;
    virtual void AttributeRequestResult(
        TSdpServRecordHandle aHandle, TSdpAttributeID aAttrID,
        CSdpAttrValue* aAttrValue) = 0;
    virtual void AttributeRequestComplete(
        TSdpServRecordHandle, TInt aError) = 0;
};
```

The notifier is sent data when search operations are executed. The `NextRecordRequestComplete()` method will be called when the latest request for a matching service search is complete. The call will indicate the error status of the search in the first parameter, give a handle to the service record in the second, and give the number of service records matched in the third. The handle can then be used to request attributes from the database record, and these results are returned by `AttributeRequestResult()` and the completion status by `AttributeRequestComplete()`.

Searching for service IDs

The agent uses search pattern objects to find service IDs. Objects of the `CSdpSearchPattern` class are used to specify the search. This class has the following definition:

```
class CSdpSearchPattern : public CBase, public
MSdpElementBuilder
    {
public:
    IMPORT_C static CSdpSearchPattern* NewL();
    IMPORT_C void ConstructL();
    IMPORT_C ~CSdpSearchPattern();
    IMPORT_C TInt AddL(const TUUID &aUUID);
    IMPORT_C TInt Remove(const TUUID &aUUID);
    IMPORT_C TInt Find(const TUUID &aUUID, TInt &aPos) const;
    IMPORT_C TInt Count() const;
    IMPORT_C const TUUID At(TInt anIndex) const;
    IMPORT_C void Reset();
    inline TBool IsEmpty();
        ...
    };
```

Service IDs are added or removed from the search pattern by methods of this class. The IDs are given by the class `TUUID`. The definition of the `TUUID` class enables many different forms of UUID specification; the use of integers is one way to give them.

To use an agent, we need to go through the following steps:

- First we need to create a notifier. This is a user-defined class derived from the MSdpAgentNotifier class that defines the method we discussed above. For example, consider the definition below:

```
class AGENTNotifier: public MSdpAgentNotifier
{
    AGENTNotifier();
    ~AGENTNotifier();
    void NextRecordRequestComplete(TInt aError,
        TSdpServRecordHandle aHandle,
        TInt aTotalRecordsCount);
    void AttributeRequestResult(
        TSdpServRecordHandle aHandle,
        TSdpAttributeID aAttrID,
        CSdpAttrValue* aAttrValue);
    void AttributeRequestComplete(TSdpServRecordHandle,
        TInt aError);
}
```

We must define each of the AGENTNotifier methods to activate something in our main application when discovery is complete.

- Next, we need to create the agent. As an example, consider the code below:

```
AGENTNotifier notifier;
CSdpAgent* agent = CSdpAgent::NewLC(notifer,
    deviceAddress);
```

The device address in deviceAddress was constructed as we did it previously—either by explicit declaration or by discovery. This creates an agent that will discover services on the device whose address is specified in deviceAddress and will communicate back using the notifier object.

- As a third step, we need to create a search pattern and add the service definitions for which we need to look. We need an object of the class CSdpSearchPattern to which we add service IDs. The fragment below illustrates this:

```
CSdpSearchPattern* pattern = CSdpSearchPattern::NewL();
pattern->AddL(100);
```

Here, we have added the service whose ID is 100 to the pattern of services for which we want to look.

- Next, we install the search pattern in the agent. An example is below:

```
agent->SetRecordFilterL(*pattern);
```

- Finally, we signal the agent to start the search process. This results in the active object that defines the agent to asynchronously search the device specified for the service given in the pattern specification. The code below would start this process:

```
agent->NextRecordRequestL();
```

When this method returns, all further communication from the agent is done through the notifier via the callback methods.

When multiple service IDs are added to a search pattern, the effect is like combining these IDs together by using a Boolean OR operator. Therefore, let's say we used the following code to construct a pattern:

```
CSdpSearchPattern* pattern2 = CSdpSearchPattern::NewL();
pattern2->AddL(100);
pattern2->AddL(150);
pattern2->AddL(730);
```

The effect is to provide a pattern that will match a service whose ID is *either* 100, 150, or 730. Once a service has been selected, the application needs to further examine its ID or attributes to determine if that service is to be used.

Note that I have taken some liberties in arbitrarily assigning service ID numbers. In many cases, for established services, the ID numbers are preassigned by the Bluetooth Consortium.

Searching for service attributes

Once a service handle has been successfully obtained through a call to an MSdpAgentNotifier class object's NextRecord RequestComplete() method, we still have to make requests to the remote database to obtain the service's attributes. This time, we need a pattern specified as an object of the CSdpAttrIdMatch-List class. The definition of this class is below:

```
class CSdpAttrIdMatchList : public CBase, public
MSdpElementBuilder
{
public:
   IMPORT_C static CSdpAttrIdMatchList* NewL();
```

```
IMPORT_C static CSdpAttrIdMatchList* NewL(
    const CSdpAttrIdMatchList &aAttrMatchList);
IMPORT_C ~CSdpAttrIdMatchList();
IMPORT_C void AddL(TAttrRange aRange);
IMPORT_C void RemoveL(TAttrRange aRange);
TInt Find(TSdpAttributeID aAttrId, TInt &aPos) const;
IMPORT_C TBool InMatchList(TSdpAttributeID aAttrId,
    TInt &aPos) const;
inline TBool InMatchList(TSdpAttributeID aAttrId) const;
inline TInt Count() const;
void FindAttributesL(CSdpServRecord &aRec,
    MAttributeMatchHandler &aHandler) const;
IMPORT_C TUint EncodeL(CElementEncoder &aEncoder) const;
...
};
```

Notice that this class has many of the same methods that we found
for service ID matching—AddL(), RemoveL(), and Find(), for
instance—and this means that we build an attribute pattern in
much the same way. Notice that AddL() and RemoveL() take
a TAddrRange structure as their parameter. This is so that we
can specify ranges of attribute IDs rather than one at a time. The
InMatchList() method is used to see if an attribute ID is already
in the pattern, and the Count() method will return the number of
patterns in an object of this type.

To search for attributes, we set up an attribute ID pattern much
the same way as we did for service ID patterns. Now, however, we
need to know what service attribute IDs we are looking for. We
proceed as follows:

- First, note what we already have: we have an agent (we used it
  to do the service ID search in the first place), the notifier object
  the agent uses to communicate, and the service handle that
  was returned with the callback to the notifier's NextRecord
  RequestComplete() method that signifies the service that
  was found.

- Now, we need to create a CSdpAttrIdMatchList object.
  The code below shows an example:

```
CSdpAttrIdMatchList* attribute_pattern =
    CSdpAttrIdMatchList::NewL();
```

- Like with service ID discovery, we add the attribute IDs to the
  attribute pattern. For example, consider this statement

```
attribute_pattern->AddL(TAttrRange(0x102));
```

- Now, we can start the attribute search by using the `AttributeRequest()` method in the agent object. As an example, consider the line below:

```
agent->AttributeRequestL(serviceHandle,
    *attribute_pattern);
```

At this point, the agent releases the caller and runs asynchronously. It communicates again through the notifier, this time using the `AttributeRequestResult()` and `AttributeRequestComplete()` methods in the notifier. For every attribute found, the `AttributeRequestResult()` method is called. When there are no more attributes that match the pattern specified, the `AttributeRequestComplete()` method is called.

13.2.4 The Service Discovery Database

In the previous section, we looked at how to search a remote device's service database. Now we will look at this from the local perspective: how do we get records into the local database to begin with? For example, how would an application register services that it is offering on the local device?

We will look at this in three parts: dealing with the database itself, characterizing service attributes, and working with service database records.

Dealing with the database

Before we can manipulate records in the service database, we have to establish a connection to it. As with most resources in the Symbian OS, the Bluetooth service database is managed by a server. So, as we have before, we first connect with the server. Then we can open and manipulate the database and finish by closing both the database and the server connection.

The database server API is found in the `RSdp` class. Its definition is below:

```
class RSdp : public RSessionBase
{
public:
  IMPORT_C RSdp();
  IMPORT_C TInt Connect();
  IMPORT_C TVersion Version() const;
  IMPORT_C void ResourceCountMarkStart();
  IMPORT_C void ResourceCountMarkEnd();
  IMPORT_C TInt ResourceCount();
};
```

Here, we would use the `Connect()` method to open a server connection. We would stop this connection with the `Close()` method inherited from the `RSessionBase` class. We can get its version number from the `Version()` method (by build number, or by major and minor version numbers). The number of connections to the database server can be counted by using the `Resource-Count...()` group of methods. To start counting, we would use the `ResourceCountMarkStart()` method and, to end the counting, we would use the `ResourceCountMarkEnd()` method. Between these method calls, a call to `ResourceCount()` will return the number of connections to the database. This resource count is a count of open subsessions, that is, the number of applications opening and manipulating the service database at the moment a call is made. This count can be used to monitor the load on a device, for example, or simply to log database use.

The database itself is characterized by the `RSdpDatabase` class. The definition for this class is below:

```
class RSdpDatabase : public RSdpSubSession
{
public:
  IMPORT_C RSdpDatabase();
  IMPORT_C TInt Open(RSdp &aSession);
  IMPORT_C void Close();
  IMPORT_C void CreateServiceRecordL(const TUUID &aUUID,
     TSdpServRecordHandle &aHandle);
  IMPORT_C void CreateServiceRecordL(
     CSdpAttrValueDES &aUUIDList, TSdpServRecordHandle &aHandle);
  IMPORT_C void UpdateAttributeL(TSdpServRecordHandle aHandle,
     TSdpAttributeID aAttrID, CSdpAttrValue &aAttrValue);
  IMPORT_C void UpdateAttributeL(TSdpServRecordHandle aHandle,
     TSdpAttributeID aAttrID, TUint aUintValue);
  IMPORT_C void UpdateAttributeL(TSdpServRecordHandle aHandle,
     TSdpAttributeID aAttrID, const TDesC16 &aDesCValue);
  IMPORT_C void UpdateAttributeL(TSdpServRecordHandle aHandle,
     TSdpAttributeID aAttrID, const TDesC8 &aDesCValue);
  IMPORT_C void DeleteAttributeL(TSdpServRecordHandle aHandle,
     TSdpAttributeID aAttrID);
  IMPORT_C void DeleteRecordL(TSdpServRecordHandle aHandle);
   ...
};
```

There is a lot of declarative jumble in that definition; the core methods are as follows:

- The `Open()` method opens a database, and the `Close()` method closes it down.
- The `CreateServiceRecordL()` methods create service records in the database. The `DeleteRecordL()` method removes service records from the database.

- The UpdateAttributeL() methods update attributes in a service record. The DeleteAttributeL() method removes attributes from a service record.

The code fragment below illustrates how we might connect to the database server, open the database, and then shut things down again:

```
RSdp database_svr;
RSdpDatabase database;
TInt result;

result = database_svr.Connect();
User::LeaveIfError(result);

result = database.Open(database_svr);
User::LeaveIfError(result);

...  // use the database
database.Close();
database_svr.Close();
```

Characterizing service attributes

Service attributes are complicated beasties. They are easily visualized (see Figure 13.2), but the open flexibility and typing requirements make the API a little cumbersome. However, the Symbian OS designers have taken care to make the API as usable as possible.

An attribute's value can be one of nine possible types. Seven of these are easily represented: integer, unsigned integer, Boolean, URL, string, UUID, and a nil type (used to represent an "undefined" value). The remaining two types are collections of values. A data element alternative (DEA) collection is a list of elements from which a single element will be selected (like a reference to an item in an array). A data element sequence (DES) collection is a list of elements that will be used as a list.

Each data element type is characterized by its own class. These classes are all derived from a base class: the CSdpAttrValue class. Figure 13.3 lists the classes and shows what each represents. Let's deal with these in two parts: the "simple" data types and the element collections.

Simple attribute types Rather than examining each individual class, we will look at the CSdpAttrValueInt class as a representative of the others. The class definition is given below:

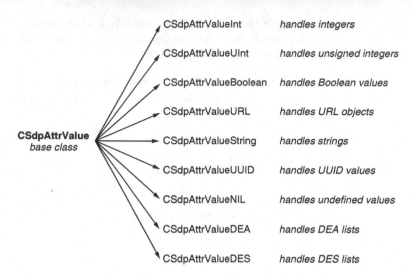

CSdpAttrValueInt	handles integers
CSdpAttrValueUInt	handles unsigned integers
CSdpAttrValueBoolean	handles Boolean values
CSdpAttrValueURL	handles URL objects
CSdpAttrValueString	handles strings
CSdpAttrValueUUID	handles UUID values
CSdpAttrValueNIL	handles undefined values
CSdpAttrValueDEA	handles DEA lists
CSdpAttrValueDES	handles DES lists

CSdpAttrValue base class

Figure 13.3 Classes that characterize attribute value types.

```
class CSdpAttrValueInt : public CSdpAttrValue
   {
public:
   IMPORT_C static CSdpAttrValueInt* NewIntL(
      const TDesC8 &aInt);
   virtual ~CSdpAttrValueInt();
   virtual TSdpElementType Type() const;
   virtual TUint DataSize() const;
   virtual TInt Int() const;
   virtual TBool DoesIntFit() const;
   virtual const TPtrC8 Des() const;
...
   };
```

This class allows the manipulation of integer attribute values in the following way:

- New values are created with the NewIntL() method. Note that this method takes a general undefined quantity as a byte buffer.

- The type of the data element is obtained by the Type() method. This method returns a value of type TSdpElementType, which is simply an enumerated set of nine values (integers) where each represents an attribute type.

- The size of the element is retrieved with the DataSize() method.

- The integer value itself is retrieved by the Int() method; this converts the byte buffer to the type described by the class, in this case integer. This is replaced by `UUID()`, for example, for the `CSdpAttrValueUUID` class.

- The `DoesIntFit()` method returns a Boolean value that indicates if the data type will fit into an integer word size.
- The `Des()` method returns the value as a general byte buffer.

Creating an integer attribute is simple; it is executed with one call:

```
CsdpAttrValueInt *intattribute;

intattribute = CSdpAttrValueInt::NewIntL(50);
```

In this example, we have created an attribute whose integer value is 50.

Attribute lists   Attribute lists are a bit more complicated. They must be built, either from simple types or from other lists. The interface, quite frankly, is a little odd; however, when it is written in a certain way, it makes sense.

Both of the data element list classes implement the `MSdpEle-mentBuilder` interface. This interface uses a series of return values of calls to construct a list. Rather than walk through class definitions, let's look at an example. Suppose we wanted to build a DES of integers. We might do this in the following way:

```
CSdpAttrValueDES* integerDES =
    CSdpAttrValueDES::NewDESL(NULL);
integerDES
    ->StartListL()
        ->BuildIntL(TServAttrInt<TInt8>(23))
        ->BuildIntL(TServAttrInt<TInt8>(1))
    ->EndListL();
```

First of all, note that this is actually only two C++ statements. The first is a declaration; the second is a series of function calls that builds a list. The indentation and formatting makes the statement easier to read and understand. Second, this code builds a DES made up of two integers: 23 and 1. The result is one attribute—held in the variable `integerDES`—whose value is a list.

Lists are built following the pattern of the above code. A list is started with a call to `StartListL()` and completed with a call to `EndListL()`. To add something to the list, it must be enclosed in a call to a `BuildtypeL()` method, where the `type` is set up to specify an attribute value type. If you are building a nested data element list, you must also include nested calls to `StartListL()` and `EndListL()`.

For example, let's say we wanted to build an attribute that contained a list of Bluetooth addresses. Each address is a 48-bit integer, so we can encapsulate it in two 32-bit integers. We might create this attribute as follows:

```
CSdpAttrValueDES* addresslist =
CSdpAttrValueDES::NewDESL(NULL);
addresslist
    ->StartListL()
        ->BuildDESL()
            ->StartListL()
                ->BuildIntL(TServAttrInt<TUint32>(TUint32(0x02)))
                ->BuildIntL(TServAttrInt<TUint32>(TUint32(0x817211d)))
            ->EndListL()
        ->BuildDESL()
            ->StartListL()
                ->BuildIntL(TServAttrInt<TUint32>(TUint32(0x0f)))
                ->BuildIntL(TServAttrInt<TUint32>(TUint32(0x620300f)))
            ->EndListL()
    ->EndListL();
```

This code builds an attribute whose value is a list with two nested lists. Each nested list is the two 32-bit integers that together comprise a Bluetooth address.

Working with service records

Service records are identified by their *handle*—a 32-bit integer defined as the class `TSdpServRecordHandle`. These handles are used as keys into the service database. Records are created and deleted by the `CreateServiceRecordL()` and `DeleteRecordL()` methods from the `RSdpDatabase` class. They are created with a UUID or a list of UUIDs that identify them in the database. Once created, the attributes of a record can be updated and modified by using the `UpdateAttributeL()` and `UpdateAttributeL()` methods from the `RSdpDatabase` class.

As an example, let's say we wanted to create an image service record with four attributes—the ones given in Figure 13.2. We could use the code below:

```
#define IMAGE_SERVICE_ID 0x10ff

TSdpServRecordHandle recordHandle = 0;
TUUID image_service_UUID(IMAGE_SERVICE_ID);
database.CreateServiceRecordL(image_service_UUID,
    recordHandle);
```

```
// Now build the attributes
_LIT8(KJPEG,"JPEG");
CSdpAttrValueString* image_format_attribute =
    CSdpAttrValueString::NewStringL(KJPEG);
CSdpAttrValueInt* image_width_attribute =
    CSdpAttrValueInt::NewIntL(320);
CSdpAttrValueInt* image_height_attribute =
    CSdpAttrValueInt::NewIntL(240);
CSdpAttrValueInt* pixel_depth_attribute =
    CSdpAttrValueInt::NewIntL(8);

#define IMAGE_FORMAT_ID 0x10f0
#define IMAGE_WIDTH_ID 0x10f1
#define IMAGE_HEIGHT_ID 0x10f2
#define PIXEL_DEPTH_ID 0x10f3

// Apply the attributes to the records
database.UpdateAttributeL(recordHandle, IMAGE_FORMAT_ID,
    *image_format_attribute);
database.UpdateAttributeL(recordHandle, IMAGE_WIDTH_ID,
    *image_width_attribute);
database.UpdateAttributeL(recordHandle, IMAGE_HEIGHT_ID,
    *image_height_attribute);
database.UpdateAttributeL(recordHandle, PIXEL_WIDTH_ID,
    *pixel_width_attribute);
```

Note a few things about this example. First, when a service record is created in the database, the record handle given as a parameter is filled in with a real value. This means that the value given to the record handle in the code—the value 0—is a "blank" value, a placeholder. Second, let me reiterate that I have arbitrarily assigned ID numbers; these are typically preassigned by the Bluetooth Consortium.

13.2.5 Some Perspective

At this point, you should catch your breath and review the last several pages. Some perspective on device and service discovery is in order.

It should now be quite clear that these discovery methods add a significant new layer of complexity to Bluetooth communications. While the models used define a flexible and adaptive system for all sorts of devices and services, searching for devices and probing service databases can be complex and time-consuming. From the searching device's point-of-view, we have a four-stage process: setup the query, make the query, wait for the query to return, process the query's results. This four-stage process is used for device discovery, for service discovery, and for each attribute that we need to process. On a memory and CPU limited device, this can amount to a big problem.

Consider an example. Suppose you and your Bluetooth-enabled computer enter a laboratory with a need to take a picture from a digital camera—one you have with you—and to print it on a printer. You know that you have a Bluetooth-enabled camera, but you do not know if a Bluetooth printer is in the room. There are five other Bluetooth devices in the room, however. While your computer can connect directly to the camera—you already have the address preconfigured in the application you are using—you must attempt to discover a printer. So, when your computer commences device discovery, it will have to examine six device replies (the camera will probably reply as well) to find printer attributes. If it finds printer attributes in a service, your computer will have to probe further to determine if it can use the printer. Hopefully, the right printer is one of the first to reply to the device discovery probe and not the last one!

While discovery does indeed appear to be a lot of work, note that we do not have much of a choice here. In a general Bluetooth environment, devices move in and out of a network's range regularly. Applications provide increasingly customized services, and devices can make few assumptions.

So programmers might have to be innovative and sparing as they implement generalized applications. It is also helpful if we can strike some kind of compromise between full device and attribute discovery and using a complete set of assumptions. That compromise can be found in the concept of class settings.

13.2.6 Class Settings: Some Middle Ground

There is, in fact, a middle ground that is helpful as we try to minimize discovery. The Bluetooth specification defines two types of coarse, descriptive characterizations for a device: the *major* and *minor class settings*. These settings are actually returned to the device with the `TInquirySockAddr` object at device discovery.

You can use these class settings as early indicators of the type of the remote device. Using these settings, you might be able to tell the difference between a printer and digital camera. You still need to check the printer for specific requirements, but you can stop certain types of discovery by using these coarse class settings.

You can use methods from the `TInquirySockAddr` class to examine these class settings:

```
inline TUint16 MajorServiceClass() const;
inline void SetMajorServiceClass(TUint16 aClass);
```

```
inline TUint8 MajorClassOfDevice() const;
inline void SetMajorClassOfDevice(
    TUint8 aMajorClassOfDevice);
inline TUint8 MinorClassOfDevice() const;
inline void SetMinorClassOfDevice(
    TUint8 aMinorClassOfDevice);
```

The class settings are simply integers—codes predefined by the
Bluetooth consortium. Notice that you can set your class settings as
well. Also notice from the above methods that class settings apply
to device characterization as well as to service characterization.

13.3   Communicating over Bluetooth

Now that we know how to get device addresses and service descriptions, we can examine how the Symbian OS supports Bluetooth
communication. Here we will revel in the modularity of the Symbian design, because communicating over Bluetooth is based on
the now familiar model of socket communication. We will tackle
this using our five-stage pattern for covering sockets.

13.3.1   Initializing the System for Bluetooth

To initialize the Symbian OS for Bluetooth communications, we
need to connect to the socket server and make it load the Bluetooth
drivers in which we are interested. This looks very much like the
sequence we used to start up IrDA socket communications. The
code fragment below illustrates this.

```
// Start comm server if necessary
result = StartC32();
if (result != KErrNone && result != KErrAlreadyExists)
    User::Leave(result);

// Connect to the socket server
result = socksvr.Connect();
if (result != KErrNone) User::Leave(result);

// Load the protocol
result = socksvr.FindProtocol(_L("BtLinkManager"),
    protocolInfo);
User::LeaveIfError(result);
```

Here, we start the socket server, connect to it, and look for the
LMP driver. Loading this driver will force the loading of the other
protocol modules as necessary.

If we are to enable remote devices to discover the local device's features, we must also initialize the system for discovery as we discussed in detail previously in this chapter. If the application is to do service database manipulation, some special care must be taken to keep the database server up and listening. When the last connection to the service database is closed, the server shuts down even if an SDP connection is open. This means that an application must take care to keep connections (database subsessions) open until all database manipulation is completed.

It is useful for a Bluetooth device to have a name. We can get and set the name of a device through the host resolver. The definitions below show the methods that are used to do this:

```
TInt GetHostName(TDes &aName);
void GetHostName(TDes &aName,TRequestStatus &aStatus);
TInt SetHostName(const TDesC &aName);
```

We have seen these before with the RHostResolver definition. The GetHostName() method will retrieve the name of the local device, placing it in the aName parameter. The SetHostName() method will set the name on the local device.

13.3.2 Opening and Configuring a Bluetooth Socket

Opening and configuring a Bluetooth socket looks almost like using any other socket. Assuming we have the information we need—a device address and a service identifier—opening and configuring a socket is quite standard.

Consider the code below from the TodoX example.

```
TBool TodoXferBt::OpenL()
{
  TInt result;

  result = sock.Open(socksvr, KBTAddrFamily,
                     KSockSeqPacket, KL2CAP);
  User::LeaveIfError(result);

  return true;
}
```

The socket used here is again from the RSocket class. Notice that we have used KBTAddrFamily for the address family. The socket type specification changes based on the protocol that is being used. We must use KSockStream if we use RFCOMM; we use KSockSeqPacket if we use L2CAP.

We can configure a socket at three different levels using Ioctl() calls:

- Low-level configuration, i.e., levels of protocol below L2CAP, can be configured through Host Controller Interface (HCI) commands to the Ioctl() method for a socket.

- There are also Ioctl() calls that will configure settings for the L2CAP protocol level.

- Settings for RFCOMM sockets can also be done through Ioctl(). RFCOMM sockets also have options that can be retrieved through the GetOpt() method of the RSocket class.

13.3.3 Connecting Client Sockets

Clients connect to servers using the RSocket::Connect() method. As we have seen before, this method needs a valid address and service specification to which to connect the socket. The service specification is set in the address object. This object can take one of several forms, all of which are derived through the inheritance tree from the TSockAddr class:

- It can be a TBTSockAddr object. This class has a SetBTAddr() method to set the Bluetooth device address directly, and a SetPort() method (from TSockAddr) to set the service specifier.

- It can be a TInquirySockAddr object, since this is the class of the information that results from device discovery. There is no need to set the device address but the service ID must be set with the SetPort() method.

- It can be a protocol-specific address, defined as either a TL2CAPSockAddr object or a TRfcommSockAddr object, specifying L2CAP or RFCOMM protocols, respectively. This class borrows methods to set the device address and service specifiers from the TBTSockAddr class.

We should make an observation here about service IDs. The L2CAP layer is meant to implement multiple services multiplexed and identified by service specifiers. RFCOMM is meant to implement serial communication behavior. Serial communication does not need multiple service specification; therefore, RFCOMM uses only one service ID, whose integer value is 3.

Once our socket is created, the call to Connect() looks the same as with other protocols. The code below is from the TodoX example:

```
addr.SetPort(15);
sock.Connect(addr,status);

iSendingState = ESC;
SetActive();
```

The call to `Connect()` is asynchronous, and `TodoX` uses an active object for the Bluetooth exchange. Therefore, we also set up the connection state, and we call `SetActive()`. Notice here that we have specifically set up the service specifier value as 15, chosen arbitrarily.

13.3.4   Binding Server Sockets

Message servers (i.e., receivers) go through the usual procedure in setting up a listener for Bluetooth connections: bind an opened socket to a local address, set up a listening queue on that socket, and open a "blank" socket to connect to an incoming connection.

For Bluetooth servers, we must bind the listening socket to a specific service ID. We do not need to specifically set the Bluetooth device address, which means the server will connect to any device, but we must set the address and listen only for connections on a specific port.

The code below from the `TodoX` example has a familiar pattern:

```
void TodoXferBt::ConfigureReceiver()
{
    TInt result;

    // ... configure security ...

    result = iListener.Open(socksvr, KBTAddrFamily,
        KSockSeqPacket, KL2CAP);
    User::LeaveIfError(result);
    addr.SetPort(15);
    result = iListener.Bind(addr);
    User::LeaveIfError(result);
    result = iListener.Listen(5);
    User::LeaveIfError(result);
}
```

This example sets up a listener socket for any device on port 15, with a listener queue size of 5.

To receive a connection, the service must call the listening socket's `Accept()` method with a "blank" socket. When `Accept()` returns, the socket will be defined and the two endpoints will have a data channel over which they can communicate.

13.3.5 Exchanging Data

As two devices are poised to send data between them, each side has a connected socket to use for the data transmission. At this point, the standard API for socket communication is used. The protocol issues—including initiation and termination—are still valid and are not specialized because we are using Bluetooth.

13.3.6 Closing a Socket

Bluetooth sockets are closed in the normal manner, by draining the socket of pending I/O requests, shutting down the socket, and then shutting down the socket server.

13.4 The Bluetooth Security Manager

One of the benefits of designing the Bluetooth protocol suite after other protocols had been designed and tested is that its designers could include features and details that the other protocol suites lacked. One of these details is security. Bluetooth pays attention to security issues in situations where other protocols do not. Bluetooth protocols negotiate certain security settings when incoming connections are made to devices. Specifically, two connecting devices will negotiate whether authentication, authorization, and encryption are required.

The Symbian OS implements this negotiation through the use of a *security manager*. The security manager is a server that protects and manages the resources associated with incoming connections. The RBTMan class encapsulates the functionality of the security manager. This manager maintains a database of security settings, characterized in the Symbian OS by the RBTSecuritySettings class. A specific collection of settings is handled by the TBTServiceSecurity class. To control the security manager, an application must first connect to it, open the security database through an RBTSecuritySettings object, and then set up a policy on a connection over a specific service specifier by registering a TBTServiceSecurity object.

The TBTServiceSecurity class has the following definition:

```
class TBTServiceSecurity
  {
public:
  IMPORT_C TBTServiceSecurity(TUid aUid,TInt aProtocolID,
    TInt aChannelID);
  IMPORT_C TBTServiceSecurity(
    const TBTServiceSecurity &aService);
```

```
          IMPORT_C TBTServiceSecurity();
          IMPORT_C void SetUid(TUid aUid);
          IMPORT_C void SetProtocolID(TInt aProtocolID);
          IMPORT_C void SetChannelID(TInt aChannelID);
          IMPORT_C void SetAuthentication(TBool aPreference);
          IMPORT_C void SetAuthorisation(TBool aPreference);
          IMPORT_C void SetEncryption(TBool aPreference);
          IMPORT_C void SetDenied(TBool aPreference);
          IMPORT_C TBool AuthorisationRequired() const;
          IMPORT_C TBool EncryptionRequired() const;
          IMPORT_C TBool AuthenticationRequired() const;
          IMPORT_C TBool Denied() const;
          IMPORT_C TUid Uid() const;
          IMPORT_C TInt ProtocolID() const;
          IMPORT_C TInt ChannelID() const;
      private:
      ...
      };
```

A set of service settings is identified by a UID and the service
specifier and protocol over which it is defined. Using the above
class interface, settings can be turned on or off for authentication,
authorization, and encryption. We can even flat out deny a specific
protocol connection through these settings. There are also methods
to determine the security settings for a particular connection.

   We might establish a set of security specifications as in the
following example:

```
TBTServiceSecurity securityspecs;
TUid specsUID;
specsUID.iUid = 0x01ff; //chosen arbitrarily

securityspecs.SetUid(specsUID);
securityspecs.SetChannelID(15);
securityspecs.SetProtocolID(KSolBtL2CAP);

securityspecs.SetAuthentication(EFalse);
securityspecs.SetAuthorisation(EFalse);
securityspecs.SetEncryption(ETrue);
```

The code above sets up a security specification for connections
over L2CAP using a service ID of 15. The specification stipulates no
authentication or authorization is necessary, but encryption must
be used.

   The RBTSecuritySettings class has the following definition:

```
class RBTSecuritySettings : public RBTManSubSession
    {
public:
    IMPORT_C TInt Open(RBTMan& aSession);
    IMPORT_C void Close();
```

```
    IMPORT_C void RegisterService(
        const TBTServiceSecurity &aService,
        TRequestStatus &aStatus);
    IMPORT_C void UnregisterService(
        const TBTServiceSecurity &aService,
        TRequestStatus &aStatus);
    ...
};
```

Using this class, an application can open and close the security database and register and unregister a set of security specifications. The RBTMan class has a rather simple definition:

```
class RBTMan : public RSessionBase
{
public:
    IMPORT_C RBTMan();
    IMPORT_C TInt Connect();
    IMPORT_C TVersion Version() const;
};
```

An application can use this class to connect to the server and tell its version. Via an inherited method from the RSessionBase class, a security manager session is closed with a Close() method call.

Given that we have the security specifications we used in previous examples, we might enter them into the security database with the code below:

```
RBTMan security_manager;
RBTSecuritySettings security_database;
TBTServiceSecurity securityspecs;
TRequestStatus status;
TInt result;

// ... define the security specifications for L2CAP/service 15

result = security_manager.Connect();
User::LeaveIfError(result);
Result = security_database.Open(security_manager));
User::LeaveIfError(result);

security_database.RegisterService(securityspecs, status);
User::WaitForRequest(status);
```

Notice that the RegisterService() method is an asynchronous call that requires us to wait for a result. The UnRegisterService() method is also asynchronous. Most security settings are imposed by the server—the recipient of a connection. The settings are negotiated as the connection is being made, and the client will automatically adjust its settings to match those demanded by the server. There is a way for the client to request settings: it must call the `Ioctl()` method for the socket being used as the connection. An example is below:

```
sock.Ioctl(KHCIAuthRequestIoctl, status, NULL, KSolBtHCI);
User::WaitForRequest(status);
```

This sets the outgoing socket connection to specifically request that authentication be used. Note that, in a settings negotiation, either side may reject the settings proposed by the negotiating partner.

13.5   An Example: Bluetooth Instant Messaging

To complete this chapter, I would like to work through one more example. Suppose we wanted to implement an application that would send short text messages between two Bluetooth devices—a kind of Bluetooth instant messenger. Let's design and construct an application to do this and see what it entails.

13.5.1   Designing the Application

The Bluetooth Instant Messenger (BTIM) application is simple in concept and composed of three parts:

- *The user interface:* Obviously, any application for a Symbian OS device must have a user interface. While it is not really the concern of this chapter, suffice it to say that we must have a simple and effective interface. An example interface is shown in Figure 13.4.

- *The sender:* This is an active object that engages a receiver in a protocol to send a message over Bluetooth. This message sending "protocol" is simply a text string that is acknowledged by the receiver. The state diagram for this active object is in Figure 13.5.

- *The receiver:* This is an active object that acts as a kind of display server. It fields connections from senders, engages in a message protocol over Bluetooth, and writes the received message to the receiving device's display. The state diagram for the server's protocol is in Figure 13.6.

Note that there are two active objects at work concurrently in this application. The message sender's client works with a remote receiver's server to get a message to the remote device's display. However, each device in the BTIM application can be both a sender and a receiver, hence the need for two active objects.

Figure 13.4 The BTIM user interface.

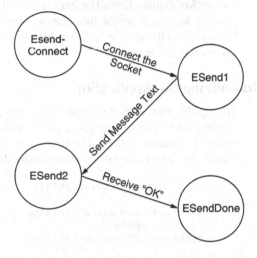

Figure 13.5 State diagram for the sender's active object.

Consider the act of sending a message. Each message must
have a destination attached. However, as is usually the case with
Bluetooth, it is not sufficient to set the receiver device once and
have this receiver be used for each message we send. Instead, we
must set the receiver for each message that goes out. This means
device discovery must be performed for each message that is sent.

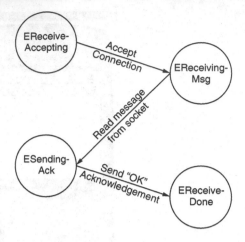

Figure 13.6 State diagram for the receiver's active object.

Consider how BTIM would receive messages. Receiving means an infinite iteration of accepting a socket connection, taking a text message over this socket, and writing this text to the display. The receiver will have to pull the name of the sender's device from the socket connection. The receiver will also have to choose the options to negotiate for this connection; in the implementation, I have chosen the easy way: no authentication, no authorization, and no encryption is used.

13.5.2   Initializing the Application

The application is quite simple. The interface is a container with a single textbox (an `CEikTextListBox` object) inside. The receiver object is created at the same time the interface is constructed and initialized. The code below shows how this is done:

```
void CBTIMAppUi::ConstructL()
{
    // Allow base class (CEikAppUi) to perform necessary
    // construction
    CQikAppUi::ConstructL();

    // Build the container
    iContainer = CBTIMContainer::NewL();

    // The container is added to the control stack (for key
    // event handling).
    AddToStackL(iContainer);

    // Start the receiver
    iReceiver = BTIMReceiver::NewL(this);
```

```
        iReceiver->Init();
        iReceiver->OpenL();
        iReceiver->Configure();
        iReceiver->StartReceive();
}
```

So after the interface has been built, we instantiate and initialize the receiver object. The call to the StartReceive() method initiates the parallel execution of the active object thread.

The interface destructor is below:

```
CBTIMAppUi::~CBTIMAppUi()
{
    iReceiver->Close();
    delete iReceiver;
    RemoveFromStack(iContainer);
    delete iContainer;
}
```

The destructor of the CBTIMAppUi object destroys the receiver object when it destroys the user interface container.

13.5.3 The Sender Object

The implementation of the sender object takes the form of the BTIMSender class and follows our five-stage definition for sockets. In the BTIM application, sending a message happens in response to the user tapping a button on the application toolbar. In response to this button tap, we call the SendMessage() method, whose code is below:

```
void CBTIMAppUi::SendMessage()
{
    TBuf<40> msg;
    CEikDialog* dialog =
        new (ELeave)
CBTIMMessageTextDialog(&msg);
    if (dialog->ExecuteLD(R_MESSAGE_TEXT_DIALOG)) {
        iSender = BTIMSender::NewL(this);
        iSender->Init();
        iSender->OpenL();
        iSender->Configure();
        iSender->SendMsg(msg);
        iSender->Close();
    }
}
```

We pop up a dialog to capture the message text, and then go through the five stages of socket usage.

Initializing the socket

We initialize a socket by starting and connecting to the socket server, loading the proper protocol, and opening a host resolver socket for device discovery. The Init() method is below:

```
TInt BTIMSender::Init()
{
    TInt result;
    TUint nProtocols;
    TNameEntry nentry;
    THostName hostname;

    // Start comm server if necessary
    result = StartC32();
    if (result != KErrNone && result != KErrAlreadyExists)
        User::Leave(result);

    // Connect to the socket server
    result = socksvr.Connect();
    if (result != KErrNone) User::Leave(result);

    // Load the protocol
    result = socksvr.FindProtocol(_L("BTLinkManager"),
        protocolInfo);
    User::LeaveIfError(result);

    // get the resolver ready
    result = resolver.Open(socksvr,
        protocolInfo.iAddrFamily, protocolInfo.iProtocol);
    User::LeaveIfError(result);

    return ETrue;
}
```

Opening the Bluetooth connection

For the sender, the OpenL() method simply involves opening the socket that we will use to send data to a receiver. The OpenL() method is below:

```
TBool BTIMSender::OpenL()
{
    TInt result;

    result = sock.Open(socksvr, KBTAddrFamily,
                        KSockSeqPacket, KL2CAP);
    User::LeaveIfError(result);

    return ETrue;
}
```

Note that we are using the L2CAP protocol, so I use the `KBTAddr-Family` address type and a socket type of `KSockSeqPacket`.

Configuration and device discovery

There really is no need for further configuration for a Bluetooth socket beyond the parameters given when the socket is opened, so I chose to do device discovery at configuration time. The `Configure()` method code is below:

```
void BTIMSender::Configure()
{
    TInt result;
    TNameEntry tnentry;

    // discover the device
    addr.SetIAC(KGIAC);
    addr.SetAction(KHostResInquiry);
    resolver.GetByAddress(addr, tnentry, status);
    User::WaitForRequest(status);

    // discover the service we want
    if (status == KErrNone) {
        tnentry.setName(SelectionUI(tnentry));
    } else {
        iAppUi->ShowErrMessage(_L("Cannot discover any other"),
                               _L("Bluetooth devices."));
        User::Leave(status.Int());
    }
}
```

This is fairly standard device discovery, using by-address discovery and setting up an unlimited query. The response comes back in the `tnentry` variable.

If there is a single device that needs to be discovered, we can pick the first response and use that one as the destination to which to send the message. However, if multiple devices have responded, the user must pick one. This is a common task, and the Symbian OS has provided a device selection user interface to perform it.

This device selection user interface is displayed by using an object from the `RNotifier` class and some selection filter classes. Consider the example code below:

```
TInt result;
TRequestStatus status;
RNotifier notifier;
TBTDeviceSelectionParams selectionFilter;
TUUID targetServiceClass(0x2345); // arbitrary, example ID
TBTDeviceResponseParams response;
TPtrC name;
```

```
// Connect to the notifier server
result = notifier.Connect();
User::LeaveIfError(result);

// Set up the parameters
selectionFilter.SetUUID(targetServiceClass);
TBTDeviceSelectionParamsPckg pckg(selectionFilter);
TBTDeviceResponseParamsPckg responsePckg(response);

// Start up the notifier
notifier.StartNotifierAndGetResponse(status,
    KDeviceSelectionNotifierUid, pckg, responsePckg);
User::WaitForRequest(status);

// Handle the notification
if (status.Int() == KErrNone) {
    if (resultPckg.IsValidDeviceName()) {
        name.Set(resultPckg().DeviceName());
    }
}

// Shut down the notifier
notifier.CancelNotifier(KDeviceSelectionNotifierUid);
notifier.Close();
```

Notice that we set up all the data, then call the `StartNotifierAndGetResponse()` method for the `RNotifier` object. By sending it the `KDeviceSelectionNotifierUid`, we get the proper dialog. Once the user has selected a device name, the above code extracts it to the `name` variable.

Sending the message

We engage in the message exchange protocol when the `SendMsg()` method is called with a text message as the parameter. Its code is below:

```
void BTIMSender::SendMsg(TDesC &aMsg)
{
    buffer.Copy(aMsg);

    addr.SetPort(BTIM_SENDING_PORT);
    sock.Connect(addr, status);
    iConnectionState = ESendConnect;
    SetActive();
}
```

In this code, we copy the message to an 8-bit buffer, set the address sending specifier to a specific value (thereby avoiding the hassle of service discovery), then try to connect the socket to the remote device.

The RunL() method implements the message exchange protocol. Its code is as follows:

```
void BTIMSender::RunL()
{
    TInt pos,err,i,result;

    switch (iConnectionState) {
        case ESendConnect:
            if (status == KErrNone) {
                iAppUi->SetProgress(_L("Sending Message"));
                Send(buffer);
                iConnectionState = ESend1;
            } else {
                // handle the error
            }
            break;

        case ESend1:
            if (status == KErrNone) {
                iAppUi->SetProgress
                    (_L("Awaiting acknowledgement"));
                Receive(buffer);
                iConnectionState = ESend2;
            } else {
                // handle the error
            }
            break;

        case ESend2:
            if (status == KErrNone) {
                if (buffer != _L8("OK")) {
                    iConnectionState = ESendError;
                } else {
                    iConnectionState = ESendDone;
                }
            } else {
                // handle the error
            }
            break;
    }

    if (iConnectionState == ESendDone) {
        socksvr.Close();
        sock.Close();
        delete this;
    } else if (iConnectionState == ESendError) {
        // handle the error
    }
}
```

This code uses the same Send() and Receive() methods as the TodoX example; the format of each message includes the length of the message as the first byte. Notice that when the object is done sending the message, it deletes itself. This is so the BTIM application object can initiate a message send operation and then leave the sending work to the active object.

13.5.4   The Receiver Object

The implementation of the receiver is via the `BTIMReceiver` class and follows the five-stage implementation pattern to which we are accustomed. The sequence of starting and terminating a receiver was already given in the code for the interface construction.

Initializing the receiver connection

Initialization of the receiver is much like that for the sender, with the exception that we do not need a host resolver. Receivers do not do device discovery. Therefore, like the sender, we start the communication server, connect to the socket server, and load the right protocol module. This code is below:

```
TInt BTIMReceiver::Init()
{
    TInt result;
    TUint nProtocols;
    TNameEntry nentry;
    THostName hostname;

    // Start comm server if necessary
    result = StartC32();
    if (result != KErrNone && result != KErrAlreadyExists)
            User::Leave(result);

    // Connect to the socket server
    result = socksvr.Connect();
    if (result != KErrNone) User::Leave(result);

    // Load the protocol
    result = socksvr.FindProtocol(_L("L2CAP"),
        protocolInfo);
    User::LeaveIfError(result);
    return ETrue;
}
```

Notice that we load the L2CAP protocol module instead of the LMP module. We need the LMP module for device discovery but not for socket connections.

Opening the Bluetooth connection

The OpenL() method opens both the listener socket and the first blank socket for communicating with the remote device. The code is below:

```
TBool BTIMReceiver::OpenL()
{
    TInt result;

    result = iListener.Open(socksvr, KBTAddrFamily,
                KSockSeqPacket, KL2CAP);
    User::LeaveIfError(result);
    result = iServiceSocket.Open(socksvr, KBTAddrFamily,
                KSockSeqPacket, KL2CAP);
    User::LeaveIfError(result);

    return true;
}
```

Configuring the receiver socket

Configuration of the receiver socket must do two things: it must configure the listening socket, and it must set up the security parameters for incoming connections. The code to do this is below:

```
void BTIMReceiver::Configure()
{
    TInt result;
    RBTMan manager;
    RBTSecuritySettings secdatabase;
    TBTServiceSecurity settings;
    TUid settingsUID;

    // Set up the listening socket
    addr.SetPort(BTIM_SENDING_PORT);
    result = iListener.Bind(addr);
    User::LeaveIfError(result);
    result = iListener.Listen(5);
    User::LeaveIfError(result);

    // Connect and open the database
    result = manager.Connect();
    User::LeaveIfError(result);
    result = secdatabase.Open(manager);
    User::LeaveIfError(result);

    // Set up the settings
    settingsUID.iUid = 0x01ff;
    settings.SetUid(settingsUID);
    settings.SetChannelID(BTIM_SENDING_PORT);
    settings.SetProtocolID(KSolBtL2CAP);
    settings.SetAuthentication(EFalse);
    settings.SetAuthorisation(EFalse);
    settings.SetEncryption(EFalse);

    // Register the settings
    secdatabase.RegisterService(settings, status);
    User::WaitForRequest(status);
}
```

As we stated above, the security settings do not use authentication, authorization, or encryption.

Receiving a message

The receiver object starts receiving when the StartReceiver() method is called. This method simply makes an Accept() call and initiates the active object thread execution. The code is as follows:

```
void BTIMReceiver::StartReceive()
{
    TInt result;

    iListener.Accept(iServiceSocket, status);

    iConnectionState = EReceiveAccepting;
    SetActive();
}
```

The RunL () method implements the message receipt protocol.

```
void BTIMReceiver::RunL()
{
    TInt pos,err,i,result;

    switch (iConnectionState) {
        case EReceiveAccepting:
            if (status == KErrNone) {
                iAppUi->SetProgress(_L("Establishing protocol"));
                Receive(buffer);
                iConnectionState = EReceivingMsg;
            } else {
                // handle the error
            }
            break;

        case EReceivingMsg:
            if (status == KErrNone) {
                iAppUi->SetProgress
                    (_L("Awaiting acknowledgement"));
                buffer.Copy(_L8("OK"));
                Send(buffer);
                iConnectionState = ESendingAck;
            } else {
                // handle the error
            }
            break;

        case ESendingAck:
            if (status == KErrNone) {
                if (buffer != _L8("OK")) {
                    iConnectionState = EReceiveError;
                } else {
                    iConnectionState = EReceiveDone;
                }
            } else {
                // handle the error
            }
            break;
    }

    if (iConnectionState == EReceiveDone) {
        iServiceSocket.Close();
        StartReceive();
    } else if (iConnectionState == EReceiveError) {
        // handle the error
    }

}
```

The receiver uses Send () and Receive () methods as the sender does to send and receive strings. Note that when a message receipt is done, an application method is called to display the text, the service socket is closed, and the process is started again through a call to `StartReceive()`. This is why the service socket is opened in that method rather than in the `OpenL()` method.

13.6   Summary

In this chapter, we discussed the support that the Symbian OS gives to Bluetooth protocols and how we are to use the APIs that result. This has been a long chapter, with much space devoted to a key element of Bluetooth technology: device and service discovery. The Symbian OS supports the rest of the Bluetooth protocol suite through extensions to the socket model. Socket support looks very much like the support for other protocol suites. We also spent time on a large example: Bluetooth instant messaging.

In the next chapter, we take on a bridge of sorts: telephony. It is not really a transport technology nor a content technology. However, it addresses a distinctive feature of Symbian OS devices, one that demonstrates the convergence of computing and communication.

14

Telephony

The convergence of telephony and handheld computing devices has had a long history. As soon as the first devices sported a serial port, telephony services could be accessed by connecting a modem and sending it commands to dial or answer phone calls. As integrated devices were developed, control over telephony functions became a more crucial issue for Symbian designers. Telephony functionality was inextricably bound to Symbian OS devices with the Ericsson R380 and Nokia 9210/9290. These devices demonstrate how telephony communication and computing capability—integrating data and voice capability—can be mutually beneficial.

This chapter will examine how Symbian OS supports telephony. In a way, this chapter represents a transition from transport technologies to content technologies. It lies between the two; telephony is neither transport nor content, yet can be used for both. The wide variety of telephony functions and uses are provided by the Symbian OS ETel telephony model.

This chapter will review the details of Symbian OS telephony services. To fully appreciate the ETel model, it is pertinent that we start by examining all of the different situations it was designed to address. We will then take an overview look at the structure of the API. Then we will dig into the details of ETel by looking at the four main objects in its design. And finally we will wrap up by looking at faxing as a special case of telephony.

14.1 The Various Forms of Telephony

Communication using a conventional analog telephone basically takes two forms: data and voice communication. Data communication over a telephone is handled by a modem, the digital-to-analog converter we discussed in Chapter 4. Fax messages are image files converted to digital format; faxes are sent between computers and fax machines using fax modems. The computer controls the modem by using a set of commands. The Hayes command set, for example, is by far the most widely used set of commands for modems. Hayes-format commands take the form of "AT" commands: the character sequence "AT" followed by characters to command the modem to do certain tasks. To initialize a modem and cause it to dial a number, for example, we might give it the following command string:

```
ATQ0E1DT555-3454
```

This string tells the modem to send result codes back to the computer in response to commands, echo back the commands sent to the modem, and tone-dial the number 555-3454.

Voice communication via telephone is effectively a peer-to-peer connection, where the "address" of the remote device is the telephone number being dialed. The telephone number is accepted by the telephone network switching infrastructure and a stable connection is made between the local and remote devices, until one or both terminate the connection by "hanging up". A telephone can handle several telephone lines; each line can typically multiplex several phone calls at once.

Telephone networks can be wired (so-called "landline" networks) or wireless (often termed "cellular" networks—I prefer the term "mobile"). Of the possible equipment (or handset) and switching network combinations, digital choices have emerged as the most promising for the future. A GSM phone is a good example of digital phone equipment using a digital connection network. As we discussed briefly in Chapter 4, GSM is a packet-based protocol that sends data packets of a fixed size for a fixed time interval. The phone handset must also be a digital device to use the digital network, and some offer the capability of being controlled by a computer. My Nokia 8290 handset, for example, has an infrared port that allows it to accept commands from an external device.

14.2   A Structural Overview

The model Symbian OS uses is abstract enough to provide the application programmer with a consistent, standard interface, no matter what kind of device is being used.

The first thing to point out about this model is that telephony functionality on Symbian OS is viewed as a resource and, as with all resources on Symbian OS, there is a server to protect and manage it. As a first step to using a telephony device, then, an application needs to connect to the root telephony server.

The remainder of the Symbian telephony model closely follows experience in using telephones. Figure 14.1 shows a diagram of this Symbian view. The model looks at telephony as a collection of *phones*. Each phone is an abstraction of a telephony device (e.g., a modem or a GSM phone). Through this abstraction, we can access a device's status and capabilities and be notified if changes occur to a device's properties. A phone can have one or more *lines*. An application can access the status and capabilities of a line, just as it can for a phone, and can be notified if any of these change.

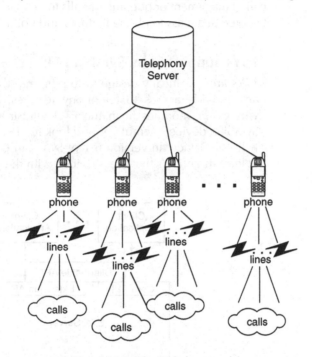

Figure 14.1   The ETel phone model.

The actual use of a line from a phone is designated as a *call*. A line can have zero or more active calls. A call can dial a number, wait for an incoming connection, and be terminated. As with lines, an application can get status and capabilities information for a call and be notified of changes to a call.

These abstractions combine to form the ETel model. The heart of this model's implementation is in the TSY module. By integrating the specific implementation of this model for a particular phone type into a module, Symbian OS designers ensured that the API for this functionality would remain the same across different phones, and the application programmer is free from worrying about the implementation specifics for a particular phone. In addition, when a new phone must be integrated into this framework, it amounts to a new TSY module implementation.

It is important to note what ETel is *not*. It *is* a phone access model; it *is not* a model for anything beyond phone access. For example, while ETel supports phone dialing, it does not support address translation when dialing—for example, the altering of the address dialed to reflect location information. As another example, ETel supports call connection and termination, but it does not support call management or queuing of calls to be made. ETel is specifically targeted at access to phone features and nothing more.

TSYs Supported by Symbian OS

TSYs are specifically designed to plug into the telephony server and provide access to telephony features. Figure 14.2 shows where TSY modules fit in the ETel infrastructure. Search your Symbian device or emulator and look for TSY modules provided with the device. In version 6.1 of Symbian OS, you should find at least three TSYs that are provided with the distribution.

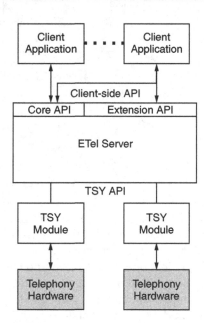

Figure 14.2 ETel structural diagram.

14.3 Components of the ETel Model

The ETel model has four components: the root telephony server, the phone component, the line component, and the call object. These are depicted in Figure 14.1.

14.3.1 The Root Server

The root server manages access to the telephony system. It is implemented by the RTelServer class. We will examine the definition of this class in several pieces.

As with all resources managed by servers, before telephony can be used we must connect to the telephony server. We do this with the Connect() function, defined below:

```
IMPORT_C TInt Connect(TInt aMessageSlots
    =KDefaultMessageSlots);
```

Using this function, we connect to the telephony server and specify how many message slots we need. Recall from Chapter 8 that a single message slot is a communication channel in one direction. The default number of slots assigned is 32. The RTelServer class is a subclass of the RSessionBase class, and therefore inherits the Close() function, which is used to shut down an active telephony server session.

Once a connection is established, the TSY module that is needed should be loaded. TSY modules can be manipulated through the functions defined below:

```
IMPORT_C TInt LoadPhoneModule(
    const TDesC &aFileName) const;
IMPORT_C TInt UnloadPhoneModule(
    const TDesC &aFileName) const;
```

The first function loads a TSY module, and the second function removes a TSY module. The TSY modules are specified by name via a string to the parameter of each function. The name should be specified without the .tsy suffix; the system will supply this as necessary. For example, we could load the GSM TSY module as gsmbsc.tsy or gsmbsc; either form will work.

Once the appropriate TSY module has been loaded, we can make queries about its properties. These queries take the form of telephony server functions, defined below:

```
inline TVersion Version() const;
IMPORT_C TInt EnumeratePhones(TInt &aNoOfPhones) const;
IMPORT_C TInt GetPhoneInfo(const TInt aIndex,
    TPhoneInfo &aInfo) const;
```

The first function retrieves the version number of the TSY module and returns that version as either a build number or a combination of major and minor version numbers. The `EnumeratePhones()` function will return in its parameter the total number of phones supported by TSY modules loaded by the telephony server. These supported phones can be accessed as an array; a particular phone is chosen by index number. The `GetPhoneInfo()` function will take an index number and return a structure containing the information on the phone from the array of phones supported by the telephony server. This information structure is defined by the `TPhoneInfo` struct given below:

```
struct TPhoneInfo
{
    TNetworkType iNetworkType;
    TName iName;
    TUint iNumberOfLines;
    TUint iExtensions;
};
```

The information given in this structure specifies the type of network of which the phone is a part (an enumerated type, specifying mobile, analog, or digital), the name of the phone, the number of lines supported by the phone, and the number of extensions the phone TSY module supports.

TSY information can be obtained from a telephony server using the functions below:

```
IMPORT_C TInt GetTsyName(const TInt aIndexOfPhone,
    TDes &aTsyName) const;
IMPORT_C TInt IsSupportedByModule(const TDesC &aTsyName,
    const TInt aMixin, TBool &aResult) const;
IMPORT_C TInt GetTsyVersionNumber(const TDesC &aTsyName,
    TVersion &aVersion) const;
```

The name of the TSY that supports the phone at a certain spot in the phone list is retrieved by the first function. The name of the TSY for the phone at the position given in the first argument is retrieved into the second argument. The second function returns a Boolean value that determines if extended functionality is supported by a TSY. All TSY modules are assumed to support a minimal set of telephony functionality. The `IsSupportedByModule()` module will set the Boolean variable in the third argument to reflect if the TSY in the first argument supports the extra functionality specified in the second argument. The second argument is a bitmask of extended functionality constants. Finally, the version number of the TSY module is retrieved by the third function.

A client of the telephony server can designate itself as a client of highest priority by using the function below:

```
IMPORT_C TInt SetPriorityClient() const;
```

Only one client can be designate itself as a high priority client.

Let's take an example. Let's say we have a PhoneCall class that will initialize a phone and make a voice phone call. The definition for this class might look like this:

```
class PhoneCall : public CActive
{
    enum TCallState {EDialing, EDone, EError};
public:
    PhoneCall();
    ~PhoneCall();

public:
    // Static construction
    static PhoneCall* NewLC();
    static PhoneCall* NewL();

public:
    void ConstructL();

    void Init();
    void MakeCall(TDesC &aTelephoneNumber);

    void DoCancel();
    void RunL();

private:
    RTelServer telserver;
    RPhone gsmphone;
    RLine phoneline;
    RCall phonecall;

    TRequestStatus callstatus;
    TCallState iCallState;
};
```

Notice that this class is an active object and uses the `iCallState` variable to track its communication state and the `callstatus` variable to monitor its I/O progress.

Now, consider the definition of the `Init()` function as it applies to the telephony server. Here, we want to deal with a voice call over a GSM phone.

```
void PhoneCall::Init()
{
    RTelServer::TPhoneInfo phoneinfo;
    RPhone::TLineInfo lineinfo;
    RPhone::TCaps capabilities;
    RLine::TCaps lcapabilities;
    TInt result;
    TInt phones,lines,calls;
    TBuf<25> name;

    // Connect to the telephony server
    result = telserver.Connect();
    User::LeaveIfError(result);

    // Load the right TSY
    result = telserver.LoadPhoneModule(_L("gsmbsc.tsy"));
    User::LeaveIfError(result);

    // Get information about phones from the server
    result = telserver.EnumeratePhones(phones);
    User::LeaveIfError(result);
    if (phones == 0) User::LeaveIfError(KErrNotSupported);

    // ... other code to init phones, lines, and calls
}
```

We connected to the telephony server and loaded the GSM TSY module. If no phones were supported (for example, if no GSM phone could be found via the infrared port), this code would abort with an error code.

14.3.2 The Phone Component

When access to the telephony server is granted, a phone supported by the telephony server must be selected. Phones are characterized by the RPhone class. This class definition is long; we will take a piecemeal walk through it.

RPhone class functions

Once a session has been established with the telephony server, a subsession with a phone must be established through an RPhone object. As you might expect, we use `Open()` and `Close()` functions for this:

```
IMPORT_C TInt Open(RTelServer &aSession,
    const TDesC &aName);
IMPORT_C void Close();
```

The session variable for an established telephony server session and the name of a phone with which to open a subsession is passed to the `Open()` function. This name is retrieved from `RTelServer` object's `GetPhoneInfo()` function.

When a phone subsession has been successfully opened, the phone must be initialized. This is done through an `Initialise()` function as below:

```
IMPORT_C TInt Initialise();
IMPORT_C void Initialise(TRequestStatus &aStatus);
```

This function is available in synchronous (the first version) and asynchronous (the second version) varieties. The asynchronous version also has a function to cancel the initialization:

```
IMPORT_C void InitialiseCancel();
```

Initializing is allowed to be asynchronous, because it may take some time to set up the telephony device (this is especially true of a modem).

When a phone subsession exists and the device has been initialized, there are several queries that we can make of a telephony device:

- We get the device's capabilities through the following function:

```
IMPORT_C TInt GetCaps(TCaps &aCaps) const;
```

These capabilities are returned in the `TCaps` structure. This structure comprises a bitstring, whose bit positions denote a specific capability. These capabilities include voice transmission, the ability to transmit fax data using various fax standards, and the ability to automatically sense when data is transferred over the modem interface.

- The status of the telephony device can be retrieved using the following function:

```
IMPORT_C TInt GetStatus(TStatus &aStatus) const;
```

This information is most useful for a modem. The TStatus structure holds information about the status of a connection: if one has been made and how far that connection has progressed.

- Information about the phone lines supported by a particular RPhone object can be obtained using the following functions:

```
IMPORT_C TInt EnumerateLines(TInt &aCount) const;
IMPORT_C TInt GetLineInfo(const TInt aIndex,TLineInfo
                          &aLineInfo) const;
```

Following the pattern of the RTelServer class, Enumerate-Lines() will return a count of the lines supported on the RPhone object queried and GetLineInfo() will return a structure with the information about a phone line connected to it. The TLineInfo structure is defined as follows:

```
struct TLineInfo
{
  RCall::TStatus iStatus;
  TUint32 iLineCapsFlags;
  TName iName;
};
```

It contains the status of the call going across a line, the capabilities of that line, and the name of the line.

- Finally, information on the phone itself—the same information that was available from the RTelServer object—is retrieved using the function below:

```
IMPORT_C TInt GetInfo(TPhoneInfo &aPhoneInfo) const;
```

Look Up These Constants

While I am certainly breezing through all these structures and constants, complete definitions can be found in \Symbian\6.1\Quartz\Epoc32\Include\etel.h. You are *urged* to examine this file as the complete reference point for ETel definitions.

When using a telephone device, changes in capabilities or functionality can occur. Symbian OS provides two functions to notify applications about any changes.

```
IMPORT_C void NotifyCapsChange(TRequestStatus &aStatus,
    TCaps &aCaps);
IMPORT_C void NotifyCapsChangeCancel() const;
```

```
IMPORT_C void NotifyModemDetected(TRequestStatus &aStatus,
    TModemDetection &aDetection);
IMPORT_C void NotifyModemDetectedCancel() const;
```

Each function is asynchronous and comes with a corresponding cancellation function. The first notifier signals the caller when the telephony device's capabilities change; the second signals when a modem change has been detected. These functions are best used by callers that are active objects themselves, so that device notification can be combined and watched along with other notification functions (e.g., I/O notification or line changes).

More on the *PhoneCall* example

Let's continue the PhoneCall class example. We need to expand the implementation of the Init() function to encompass initializing phones. The result is below:

```
void PhoneCall::Init()
{
    RTelServer::TPhoneInfo phoneinfo;
    RPhone::TLineInfo lineinfo;
    RPhone::TCaps capabilities;
    RLine::TCaps lcapabilities;

    TInt result;
    TInt phones,lines,calls;
    TBuf<25> name;

    // ...code to initialize the telephony server connection

    // Get the information on the phone we need
    result = telserver.GetPhoneInfo(0, phoneinfo);
    User::LeaveIfError(result);
    name.Copy(phoneinfo.iName);

    // Open the phone and get its capabilities
    result = gsmphone.Open(telserver, name);
    User::LeaveIfError(result);
    result = gsmphone.GetCaps(capabilities);
    User::LeaveIfError(result);
    if (capabilities.iFlags & RPhone::KCapsVoice == 0)
        User::LeaveIfError(KErrNotSupported);

    // ... other code to init lines and calls
}
```

Note that the phone is automatically initialized when opened. So we do not need to call Initialise() from this initialization code. In the code above, we retrieve the name of the first phone from the telephony server and open it up. On a Nokia 8290 phone (a GSM phone used in the United States), the name of this first phone is GsmPhone1. We conclude this code by making sure that the phone we obtained can indeed support voice capability.

14.3.3 The Line Component

Once a subsession with a phone has been established, we need to establish a subsession over a particular line. The line implementation is captured by the RLine class. Again, since the definition is large, I will pick it apart and look at it in pieces.

As with RPhone objects, RLine object subsessions are opened and closed. The functions to do this are below:

```
IMPORT_C TInt Open(RPhone &aPhone,const TDesC &aName);
IMPORT_C TInt Open(RTelServer &aServer,
   const TDesC &aName);
IMPORT_C void Close();
```

Notice that we can open a session using either an RTelServer object or an RPhone object. The name of the telephony line to use must also be given; this should match a line name retrieved from the RTelServer or RPhone object being used.

Once a subsession has been established, we can make several queries of an RLine object:

- We can get a line's capabilities the same way we did with an RPhone object, using the same TCap structure:

  ```
  IMPORT_C TInt GetCaps(TCaps &aCaps) const;
  ```

- We can get the status of a line using two functions:

  ```
  IMPORT_C TInt GetStatus(RCall::TStatus &aStatus) const;
  IMPORT_C TInt GetHookStatus(RCall::THookStatus
                              &aHookStatus) const;
  ```

  The first function returns the status of a call that might occur over the line. This status is an enumeration that depicts a call as idle or in one of a number of states of making a call—from ringing through answering to hanging up. The hook status is a more general view of a call, returning an enumeration that indicates either "on hook" (meaning a disconnected line) or "off hook" (meaning a call in progress).

- Information about calls opened on a line can be retrieved using the functions below:

```
IMPORT_C TInt EnumerateCall(TInt &aCount) const;
IMPORT_C TInt GetCallInfo(TInt aIndex,
    TCallInfo &aCallInfo) const;
```

As with other telephony objects, the first function gives the number of calls allowed on a line. The second function gets information on a specific call. The `TCallInfo` structure is defined below:

```
struct TCallInfo
{
    TName iCallName;
    RCall::TStatus iStatus;
    TUint32 iCallCapsFlags;
};
```

This gives the name of the call, its status, and its capabilities.

- Finally, information about a line itself can be obtained using the function below:

```
IMPORT_C TInt GetInfo(TLineInfo &aLineInfo) const;
```

This information includes the status of the current call (if there is one) and the name of the last call that was made on this line.

As with `RPhone` objects, `RLine` objects can be notified when aspects of a line change. There are many different properties that can change, and this is reflected in the number of notification functions that are defined for the `RLine` class. These are below:

```
IMPORT_C void NotifyIncomingCall(TRequestStatus &aStatus,
    TName &aName);
IMPORT_C void NotifyIncomingCallCancel() const;
IMPORT_C void NotifyHookChange(TRequestStatus &aStatus,
    RCall::THookStatus &aHookStatus);
IMPORT_C void NotifyHookChangeCancel() const;
IMPORT_C void NotifyStatusChange(
    TRequestStatus &aStatus,RCall::TStatus &aLineStatus);
IMPORT_C void NotifyStatusChangeCancel() const;
IMPORT_C void NotifyCallAdded(TRequestStatus &aStatus,
    TName &aName);
IMPORT_C void NotifyCallAddedCancel() const;
```

There are four notification functions, each with its own cancellation function. Each is also asynchronous and requires a status variable for monitoring. In addition, each function has a second parameter that will be filled in by the telephony server when notification is made. The NotifyIncomingCall() function will notify when an incoming call is detected and will return the name of the incoming call (calls have names—see the next section). NotifyHookChange() will notify when there has been a change in the hook status of a line and the current hook status is returned. The NotifyStatusChange() function will notify interested parties about changes in line status, returning a TStatus structure from the RCall class that reflects the status of a line. Finally, the NotifyCallAdded() function will notify when a call is added to the line. This occurs when a new call has been created (see next section) and its properties are added to the line in question. Adding a call does not necessarily mean that a phone call has actually been made, just that the call object is associated with the current line.

Let's continue to flesh out the PhoneCall class example. Initializing a line for a phone means getting its name and opening a subsession, as below:

```
void PhoneCall::Init()
{
    RTelServer::TPhoneInfo phoneinfo;
    RPhone::TLineInfo lineinfo;
    RPhone::TCaps capabilities;
    RLine::TCaps lcapabilities;

    TInt result;
    TInt phones,lines,calls;
    TBuf<25> name;

    // ... code to init telephony server and phone

    // Get the info on the line we need
    result = gsmphone.GetLineInfo(2, lineinfo);
    User::LeaveIfError(result);
    name.Copy(lineinfo.iName);

    // Open the line and get its capabilities
    result = phoneline.Open(gsmphone, name);
    User::LeaveIfError(result);
    result = phoneline.GetCaps(lcapabilities);
    User::LeaveIfError(result);
    if (lcapabilities.iFlags & RLine::KCapsVoice == 0)
            User::LeaveIfError(KErrNotSupported);

    // ... code to init call
}
```

This example chooses the third line available on the phone and checks its capabilities. On my Nokia 8290 phone, this third line is the voice line (the first two are fax and data), and the name of this line is Voice.

14.3.4 The Call Object

Having established a session with the telephony server and opened subsessions to a phone and a line, we can finally open and manage a call. Calls are described by the RCall class. Before we launch into how to use this class, I should point out a few things about calls.

- *Calls have names.* As with other telephony components, a call has a name. The name of a call is typically generated by the OS and returned when a call subsession is created. A "fully qualified" call name is one that includes call, line, and phone information. in the format PhoneName::LineName::CallName.

- *Opening a call subsession does not connect a call.* As with phones and lines, a call subsession must be opened before we can use a call. Opening a subsession allows the telephony server to allocate memory and resources for a call but does not manipulate the call in any way.

- *Calls can be incoming as well as outgoing.* In addition to instructing the telephony server to make a call, we can instruct the server to answer a call. This is especially useful when receiving faxes.

Opening a call subsession

A call subsession must be opened before the call can be manipulated. A new subsession is opened with the following functions:

```
IMPORT_C TInt OpenNewCall(RTelServer &aServer,
    const TDesC &aName,TDes &aNewName);
IMPORT_C TInt OpenNewCall(RTelServer &aServer,
    const TDesC &aName);
IMPORT_C TInt OpenNewCall(RPhone &aPhone,
    const TDesC &aName,TDes &aNewName);
IMPORT_C TInt OpenNewCall(RPhone &aPhone,
    const TDesC &aName);
IMPORT_C TInt OpenNewCall(RLine &aLine,TDes &aNewName);
IMPORT_C TInt OpenNewCall(RLine &aLine);
```

A new call can be opened by referencing an open telephony server session, a phone subsession or a line subsession. If a server session is referenced, the fully qualified name of the call must be given so that the OS can derive the phone and line to use. If a phone subsession is referenced, the line name must be passed. If a line is referenced, there is no need to further specify anything. Notice that some calls come with a second parameter; this parameter is filled in with the name of the call if it is provided.

Subsessions can be opened with existing calls, i.e., calls in progress. This is done by applications that want to work with calls already received or started by other applications. For example, if one application placed a voice call, a second application could implement a call timer. To hang up after a certain time period, the timer application would have to open the existing call. We can do this using the functions below:

```
IMPORT_C TInt OpenExistingCall(RTelServer &aServer,
    const TDesC &aName);
IMPORT_C TInt OpenExistingCall(RPhone &aPhone,
    const TDesC &aName);
IMPORT_C TInt OpenExistingCall(RLine &aLine,
    const TDesC &aName);
```

In all cases, the second parameter must contain the name of the call to open. As with the OpenNewCall() function, the format of the name will change depending on the type of reference made. For a telephony server reference, for example, the name must be fully qualified as PhoneName::LineName::CallName.

As an example, we can complete the PhoneCall::Init() function. Here, we simply open a new call subsession by referencing the line subsession (the simplest way):

```
void PhoneCall::Init()
{
    RTelServer::TPhoneInfo phoneinfo;
    RPhone::TLineInfo lineinfo;
    RPhone::TCaps capabilities;
    RLine::TCaps lcapabilities;
    TInt result;
    TInt phones,lines,calls;
    TBuf<25> name;

    // ... code to init server, phone, and line

    // Open a new call
    result = phonecall.OpenNewCall(phoneline, name);
    User::LeaveIfError(result);
}
```

On my Nokia phone, this call is assigned the name VoiceCall1.

Although it may seem like a long journey, eventually all sessions and subsessions will be opened and initialized. At this point, we still have not made a call, but the system is ready for this next step.

Calls are made in one of two ways. They can be dialed by the Symbian OS device or they can be connected to an already dialed call. To dial a call, we would use one of the following functions:

```
IMPORT_C TInt Dial(const TTelNumberC &aTelNumber) const;
IMPORT_C TInt Dial(const TDesC8 &aCallParams,
    const TTelNumberC &aTelNumber) const;
IMPORT_C void Dial(TRequestStatus &aStatus,
    const TTelNumberC &aTelNumber);
IMPORT_C void Dial(TRequestStatus &aStatus,
    const TDesC8 &aCallParams,
    const TTelNumberC &aTelNumber);
```

The first two functions are synchronous; the second two are asynchronous. All functions take a parameter of the type TTelNumberC—a typedef for a TDesC string. There are also two functions—one in each pair—that includes a specification of call parameters. This is a generic byte buffer specific to each TSY module. Note that if the asynchronous dial functions are used, we can use the following function to cancel the dialing operation:

```
IMPORT_C void DialCancel() const;
```

To connect to a previously dialed call, the following functions may be used:

```
IMPORT_C TInt Connect() const;
IMPORT_C TInt Connect(const TDesC8 &aCallParams) const;
IMPORT_C void Connect(TRequestStatus &aStatus);
IMPORT_C void Connect(TRequestStatus &aStatus,
    const TDesC8 &aCallParams);
```

As with the dialing functions, connection functions come in synchronous or asynchronous varieties and can include call parameters. If an asynchronous connection call was used, we can cancel it using the following function:

```
IMPORT_C void ConnectCancel() const;
```

To illustrate this, let's define the MakeCall() function from our PhoneCall example. For this definition, I have decided to make the

PhoneCall class an active object, and I can use an asynchronous version of the Dial() function:

```
void PhoneCall::MakeCall(TDesC &aNumber)
{
    phonecall.Dial(callstatus, aNumber);
    iCallState = EDialing;
    SetActive();
}
```

Since we have already set up the telephony system, this is a simple implementation. The number is a string and we return from this function right away while the system dials the call. When the call is dialed, the status variable will change state and the active object's RunL() function will be called. We can field this change by including the following code in the RunL() function:

```
switch (iCallState) {
    case EDialing:
        if (callstatus == KErrNone) {
            // handle the successful call
        } else {
            // handle the call error
        }
        break;
```

This is just like the active object code we have seen before.

Answering a call

If we have successfully created all the sessions and subsessions we need, answering an incoming call is straightforward. One of the functions below should be used:

```
IMPORT_C TInt AnswerIncomingCall() const;
IMPORT_C TInt AnswerIncomingCall(
    const TDesC8 &aCallParams) const;
IMPORT_C void AnswerIncomingCall(TRequestStatus &aStatus);
IMPORT_C void AnswerIncomingCall(TRequestStatus &aStatus,
    const TDesC8 &aCallParams);
```

The first two versions are synchronous; the second two are asynchronous. Each pair has one version that gives a general buffer variable set by the system when a call comes in. The asynchronous versions of this function can be cancelled with the function below:

```
IMPORT_C void AnswerIncomingCallCancel() const;
```

Once a call has been answered, the application is free to do what it wants with the open phone call. If this is a data call, the application might want to access the data port directly for a time. For example, if we are making a call with a modem to transfer some data, we might want the telephony server to take care of dialing the phone number and connecting to the opposite side, but we will then want control to pass our data. We do this by "loaning" the data port to the application using the following functions:

```
IMPORT_C TInt LoanDataPort(TCommPort &aDataPort) const;
IMPORT_C void LoanDataPort(TRequestStatus &aStatus,
    TCommPort &aDataPort);
```

This function comes in synchronous and asynchronous versions. Both versions return information on the data port that is involved in the loan. The TCommPort structure contains the CSY module's filename and the name of the data port itself. As usual, if the asynchronous version is used, we can cancel the loan by using the function below:

```
IMPORT_C void LoanDataPortCancel() const;
```

Once the data port has been used for the transmission of data (e.g. using sockets), it can be returned to the telephony server using the function below:

```
IMPORT_C TInt RecoverDataPort() const;
```

Notifications and call information

For a call, there are a few notifications that the system can give an application. The intent to receive these notifications can be registered or cancelled with the following functions:

```
IMPORT_C void NotifyHookChange(TRequestStatus &aStatus,
    THookStatus &aHookStatus);
IMPORT_C void NotifyHookChangeCancel() const;
IMPORT_C void NotifyStatusChange(TRequestStatus &aStatus,
    TStatus &aCallStatus);
IMPORT_C void NotifyStatusChangeCancel() const;
IMPORT_C void NotifyCallDurationChange(
    TRequestStatus &aStatus, TTimeIntervalSeconds &aTime);
IMPORT_C void NotifyCallDurationChangeCancel() const;
```

There are three changes in status that can be signaled to an application: the hook status, the call phase status, and the call duration. The hook status is the status of a call's connection (on-hook/off-hook). Remember that the remote device or the switching network can terminate a call at any time without asking for permission or giving prior warning. The call phase status is a representation of the state of a call as it passes through its "life cycle": idle, dialing, ringing, answering, connecting, connected, or hanging up. The call duration is the time, in seconds, that the call has been active. This is notified to a registrant every second (useful to know as most calls carry a connect charge based on the duration of the call).

Information about the duration of a call—the time between off-hook and on-hook status changes—can be derived from the following call:

```
IMPORT_C TInt GetCallDuration(
    TTimeIntervalSeconds &aTime) const;
```

Complete information about a call in progress can be obtained through the GetInfo() function:

```
IMPORT_C TInt GetInfo(TCallInfo &aCallInfo) const;
```

This function returns a structure that depicts information about the call:

```
class TCallInfo
{
  public:
    IMPORT_C TCallInfo();
    TName iCallName;
    TName iLineName;
    THookStatus iHookStatus;
    TStatus iStatus;
    TTimeIntervalSeconds iDuration;
};
```

This can be derived at any time for an active call subsession.

Call ownership

To avoid problems with multiple clients accessing the same call, Symbian OS designates a specific client as the *owner* of a call. This ownership is initially passed to the client that connected to a phone call first, but it can be transferred to another client. For example, one contact manager client may be responsible for setting up a data call while another client is responsible for the actual data transfer.

The transfer of call ownership is managed by the following functions:

```
IMPORT_C TInt TransferOwnership() const;
IMPORT_C void AcquireOwnership(
    TRequestStatus &aStatus) const;
IMPORT_C void AcquireOwnershipCancel() const;
```

The owner of a call signals its desire to transfer the ownership by calling `TransferOwnership()`. A potential receiver of that ownership transfer calls `AcquireOwnership()`; this call is asynchronous and blocks until the `TransferOwnership()` function is called. Cancellation of the `AcquireOwnership()` function is done through `AcquireOwnershipCancel()`.

The ownership status of a call can be retrieved by the following function:

```
IMPORT_C TInt GetOwnershipStatus(
    TOwnershipStatus &aOwnershipStatus) const;
```

The call returns a variable that is an enumeration specifying the ownership.

Terminating a call

Call termination, that is, "hanging up" the phone, is accomplished through the functions below:

```
IMPORT_C TInt HangUp() const;
IMPORT_C void HangUp(TRequestStatus &aStatus) const;
```

These functions will terminate the call immediately. The asynchronous function can be cancelled using the function below:

```
IMPORT_C void HangUpCancel() const;
```

14.4   A Special Case Phone Call: Faxing

A fax call is a phone call with some special properties. It is a data call with some structure (faxing is done in "page" units). Special support for faxing is built into Symbian OS.

Faxing is supported through the `RFax` class. The definition of this class is below:

```
class RFax : public RTelSubSessionBase
{
public:
  IMPORT_C RFax();
  IMPORT_C TInt Open(RCall& aCall);
  IMPORT_C void Close();

  IMPORT_C void Read(TRequestStatus &aStatus, TDes8 &aDes);
  IMPORT_C void Write(TRequestStatus &aStatus,
      const TDesC8 &aDes);
```

```
            IMPORT_C void WaitForEndOfPage(
                TRequestStatus &aStatus) const;
            IMPORT_C TInt TerminateFaxSession() const;

            IMPORT_C TInt GetProgress(TProgress &aProgress);
            ...
        };
```

A fax subsession is based on a call subsession. The normal way to handle this is to create a call subsession and to connect using this call (either by initiating or answering a call). We would then perform a fax operation by using the established call object in the `RFax::Open()` function. This establishes the fax data protocol with the remote side.

Once the fax call is established, faxes can be sent or received using the `Read()` and `Write()` functions. These functions take image data and transfer that data using fax protocols. These functions are asynchronous.

The end of a received page can be retrieved through the `WaitForEndOfPage()` function. Because this function is also asynchronous, the `Read()` function can be used in parallel with this function (using different status variables) to read data but terminate images as the ends of pages arrive.

The fax session can be terminated with the `TerminateFaxSession()` function. This function terminates the fax protocol but not the call itself.

Information about faxing can be manipulated in two ways. First, the `RFax` class above has a function to retrieve information about a fax in progress. A call to the `GetProgress()` function will return a `TProgress` structure, defined below:

```
        struct TProgress
        {
            TTime iLastUpdateTime;
            TBuf<20> iAnswerback;
            TFaxPhase iPhase;
            TFaxResolution iResolution;
            TFaxCompression iCompression;
            TInt iECM;

            TInt iPage;
            TInt iLines;
            TInt iSpeed;
        };
```

This structure gives all the information available about a fax-in-progress.

Fax settings are retrieved and set through the `RCall` class. The two functions below work with these:

```
IMPORT_C TInt GetFaxSettings(
    TFaxSessionSettings &aSettings) const;
IMPORT_C TInt SetFaxSettings(
    const TFaxSessionSettings &aSettings) const;
```

These functions get and set the settings that govern fax calls: the fax protocol class, the speed of the transfer, the resolution and compression settings, and so forth.

14.5 Summary

In this chapter, we have taken a look at how Symbian OS supports telephony. Symbian OS views telephony in terms of four components: a telephony server, a phone, phone lines defined for a phone, and finally a call made over a phone line. We reviewed how to set up the structure so that we can use phone calls, and we looked at making and answering calls. We defined how applications can be notified when changes in the phone system and settings are made and we reviewed faxing as a special case of a phone call.

The next chapter will focus on a very important part of Symbian OS: messaging. Messages are at the heart of communication, and Symbian OS has built a large yet flexible infrastructure around them. We will look at this infrastructure next.

15

Sending and Receiving Messages

In everyday life, messages can take many forms. There are verbal and non-verbal messages; messages are written on paper and heard via audio devices; messages can be notes passed in secret or signs on a billboard. Delivery of messages can sometimes be a chancy thing: if you have ever had to rely on a family member to deliver a telephone message, you know what I mean! Even with this wide assortment of message types and delivery functions, humans are able to send and receive these messages fairly easily. We have, in fact, developed an internal system that processes different message types using the same processes, implemented by a tool specialized to each message.

As we have seen, electronic messaging is also a very diverse area. There are many message types and delivery takes many different forms (e.g., delivering email over a PPP network connection is very different than sending an SMS message to a mobile phone). So it should come as no surprise that designing a single framework that will characterize and work with all message forms is quite a challenge. The designers of Symbian OS took on this challenge with EPOC Release 5 and its email system and sharpened their skills through subsequent Symbian OS releases. In the current release of the OS, they have built a messaging system that can not only handle several disparate message types but can accommodate future messaging needs as well.

This chapter overviews the message framework of Symbian OS. We start with an overview—a survey of messaging components and requirements. We then begin looking at the message system API by examining the message server that manages the message store resource. We will then examine the classes that characterize messages themselves. We follow this by looking at "send-as messaging", which forms the heart of the ability to send messages, and "watchers", the functionality for receiving messages. We will wrap up the chapter by looking at four specific message types and how the messaging system deals with them.

15.1 Overview of the Architecture

Let's start by stepping back for a moment and taking an overview of how Symbian OS views messaging. As they built the messaging system, the designers were guided by the need to put together a generic framework that could handle the components of many different message types. They built a framework that viewed all messages as composed of generic components. Through the use of object orientation, each message type is handled by a separate implementation of those generic components. Symbian OS message architecture brings these implementations together under a common messaging application and a common API.

As we look at messages and their components, it is important to note where these messages come from. All Symbian OS devices have a central message store. This store contains all messages received by and created on the device on which it resides and has a specialized, hierarchical format (as we will explain later in this chapter). It can reside on any storage accessible to a Symbian OS device; message applications can change where this store resides. Originally, it resides on the C: drive of the emulator device.

Now let's look at the messaging framework by pulling apart a message and then building the framework from its component parts.

15.1.1 Dissecting a Message

Back in Chapter 5, we looked at messages as having several common characteristics. Figure 15.1 depicts these characteristics and adds a few more. Messages are composed of *delivery information* and *content* and are generally characterized by *message types*.

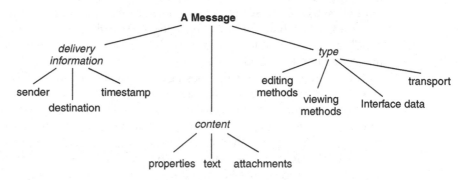

Figure 15.1 Message characteristics.

Delivery information is composed of sender information, destination information, and timestamp information. We reviewed these components back in Chapter 5 and gave several examples. Email messages, for example, contain all this information textually in the header of a message. Sender information is contained in the `Received`: and `From`: fields; destination information is kept in the `To`: field; timestamp information is found in the `Date`: field.

Content has three parts: properties, message content and possibly a set of data objects or attachments. An email message can again serve as a straightforward example. There are pieces of message header that specify certain properties of the message; the `Content-Type`: and `Content-Length`: fields, for example, indicate the MIME properties and the length of the body. The message itself is contained in the body of an email message as text. In email, data objects can also appear in the message body as MIME attachments.

Each message also has a *message type*. The type of a message is the definition of a larger class of messages that describes general characteristics of that class. A message type cannot describe the specific contents of a message, but it can describe properties of the message class. These properties include:

- *The editing function:* This property is a description of how to edit a message of a particular message type. On a Symbian OS device, this "description" takes the form of an implementation of a message editor application.

- *The viewing function:* This property describes how to view a message of a particular message type. Again, in Symbian OS, this "description" is actually an implementation of a message viewer application.

- *User interface data:* There can be certain data associated with user interfaces that deal with a certain message type. These data include items like icons and progress dialog interfaces to display for the message type.

- *The transport function:* Messages of a certain type are transported in the same way to and from their destinations or repositories. The implementation of this transport is associated with the message type and not each individual message.

Let's look at email messages again. All messages that are of the "email" class of messages might be viewed the same way in Symbian OS—through an email viewer that can present the textual message with tools to view header information as well as any attachments to the email. There is a common composition (editing) interface that you can use to compose new messages or edit draft messages. There is a set of user interface definitions—some icons for email applications to display, for example—that can be accessed. Finally, email is transported to a server via SMTP and from a server via POP3 or IMAP4. (Since there are three transport functions, one could argue that there are actually three message types for email. Indeed, Symbian OS views it this way as well.)

Now if we expand our view to other types of messages, we can see that the framework established for Symbian OS will work for any type of message we have encountered. Fax, SMS, and BIO messages all have this format, albeit with different implementations for each component. For that matter, BTIM messages from Chapter 13 could fit right into this framework but would require new implementations for API components.

BTIM Messages in Symbian OS Message Structure

Consider BTIM messages from Chapter 13. These are simple text messages that shuttle back and forth between devices over Bluetooth. This type of messaging is a prime target for incorporation into the Symbian OS messaging framework.

Consider how this might work. Instead of a separate application, we would integrate BTIM messaging into the existing framework and work with BTIM messages using the messaging application on a Symbian OS device.

Consider what this would look like. How would this look in the application? What viewer or editor might be necessary? What interface information would you need? What delivery information might be required? As we move toward designing our own BTIM components, we need to answer these basic questions.

15.1.2 Putting the Pieces Together: MTMs

Symbian OS uses *message type modules* (MTMs) to define message types. An MTM is composed of four classes that are used as base classes for specific message handling implementations. These four classes are as follows:

- The *user interface MTM* is defined as the `CBaseMtmUi` class and defines user interface capabilities, such as viewing and editing messages.

- The *client-side MTM* is defined as the `CBaseMtm` class and handles the interface between the internal representation of a message's data and the user interface MTM.

- The *user interface data MTM* is represented by the `CBaseMtmUi-Data` class and provides access to user interface data properties (e.g., icons).

- The *server-side MTM* is defined in the `CBaseServerMtm` class and provides message transport capability.

Each message type, then, has an implementation of each of these MTMs, subclassing their definitions from the classes above. Some message types can share MTMs; IMAP email and POP email, for example, can share the same user interface MTM, while having different server-side and client-side MTMs.

15.1.3 Some Perspective on this Architecture

This way of modeling messages is powerful and very effective. Through various MTM implementations, Symbian OS supports its four main message formats (email, SMS, fax, and BIO formats) as well as several formats that work behind the scenes to implement other protocols.

It is interesting to examine the disparity between the various forms of messaging under the MTM framework. Fax messaging, for instance, is vastly different from SMS messaging, yet both fit comfortably in this model. Although faxing has different delivery requirements than SMS and must be viewed as an image, where SMS can be viewed as text, both can still be integrated with the same messaging application on a Symbian OS device.

The large number of different forms of messaging results in a large number of MTM implementations. Any messaging application must be able to sift through these implementations to find the necessary MTMs as quickly as possible. Symbian OS helps in this endeavour by providing a registry of installed MTMs that are accessible to an application. This registry allows MTM components to be identified and instantiated quickly and easily.

Now consider this structure from a programmer's perspective. Imagine you are a programmer who wants to implement the sending of an SMS message as a small part of a larger application. It would be quite daunting for you to use the MTM framework in all its glory to send a "simple" SMS message. In fact, you might just reject the idea as not worth the time and effort. The designers of the MTM model understood that a complicated structure might frustrate programmers who want to do simpler tasks, so they added something to the architecture called *send-as messaging*. Send-as messaging provides a simple interface that allows applications to create outgoing messages by using a single API. By using send-as messaging, a programmer uses one interface for any message and simply informs the OS what type of message to send; the OS implementation will figure out which MTMs to use and how to send the message. This is a powerful idea and it reinforces the modularity of the MTM structure. It has proven to be an easy and effective interface. It is so effective, in fact, that many applications use it to transport data other than traditional messages. The Agenda engine, for example, uses send-as messaging to send vCalendar objects over the IR interface.

Interesting MTM Implementations

Using the Find function in your Windows Start button, look for file names that include "MTM" in your installation of Symbian OS SDK. You will find several that might look familiar, but you will also find some that do not. For example, there is an MTM module implemented as a DLL called `WAPPUSHMTM-CLIENTSERVER.DLL`. This is an implementation for messages that would show up in the messaging applications that include WAP formatted content.

Look for other messaging types that do not look familiar, and consider what they might be used for.

15.2   The Message Server

15.2.1   Message Server Functionality

Symbian OS considers the data repository for messages as a resource that can be shared between processes. Therefore, following Symbian OS standards, there is a server that protects this repository and manages access to it. The message server implements two valuable functions:

- *Access to the message data repository:* As clients request message access, the message server delegates temporary, exclusive access to message data. The message server must keep the message data repository correctly ordered and must cope with anomalous message events correctly. For example, access failures or incomplete sessions must not corrupt the message data.
- *Access to MTMs:* The message server must enable applications to identify requests, such as the sending of a message, that require protocol-specific functionality and load the appropriate MTM.

The message server accepts requests from client applications that require access to messages and MTMs. These requests are handled asynchronously, as they might require a large amount of time to perform (fax messages, for example, typically take much more time to process than email messages). Requests can include changing the structure or contents of the local folders, sending and receiving messages through different services, changing the structure or contents of remote mailboxes, and MTM-specific requests. Note that actions such as delivery and storage concepts such as local folders and remote mailboxes are all managed by the message server.

15.2.2 Storage and Message Structure

The Symbian OS message store has a specific structure shown in Table 15.1. The diagram in Figure 15.2 shows an overview of this structure. Messages are stored in folders, which are accessed as children of services. A service can be viewed as a message source; an ISP is a service, as is local, on-device storage. Folders can be user-defined or system-defined; for example, in and out boxes are defined by the system and are applicable under the local storage service. Folders can have subfolders, which can have subfolders, etc. This hierarchical organization of the storage structure means that access to messages requires a walk through the storage tree before access is granted to a message.

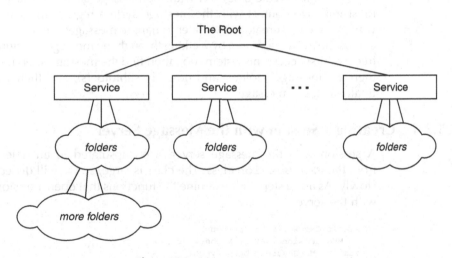

Figure 15.2 Message storage structure.

Messages themselves also have a structure. This structure is shown in the table below.

Table 15.1 Message structure

Message component	Type of data
Generic message header	Message index entry data
MTM-specific information	MTM-stream data
Message body	Rich text data in message store.
Attachments	Attachment files stored in the message's store

Message index entries have a specific format. That format is quite large, and I will not reproduce it here. Suffice it to say that both delivery and content header information is stored here and that this information varies for different MTMs. The MTM-stream date is specifically formatted for the type of MTM that is used for the message. Obviously, this information also varies for the MTMs. The message body is a rich text object (from the CRichText class) that contains text as well as formatting information. Details about attachments are found in the message header—the index portion—but the data files are stored in their own format in the message store after the message body.

15.3   Accessing Messages

To access messages, we must create and manipulate several objects. First, we must create a session with the message server. Next, we must initialize contact with the message system registry in such a way that we can create MTMs later to handle messages. Finally, we access the message system by walking through the message structure tree: we first access the system root, then find the message's service, then the message's folder (and possibly subfolders), and then we finally access a message.

15.3.1   Creating a Session with the Message Server

A session with the message server is encapsulated in an object from the CMsvSession class. The class is large, so we will dissect slowly. As a first step, let's examine the functions that open a session with the server:

```
static CMsvSession* OpenSyncL(
    MMsvSessionObserver &aObserver);
static CMsvSession* OpenAsyncL(
    MMsvSessionObserver &aObserver);
```

The first function opens a session synchronously, i.e., when the function call returns, the session has been started and is valid. The second function opens a session asynchronously. When the session is valid, the caller is informed through the `MMsvSessionObserver` object. Notice that both functions require an observer object derived from the `MMsvSessionObserver` class. This class is a base class and using it mandates that you create a subclass that uses this one as its foundation. Specifically, the subclass must implement the single function in this class:

```
void HandleSessionEventL(TMsvSessionEvent aEvent,
    TAny* aArg1, TAny* aArg2, TAny* aArg3);
```

This function will be called as events happen in the session that was created. The `TMsvSessionEvent` argument contains the event that caused the function call, and the `TAny` arguments contain any data that will be used with the event to provide more information. We will deal with this observer functionality later in this chapter.

15.3.2 Opening the Registry

The next step is to open the registry so that we can obtain MTM objects when we need them. There are three kinds of access into the registry: one to access client-side MTMs, one to access user interface MTMs, and one to access user interface data MTMs. Each access is implemented by its own class: `CClientMtmRegistry`, `CMtmUiRegistry`, and `CMtmUiDataRegistry` classes, respectively. They are derived from the same base classes and have similar definitions.

No Server-side MTM Access

Accessing the registry does not give us access to server-side MTMs. Because all outgoing functionality is encapsulated by send-as messaging, access to server-side MTMs is funneled through this system. We will see this later.

Let's look at the `CClientMtmRegistry` class as a representative. It has the following definition:

```
class CClientMtmRegistry : public CObserverRegistry
{
public:
  IMPORT_C static CClientMtmRegistry* NewL(
    CMsvSession &aMsvSession, TTimeIntervalMicroSeconds32
    aTimeoutMicroSeconds32=TTimeIntervalMicroSeconds32(30000000));
  IMPORT_C ~CClientMtmRegistry();
  IMPORT_C CBaseMtm* NewMtmL(TUid aMtmTypeUid);
  //
    ...
};
```

There is a function to create a new instance, a function to destroy an instance, and a function to create a new MTM handle. The `NewL()` function takes an active message server session object and an optional timeout parameter (without this parameter, the call times out in 30 seconds). The `NewMtmL()` function takes the UID of the type of MTM we will need. Each MTM has a UID, as shown in Table 15.2:

Table 15.2 MTM UIDs for Symbian OS version 6.1

MTM Type	UID Value	Constant Name
Text	0x10005247	KUidMsgTypeText
SMTP	0x10001028	KUidMsgTypeSMTP
POP3	0x10001029	KUidMsgTypePOP3
IMAP4	0x1000102A	KUidMsgTypeIMAP4
Fax	0x1000102B	KUidMsgTypeFax
SMS	0x1000102C	KUidMsgTypeSMS

Other MTM Registries

You can find out about the other MTM registry interfaces by browsing their definitions. The `CClientMtmRegistry` class is defined in the `mtclreg.h` file; the `CMtmUiRegistry` class is found in the `mtuireg.h` file; and the `CMtmUiDataRegistry` class is found in the `mtudreg.h` file. These definition files are found in the `\Symbian\6.1\Quartz\Epoc32\include` directory.

To make an instance of a registry class and create an MTM handle for later use, we could use the code below:

```
CClientMtmRegistry ClientMTMRegistry;
CBaseMtm* ClientMtm;

ClientMTMRegistry = CClientMtmRegistry::NewL(
    MsgSvrSession);
ClientMtm = ClientMTMRegistry ->NewMtmL(KUidMsgTypeText);
```

Notice that we had to give a message server session object (already established in the `MsgSvrSession` variable) and the type of message for which we will need the MTM. In the example above, we are intending to use client-side MTMs for text messages.

15.3.3 Accessing the Message Tree

Once we have established a valid message server session and we have access to the registry, we can access the message tree structure.

Entries in this tree structure are represented by the CMsvEntry class. All types of entries, from root entries through to messages themselves, are represented by this class. Entries are retrieved from the message tree by using functions from the CMsvSession class. Two functions from that class are relevant here:

```
inline CMsvEntry* GetEntryL(TMsvId aEntId);
inline TInt GetEntry(TMsvId aId, TMsvId &aService,
    TMsvEntry &aEntry);
```

The GetEntryL() function looks up a message tree entry by the entry's ID. In the first version of the function, the call returns a pointer to a CMsvEntry class object that represents the message being retrieved. In the second version of the function, other information is returned: the service of which the entry is a child and the header information (the index entry, a TMsvEntry object) of the entry we are retrieving. The entry ID of the root of the message tree is given by the constant KMsvRootIndexEntryId.

Let's stop for a moment and look at the characteristics of an entry in the message tree as represented by the CMsvEntry class. An entry includes the following properties:

- *an entry ID*, an object of the TMsvId class, retrieved by the CMsvEntry::EntryId() function
- *the header information*, what we earlier referred to as entry index information, obtained via the CMsvEntry::Entry() function
- *an "owning service"*, i.e., the parent of an entry, retrieved by the CMsvEntry::OwningService() function, which returns an entry ID
- *a certain number of children* (for the root and inner tree nodes), accessed by a number of functions, e.g., CMsvEntry::Children() and CMsvEntry::Count() functions
- *file storage*, determined by the Boolean CMsvEntry::HasDirectoryL() and CMsvEntry::HasStoreL() functions and retrieved by the CMsvEntry::GetFilePath() function
- *an MTM list*, set mostly by the system as entries are created

Consider an example. Let's say we need a function that would look up a node and walk through each of its children. Consider the following code:

```
void MessageExample::EntryWalk(TInt aEntryId)
{
    TInt i;
    TInt iCount;
    CMsvSession *iMessageSession;
```

```
                  CMsvEntrySelection* iChildren;
                  CMsvEntry* iRootEntry;
                  CMsvEntry *child;

                  // Open a session with the message server
                  iMessageSession = CMsvSession::OpenSyncL(*this);
                  iRootEntry = iMessageSession->GetEntryL(aEntryId);
                  iCount = iRootEntry->Count();

                  // Get the root of the hierarchy
                  iChildren = iRootEntry->ChildrenL();
                  for (i=0; i<iCount; i++) {
                      child = iMessageSession->GetEntryL((*iChildren)[i]);

                      // do something with the child

                  }
              }
```

In this code, we open a session to the message server, get the node
entry referenced by the aEntryId parameter, find its children, and
then loop through fetches of each child. If we wanted to look at
each service that the message server manages, we could call this
function with the entry ID of the root of the message tree (Kmsv-
RootIndexEntryId). Since services are direct children of the
message tree root, this would access each service. We could repeat
the process (perhaps recursively) to eventually reach each message.
As another example, if we wanted to look at each message in the
message tree inbox for the local message store, we would call this
function with the entry ID of KMsvGlobalInBoxIndexEntryId,
which is defined as the inbox ID constant.

Notice in the above code that the children of an entry are
retrieved into a CMsvEntrySelection class. This class is defined
as an array of entry IDs.

15.3.4 Viewing and Editing Messages

Once we have a message entry as a CMsvEntry object that we
want to manipulate, we need to get its interface MTM to view it or
edit it. We can follow this sequence to obtain and use this MTM:

- Obtain the header information from the entry. This will be in the
  form of a TMsvEntry object.
- Use the data from the header information to discover the MTM
  type that handles the entry. For example, the UID of the MTM
  can be found as the TMsvEntry::iMtm variable of this object.
- Request instances of the client-side MTM and user interface
  MTM objects from the registry.

- Set the context of the client-side MTM. This means that we "focus" the client-side MTM on a specific message, so that it can configure itself to obtain the right types of data (e.g., MTMs).
- Call the operation function (i.e., either viewing or editing) provided by the user interface MTM. This returns an active object to manage the asynchronous operation.
- When that operation object completes, it will signal the active object implemented by the client program.
- That active object then handles any action, such as cleanup, that is required.

From this sequence, notice that the actual operation of viewing or editing is an asynchronous operation, governed by an active object. This object is an instance of the CMsvOperation class, which is derived from the CActive class (among others). This class is used extensively by CMsvEntry objects and user interface MTMs to implement functions that require a parallel active object thread and have the possibility of cancellation. In addition to creation and cancellation of the CMsvOperation object, several other operations are possible. The definition below is taken from the definition of the CMsvOperation class:

```
virtual const TDesC8& ProgressL()=0;
IMPORT_C virtual const TDesC8& FinalProgress();
IMPORT_C virtual TUid Mtm() const;
inline TMsvOp Id() const;
inline TMsvId Service() const;
```

The progress and final disposition of the operation performed (when it completes) are available in human-readable strings from the first two functions. The Mtm() function will return the UID of the MTM that is being used for the operation. The Id() function returns the ID of the operation internal to the message server. The ID allows a client to keep track of different operations. Finally, the Service() function returns the entry ID of the service that is involved in the operation.

Now, let's follow an example that implements the above sequence. Assume we have a CMsvEntry message entry object as the variable child, from the example above. We would view this message as follows:

```
TRequestStatus status;
TMsvEntry *msginfo;
CClientMtmRegistry iMTMClientRegistry;
CMtmUiRegistry iMTMUiRegistry;
CBaseMtm *iClientMtm;
CBaseMtmUi *iMtmUi
```

```
msginfo = child->Entry();

// Create a client-side MTM
iMtmClientRegistry = CClientMtmRegistry::NewL(
    iMessageSession);
iClientMtm = iMtmClientRegistry->NewMtmL(msginfo->iType);

// Set the client MTM's context
iClientMtm->SwitchCurrentEntryL(child->EntryId());

// Extract the text message MTM UI
iMTMUiRegistry = CMtmUiRegistry::NewL(iMessageSession);
iMtmUi = iMTMUiRegistry ->NewMtmUiL(iClientMtm);

// View the message
iMtmUi->ViewL(status);
User::WaitForRequest(status);
```

In this code, we create a new client-side MTM by using the registry
to obtain one for the type of message we are looking at, as derived
from the child message. We then set the *context* of the client-side
MTM—i.e., customize it—to the current message. At this point, the
MTM interface object is focused on the right message and the right
context/message type, and we can view the message through that
interface object.

15.3.5   Other Operations on Messages

The definition of the `CBaseMtmUi` class is lengthy. It includes
functions for viewing and editing messages (as we have just seen),
copying and moving messages between folders, replying to and forwarding messages, deleting messages, and monitoring the progress
of operations. In all cases, since these operations may take a while,
the functions work like `EditL()` and `ViewL()` above, i.e., they
invoke a `CMsvOperation` active object and return a handle to it.

Just as operations for viewing and editing messages are tailored
for a specific message type, replying and forwarding messages are
also implemented differently for each message type. You would
reply to a fax differently than you would to an SMS message. These
are handled by asynchronous functions, as in the definitions below:

```
virtual CMsvOperation* ReplyL(TMsvId aDestination,
    TMsvPartList aPartlist,
    TRequestStatus &aCompletionStatus) = 0;
virtual CMsvOperation* ForwardL(TMsvId aDestination,
    TMsvPartList aPartList,
    TRequestStatus &aCompletionStatus) = 0;
```

Both functions take an entry ID of the service or folder where
the newly-created message from a successful completion should

be placed. For example, using the supplied constant, KMsv-GlobalOutBoxIndexEntryId, would place the resulting new message in the outbox to await delivery. The second parameter to these functions is a "parts list"—an integer whose bit positions determine which parts of the original message will be included in the new message. Message parts are defined by the constants that are OR'd together. The final parameter is a status variable used to monitor the progress of the active object.

Messages and services can be deleted through the functions below:

```
IMPORT_C virtual CMsvOperation* DeleteFromL(
    const CMsvEntrySelection &aSelection,
    TRequestStatus &aStatus);
IMPORT_C virtual CMsvOperation* UnDeleteFromL(
    const CMsvEntrySelection &aSelection,
    TRequestStatus &aStatus);
IMPORT_C virtual CMsvOperation* DeleteServiceL(
    const TMsvEntry &aService, TRequestStatus &aStatus);
```

The first two functions take a selection array and a status indicator. They allow messages to be deleted or undeleted from folders. The third function will delete a service, including the folders and messages that are dependent on that service.

There are four functions that implement the transfer of messages to and from remote servers. They are defined below:

```
IMPORT_C virtual CMsvOperation* CopyToL(
    const CMsvEntrySelection &aSelection,
    TRequestStatus &aStatus);
IMPORT_C virtual CMsvOperation* MoveToL(
    const CMsvEntrySelection &aSelection,
    TRequestStatus &aStatus);
IMPORT_C virtual CMsvOperation* CopyFromL(
    const CMsvEntrySelection &aSelection,
    TMsvId aTargetId, TRequestStatus &aStatus);
IMPORT_C virtual CMsvOperation* MoveFromL(
    const CMsvEntrySelection &aSelection,
    TMsvId aTargetId, TRequestStatus &aStatus);
```

The first two—CopyToL() and MoveToL()—will copy or move messages indicated by the selection array to the current context. The context is the current folder to which you have navigated in your application prior to executing one of the above functions. Since the messages will have their own context information encoded in each reference in the selection array, the system will know the context from which to transfer the message. The second two functions—CopyFromL() and MoveFromL()—do not have this information, because they transfer messages from the current context to some other context. You must provide the entry ID of that destination context in the `aTargetId` argument.

Two functions allow information to be obtained about on-going operations. Consider the definitions below:

```
IMPORT_C virtual TInt DisplayProgressSummary(
    const TDesC8 &aProgress) const;
IMPORT_C virtual TInt GetProgress(
    const TDesC8 &aProgress,
    TBuf<EProgressStringMaxLen> &aReturnString,
    TInt &aTotalEntryCount, TInt &aEntriesDone,
    TInt &aCurrentEntrySize,
    TInt &aCurrentBytesTrans) const;
```

These functions convert progress information about some asynchronous operation, information that is specific to an MTM such as message sending, to a human-readable form. The progress information that you must pass into these functions is a string obtained from an on-going `CMsvOperation` by calling its `ProgressL()` function. The nature of any information that is displayed is MTM-specific. The first function simply displays a progress message. The second function actually gets more information so you can display it in your application.

15.3.6 MTM-Specific Functions

In the implementations of different MTMs, there are bound to be functions that are specific to each MTM that do not generalize to all MTMs. For example, an email message MTM that uses POP3 would need functions to connect to and disconnect from the POP3 server. A BIO message MTM would not need a function to connect to a server because there is no server for BIO messages (they are pushed to a device). On the other hand, a BIO message MTM needs a function to process the BIO message content. This applies to SMS and fax messages as well. Each MTM implementation will require its own specialized functions.

The messaging architecture provides a way for MTM components to offer protocol-specific functionality not provided by base class interface functions. These MTM-specific functions are implemented in the MTM and assigned IDs that correspond to each protocol-specific operation offered. To call these specific functions, each MTM component implements two functions, called `InvokeSyncFunctionL()` and `InvokeAsyncFunctionL()`, that allow clients to access these operations by passing in the appropriate ID. As you can guess from their names, the first function allows an operation to be called synchronously and the second allows asynchronous access to an operation. The actual calling sequence is defined below from the `CBaseMtm` class:

```
virtual CMsvOperation* InvokeAsyncFunctionL(
    TInt aFunctionId, const CMsvEntrySelection &aSelection,
    TDes8 &aParameter,
    TRequestStatus &aCompletionStatus) = 0;

virtual void InvokeSyncFunctionL(TInt aFunctionId,
    const CMsvEntrySelection &aSelection,
    TDes8 &aParameter) = 0;
```

Each call requires the function ID as the first parameter. This is different for each MTM used. The second parameter defines the messages that are affected as a message selection array. The third parameter is a generic buffer of byte data that provides a parameter list to the function being invoked. Finally, the asynchronous call requires a status variable for monitoring.

Look Up MTM–Specific Function IDs

You can find the MTM-specific function IDs in certain header files. Under the `\Symbian\6.1\Quartz\Epoc32\include`

15.4   Creating Basic Messages: The BaseMtm Class

As we have discussed, Symbian OS supports several kinds of message types and allows new types to extend the architecture. While each message type has its own MTM and its own set of progress monitors, there is a core structure that should look familiar. All MTMs are derived from a single base MTM class: the CBaseMtm class. Each MTM subclass will inherit functions from the base class and will customize them for its own purposes. We will go over the core set before elaborating on the derived classes.

The first functions we should review are functions that determine the context of an MTM: SetCurrentEntryL() and SwitchCurrentEntryL():

```
IMPORT_C void SetCurrentEntryL(CMsvEntry* aEntry);
IMPORT_C void SwitchCurrentEntryL(TMsvId aId);
inline CMsvEntry& Entry() const;
inline TBool HasContext() const;
```

These functions change and test the entry on which later actions are performed through the MTM. The first two functions are distinguished by their parameter types. The first takes a pointer to a service, folder, or message; the second takes an entry ID number. A message client application must use one of these to set a context before using other MTM functions. The third function retrieves the context of the MTM, and the last function tests if one has been set.

When the context is set, no data is manipulated. The context is the *environment* of the message—its representative properties—but not its *contents*. Message data must be explicitly loaded and saved through the functions defined below:

```
virtual void SaveMessageL()=0;
virtual void LoadMessageL()=0;
```

To retrieve entry data, invoke the LoadMessageL() function after setting the context; any changes made to a message should be saved by calling SaveMessageL(). There is a cache that is set up for the message, which is emptied upon switching contexts; calling these functions will fill and save this cache.

A message can be created—i.e., its entry is created and the message framework established—by the `CreateMessageL()` function. This is defined below:

```
IMPORT_C virtual void CreateMessageL(TMsvId aServiceId);
```

The parameter is an entry ID for the service to which this message will belong.

Specific parts of a message can be manipulated on their own using the `CBaseMtm` class. The functions include the ones below:

- Addresses can be added to and deleted from the recipient lists of messages through the functions below:

```
inline const CDesCArray &AddresseeList() const;
virtual void AddAddresseeL(
    const TDesC &aRealAddress) = 0;
virtual void AddAddresseeL(
    const TDesC &aRealAddress, const TDesC &aAlias) = 0;
virtual void RemoveAddressee(TInt aIndex) = 0;
```

Addresses are simply strings for these function calls, and the address list is an array of strings. Addresses are removed by using indexes from this address list array. These functions are designed to allow address list manipulation with no MTM-specific knowledge.

- The subject of a message is controlled through the functions defined below:

```
IMPORT_C virtual void SetSubjectL(
    const TDesC &aSubject);
IMPORT_C virtual const TPtrC SubjectL() const;
```

These functions will set the subject and retrieve the subject. The subject itself is simply a string.

- The body of a message can only be retrieved in the `CBaseMtm` base class. Subclasses will define ways to set the body on their own. Retrieving the body of a message is accomplished by functions defined below:

```
inline CRichText& Body();
inline const CRichText& Body() const;
```

Note that these functions return a `CRichText` object. A `CRichText` class object is generic enough to handle all the different formats that a body could be in for the various types of messages we will use.

The body of a message is cached by the operating system—even after manipulation—so that access to it can be fast. To move the cache to and from file storage, we need to use one of two functions, defined below:

```
IMPORT_C void StoreBodyL(CMsvStore &aStore);
IMPORT_C void RestoreBodyL(CMsvStore &aStore);
```

StoreBodyL() and RestoreBodyL() encapsulate the retrieval and storage of this CRichText object to a CMsvStore for implementers of derived classes. If you want to read or write the body without reading or writing the entire message, this is how to do it.

- Attachments are important for several types of messages. We manipulate attachments by the following functions:

```
IMPORT_C virtual void CreateAttachmentL(
    TMsvId &aAttachmentId, TFileName &aDirectory);

IMPORT_C virtual void DeleteAttachmentL(
    TMsvId aMessageId, TMsvId aAttachmentId);
```

These functions do not actually create or delete anything more than an index entry to be filled in by the application. When CreateAttachment() is called, an index entry is created for the attachment, and the entry ID for it is returned along with the directory in which to create the attachment. Deleting an attachment with DeleteAttachmentL() must use the entry ID for a message and for the attachment ID on that message.

Without a specific type of a message to use, it is hard to give a concrete example of the above functions. But we can review the sequence of events that must occur to create a message.

- First, we must create the MTM for a message type. We would do this as we did before using the registry. Let's assume we have an MTM called theMTM, created with a KUidMsgTypeSMTP message type (email using SMTP).
- Next, we would have to create a message. Let's say we want to create a message in the local message service's outbox. We would use code like this:

```
theMTM->CreateMessage(KmsvGlobalOutBoxIndexEntryId);
```

- Next, we would want to set up the destination of the message. For example, we might use the code below:

```
theMTM->AddAddresseeL(_L("jipping@cs.hope.edu"));
```

  This sets the message to go out to my email address.

- We could set up the subject as follows:

```
theMTM->SetSubjectL(_L("Meeting at 3:00 pm"));
```

- We would then manipulate the message body as the specific type of message MTM stipulates.

- If we want to manipulate attachments, we would do so with the functions from the specific MTM.

- We can now save the message. We could use the code below:

```
theMTM->SaveMessageL();
```

  This saves the message to the outbox.

Notice how once the message has been created—and the context set by that creation—all future function calls work on that message context. There is no need in the calls to specify which message to manipulate.

15.5 Easy Sending of Messages: Send-As Messaging

By now you might be a little taken aback by the complexity of message handling and the message architecture of Symbian OS. While it is true that the architecture is big and complex—after all, it must handle messages as different as faxes and SMS messages–the designers of Symbian OS have streamlined the process we use to send messages. The sending process is relatively short and very straightforward. Let's review that process in this section.

The sending procedure is called *send-as messaging*. It is a generic process—i.e., one process for all message types—that uses a message type's MTM to guide the sending process. It is a powerful model that can be used to send messages of all types and even to transfer data in unique ways. The procedure follows the sequence we outlined in the last section.

Send-as messaging centers on the CSendAs class. The definition of this class is rather large, so we will not go through it in its entirety. Rather, we will go through the process necessary to send a message and overview the API along the way.

15.5.1 Step 1: Choose the MTM

The first step is to choose the MTM that the CSendAs object will use to send the message. This can be done in two ways: we can set the MTM directly or we can use a CSendAs object to search for the MTM we need.

The first function is the easiest, but we must know (a) which MTM we want and (b) that the MTM is available on the device we are using. To set the MTM, we need the CSendAs function defined below:

```
IMPORT_C void SetMtmL(TUid aMtmUid);
```

For this function, we need to know the UID of the MTM we intend to use. There are constants defined for this purpose for the installed MTMs; Table 15.2 has some of the predefined standard UIDs.

The second way to set the MTM is to search for it. To use this function, we need to give the CSendAs object some search criteria to help it prune the list of available MTMs. To do this, we would use following function:

```
IMPORT_C void AddMtmCapabilityL(TUid aCapabilityId,
    TBool aResponseExpected=EFalse);
```

We would add each of the necessary capabilities, which would filter the MTM list for those that have the capabilities we need. In version 6.1 of Symbian OS, there are 15 predefined UIDs for MTM capabilities. For example, if we wanted an MTM that supports subjects and attachments, we might use the code below:

```
iSendAs->AddMtmCapabilityL(KUidMtmQuerySupportSubjects);
iSendAs->AddMtmCapabilityL(
    KUidMtmQuerySupportAttachments);
```

Once the capability list has been set, the list of available MTMs can be accessed through the function defined below:

```
inline const CDesCArray& AvailableMtms() const;
```

This function returns an array of strings that indicate the MTMs that possess the capabilities stipulated.

This list of capabilities can be reset by a call to the following function:

```
IMPORT_C void ResetMtmCapabilitiesL();
```

Once an MTM has been chosen from the list of available ones, the MTM can be set for a CSendAs object by using an index into the array of available MTMs, using the function below:

```
IMPORT_C void SetMtmL(TInt aMtmIndex);
```

This function is an overloaded alternative to the SetMtmL() function we discussed above.

15.5.2 Step 2: Choose the Service to Use

Once the MTM has been chosen, we need to set the service to use for the outgoing message. To do this we use the two functions below:

```
inline const CDesCArray& AvailableServices() const;
IMPORT_C void SetService(TInt aServiceIndex);
```

The first function will return an array of strings that describe the services that are available. The second function chooses a service by selecting an index from this array of available services.

If no service is explicitly selected, a default service will be used for sending the message.

15.5.3 Step 3: Create the Message (and All Its Parts)

We begin a message by creating it through the CSendAs object. We would use one of the functions described below:

```
IMPORT_C void CreateMessageL();
IMPORT_C void CreateMessageL(TMsvId aId);
```

In both cases, a message for the current CSendAs object is created. In the first version, a blank message is created; in the second version, a message is created whose context and contents are copied from the message whose ID is given as a parameter. To create a message, the MTM for the CSendAs object must already have been set.

Once the message for the CSendAs object has been created, we can create and modify its components. The components are the same ones that we addressed with the CBaseMtm class, with similar functions.

- Message recipients are modified with one the following functions:

```
IMPORT_C const CDesCArray& RecipientList() const;
IMPORT_C void AddRecipientL(
    const TDesC &aRealAddress);
```

```
IMPORT_C void AddRecipientL(
    const TDesC &aRealAddress, const TDesC &aAlias);
IMPORT_C void RemoveRecipient(TInt aIndex);
```

The two `AddRecipientL()` functions add the string given to
the list of recipients for the message. The list can be retrieved with
`RecipientList()` as an array of strings. The `RemoveRecip-`
`ient()` function removes the recipient at the position in the list
indicated by its parameter.

- The subject of the message—as a string—is set with the following function:

```
IMPORT_C void SetSubjectL(const TDesC &aSubject);
```

Obviously, SMS and BIO messages do not have a subject.

- The body of a message is set with a rich text object using this
  function:

```
IMPORT_C void SetBodyL(const CRichText &aMessageBody);
```

- Any attachments can be modified with the following functions:

```
IMPORT_C void CreateAttachmentL(TMsvId &aAttachmentId,
    TFileName &aDirectory);
IMPORT_C void DeleteAttachmentL(TMsvId aAttachmentId);
IMPORT_C void SetAttachmentL(TMsvId aAttachmentId,
    const TDesC &aAttachmentName);
```

When an attachment is created, its entry ID is returned along
with a directory in which that the attachment must be created.
Once the file that contains the attachment has been created,
that file can be attached by the `SetAttachmentL()` function.
We must provide the attachment ID and filename to attach
to it as parameters. Finally, attachments can be deleted by
using `DeleteAttachmentL()` with the appropriate attachment entry ID.

15.5.4   Step 4: Save and Send the Message

When the message has been prepared, sending the message means
saving it into the appropriate service's message store. This means a
call to one of the functions below:

```
IMPORT_C void SaveMessageL(TBool aMakeVisible=ETrue);
IMPORT_C void SaveMessageL(TRequestStatus &aStatus,
    TBool aMakeVisible=ETrue);
```

Both versions take a Boolean value, a flag that dictates to the message server whether it is to make the message visible in the message's context. The second version is asynchronous and also takes a status variable through which an application can monitor the progress of the CSendAs object. The second version is used for messages that may take more time than an application is willing to wait, e.g., a fax page that must be rendered before being saved.

15.5.5 An Example

Let's consider a CSendAs example. Suppose we want to extend the TodoX example to send the todo-list item as an attachment to an email message. To make this extension work, it must be a subclass of the TodoXferBase class and must implement some meaningless—and therefore empty—functions. But the new class will fit into the transfer scheme nicely. We can also finally transfer a vCalendar object.

In this example, the calling sequence for this new "port" looks like this:

```
iXferPort->Init(_L("jipping@cs.hope.edu"));
iXferPort->OpenL();
iXferPort->Configure();
iXferPort->SendItem(iReader->iEntry);
iXferPort->Close();
```

Here, iXferPort is an object of the TodoXferEmail class. This looks like all the other calling sequences we have seen for this example.

In order to fit email transfer into the TodoX class hierarchy, I had to split up message sending just a bit. If you think of the email message as a "port", this will make more sense. The Init() function is defined as follows:

```
TInt TodoXferEmail::Init(TDesC &aRecipient)
{
    TInt result;

    iSendAs = CSendAs::NewL(*this);
    iRecipient.Copy(aRecipient);

    return 0;
}
```

The recipient of the email is sent as the parameter. The CSendAs object is created and the recipient stored for future use.

Opening the email message does not make sense here, so the OpenL() function has an empty definition.

Configuring the email message means setting the MTM properties of the CSendAs object. The definition of Configure() is below:

```
void TodoXferEmail::Configure()
{
    if (iSendAs) {
        iSendAs->AddMtmCapabilityL(
            KUidMtmQuerySupportAttachments);
        iSendAs->SetMtmL(KUidMsgTypeSMTP);
    }
}
```

In this code, we make sure that we can support attachments, and we set the message type to be defined as SMTP messages by using the SMTP MTM.

The SendItem() function contains the real meat of the sending process. Its definition is below:

```
void TodoXferEmail::SendItem(CAgnEntry *aEntry)
{
    CAgnTodo* iTodoItem;
    TBuf<100> dbuffer;
    TBuf8<100> buffer;
    TUint priority;
    TTime duedate;

    // Generate a file with the vCal object in it
    RFs fs;
    fs.Connect();
    RFile outputFile;

User::LeaveIfError(outputFile.Replace(fs,KOutputFile,
                    EFileWrite));
    RFileWriteStream writeStream(outputFile);
    iAppUi->iReader->WriteVCalObject(aEntry, writeStream);
    writeStream.CommitL();
    writeStream.Close();
    outputFile.Close();

    // Create message
    iSendAs->CreateMessageL(KMsvGlobalOutBoxIndexEntryId);

    if(iSendAs->QueryMessageCapability(
        KUidMtmQuerySupportAttachments) == KErrNone) {
        TMsvId messageId;
        TFileName attachment;
        TFileName srcFile;

        messageId = iSendAs->MessageId()
        iSendAs->CreateAttachmentL(messageId, attachment);
        attachment += KFileName;
```

```
CFileMan* file = CFileMan::NewL(fs);
TInt fileCopy = file->Copy(KOutputFile, attachment);
delete file;

if (fileCopy == KErrNone) {
    // Save the message, creating an email with the
    // current recording as an attachment.
    iSendAs->SetAttachmentL(messageId, KFileName);
        if    (iSendAs->AvailableServices().Count() < 1)
            User::Leave(KErrNotFound);
    iSendAs->SetService(0);
    iSendAs->AddRecipientL(iRecipient);
    iSendAs->SetSubjectL(_L("A New Todo-List Item"));
    iSendAs->SetBodyL(FormMessageLC(_L
        ("Here is the todo-list item")));
    iSendAs->SaveMessageL(ETrue);
        User::LeaveIfError(iSendAs->ValidateMessage());
}
CleanupStack::PopAndDestroy(3); // globalCharLayer,

globalParaLayer, messageBody
    } else {
        //handle the error
    }
}
```

There are several things to point out about this code:

- Notice that we are not actually including the vCalendar object as an attachment, but are including the *text representation* of the vCalendar object as the attachment. The first part of the code creates a file and dumps the vCalendar text from the todo-list item selected into that file.

- After we create an empty message in the message server outbox, we stop to check if the MTM in use can support attachments. We use the `QueryMessageCapability()` of the `CSendAs` object to test this.

- The attachment itself is created by (1) creating an empty attachment with the `CreateAttachmentL()` function, which returns a directory used to store the attachment, (2) appending the filename to this directory name, (3) copying the vCalendar text file to the file indicated by the newly created path name, and (4) telling the message server that the attachment is in the file just copied by using the `SetAttachmentL()` function.

- The rest of the message is created as we discussed earlier: we set the recipient to the previously copied string, we set the subject appropriately, and we set the body of the message to some rich text object (FormMessageLC() returns a rich text object that contains the text specified).

- Finally, saving the message puts it in the outbox, ready for sending.

When the SendItem() function is complete, an email message will exist in the outbox folder of the default email service. We can send this message by invoking the message application and using it to send the messages from the outbox, or do this programmatically by using the client-side MTM. The SendL() function below defines how to do this:

```
CMsvOperation* TodoXferEmail::SendL(
  TRequestStatus &aStatus)
{
  CMtmUiRegistry* iMtmUiRegistry;
  CBaseMtmUi* iBaseMtmUi;
  CBaseMtm* iClientMtm;
  CMsvSession* iSession;

  // extract MTM information from the SendAs object
  iClientMtm=&(iSendAs->ClientMtm());
  iSession=&(iClientMtm->Session());

  // Establish a connection with the registry
  iMtmUiRegistry=CMtmUiRegistry::NewL(*iSession,10000000);
  iBaseMtmUi=iMtmUiRegistry->NewMtmUiL(*iClientMtm);

  // Create CMsvEntrySelection with a single entry of the
  // message created ClientMtm has context set to last created
  // message, so we use that
  TMsvId entryID=iClientMtm->Entry().EntryId();
  CMsvEntrySelection* selection=new (ELeave)
    CMsvEntrySelection();
  selection->AppendL(entryID);

  // Set context to target service
  // The following reads "the id of the target service in the
  // index entry of the context of the client-side MTM"
  TMsvId serviceID=iClientMtm->Entry().Entry().iServiceId;
  iClientMtm->SwitchCurrentEntryL(serviceID);

  // And send the message by copying it to the service
  CMsvOperation* msvOperation=iBaseMtmUi->CopyToL(*selection,
    aStatus);

  return msvOperation;
}
```

The result of this function is a CMsvOperation object, which is an active object that governs the sending process. This active object uses the status variable sent as a parameter to the function for monitoring the progress. This function works by (1) using the client-side MTM to create a message selection, (2) changing the context to that of the client-side MTM, and (3) copying the message from where it is kept (in our case, the outbox) to the client-side MTM context. This causes the sending operation to initiate and attempt to send out the message selection.

Finally, "closing" the message means deleting the CSendAs object. The definition of Close() is below:

```
void TodoXferEmail::Close()
{
    delete iSendAs;
    iSendAs = NULL;
}
```

15.6   Receiving Messages

Applications can work with the messaging system and message arrival. While the message server itself handles the actual listening and transport functions, applications can register themselves to be notified upon message arrival.

Registration occurs when a connection with the message server is established. Recall from Section 15.3 that connecting with the message server requires a parameter that is an object of the MMsvSessionObserver class. As we said before, this is an abstract class that forces classes derived from it to implement a single function, shown below:

```
void HandleSessionEventL(TMsvSessionEvent aEvent,
    TAny* aArg1, TAny* aArg2, TAny* aArg3);
```

The message server will call this function from the class object passed during the server connection whenever a "message event" occurs. A code that signifies which event actually occurred is passed in the first parameter and up to three pointers to data areas that apply to the message event make up the rest of the function call's parameter list.

Session Event Types

The session events that are possible are defined by the TMsvSessionEvent enumeration. There are 21 different event types defined by this type, and they can be found in \Symbian\6.1\Quartz\Epoc32\Include\msvapi.h.

For example, suppose that an application wants to be notified when it receives SMS messages. We might create a message server session as follows:

```
iSession = CMsvSession::OpenSyncL(*this);
```

This means that the object that made this call must be subclassed from the MMsvSessionObserver class. Further, we must implement the HandleSessionEventL() function. An example of an implementation is below:

```
void TodoXferSMS::HandleSessionEventL(
   TMsvSessionEvent aEvent,
   TAny* aArg1, TAny* aArg2, TAny* aArg3)
{
    TInt i;

    switch(aEvent) {
       case EMsvEntriesCreated:
            // We are only interested in inbox messages.
            // For this event, aArg2 is the parent of
            // the created entries.
            if (*(static_Cast<TMsvId*>(aArg2)) !=
               KMsvGlobalInBoxIndexEntryId) return;

            // aArg1 will be the message selection set
            CMsvEntrySelection* entries =
                static_cast<CMsvEntrySelection*>(aArg1);
            for(i = 0; i < entries->Count(); i++) {
                DoSomething(entries->At(i));
            }
            break;

       default:
          //Ignore all other events.
          break;
   }
}
```

As we are only interested in new messages, we only pay attention to the EMsvEntriesCreated event. In addition, we are only interested in new inbox entries, so we check to make sure that the parent folder is the system inbox. When we are sure we have a new inbox entry, we get a list of entry IDs and call the DoSomething() function for each ID in the list.

For our example, this DoSomething() function must (1) validate that we have an SMS message, and then (2) load and process that message. We can define DoSomething() as follows:

```
void TodoXferSMS::DoSomething(const TMsvId &aEntryId)
{
    TInt length;
    HBufC* iMessageData;
    TPtr messageDataPtr;

    iSmsMtm->SwitchCurrentEntryL(aEntryId);

    // Validate the message as an SMS message
    TMsvPartList validationFlags(
                    KMsvMessagePartBody
                  | KMsvMessagePartDescription
                  | KMsvMessagePartOriginator );

    if (iSmsMtm->ValidateMessage(validationFlags) != 0)
      return;
    iSmsMtm->LoadMessageL();
    //Extract the message and notify the observer.
    length = iSmsMtm->Body().Read(0).Length() - 1;
    iMessageData = HBufC::NewL(length);
    messageDataPtr = iMessageData->Des();
    messageDataPtr.Copy(iSmsMtm->Body().Read(0));

    // ... now do something with the message data
}
```

After switching to the context of the message, we validate the message through the SMS MTM by checking the message body, the message's date, and the message's originator/sender. Then we load the message and extract the message body. Finally, we do whatever the application was supposed to do with the message text through the string pointer `messageDataPtr`.

15.7 More Details on Specific Message Types

15.7.1 Email Messages

Email messages are actually handled by three MTMs in Symbian OS. Incoming messages are retrieved by either the POP3 or the IMAP4 MTM; outgoing messages are handled via the SMTP MTM.

The POP3 MTM set is made up of a POP3 client-side MTM, a class that implements email retrieval, a class that holds POP3 settings, and a class that manipulates email entries in the message structure. The client-side MTM, `CPop3ClientMtm`, implements the functionality necessary to treat messages as if they were received using POP3 protocols. It is subclassed from both the `CBaseMtm` and `MEntryObserver` classes. Because of this, all message functions handle messages as if they are POP3 email messages. In addition, the `MEntryObserver` functionality allows this class to respond to operations on messages from the message server.

The POP3 MTM uses the `CImPop3GetMail` class to retrieve email from a remote host using POP3. It handles connection and disconnection and treats the remote inbox as if it was just another folder under the email service. The POP3 MTM also uses the `CImPop3Settings` class to hold the settings for the POP3 protocol exchange. Properties such as the IP address of the remote inbox server and login name/password for the POP3 protocol are specified with this class. Finally, the `TMsvEmailEntry` class is used by the POP3 MTM to characterize email messages. It is subclassed from the `TMsvEntry` class and tailored to specifically address email messages.

The IMAP4 MTM also consists of four components. Its client-side MTM is implemented by the `CImap4ClientMtm` class and has the same properties as the POP3 client-side MTM. It tailors the `CBaseMtm` functions to specifically address messages retrieved by IMAP4. It also inherits functions from the `MEntryObserver` class, so it can handle events that occur to IMAP4 messages. The MTM uses the functionality built into the `CImImap4GetMail` class to retrieve email using the IMAP4 protocol. The MTM also uses the `TMsvEmailEntry` class to manipulate specific email messages.

The SMTP MTM uses the `CSmtpClientMtm` class as its client-side MTM. This class implements the functionality to send email via SMTP; it handles connection scenarios, delivers messages, and manages the protocol. There is no implementation for the receipt of messages via SMTP. The SMTP MTM uses the `TSmtpProgress` class as a callback class to relay progress information. Progress information for SMTP operations includes the current connection state and the number of messages sent. Settings for SMTP messages and sessions are stored using the `CImSmtpSettings` class. Manipulation of SMTP messages—that is, email messages—is handled through the `TMsvEmailEntry` class as with the other protocols.

15.7.2   SMS Messages

SMS messages are handled by the SMS MTM, which is implemented by a client-side MTM, a settings class, and a progress call-back class.

The client-side MTM is implemented by the `CSMSMtmClient` class. This class provides specific support for SMS messages, including operations to access a device's service information and the scheduled sending of SMS messages. Progress information can be obtained via the `TSmsProgress` class for messaging operations. Progress information includes such things as the type of operation and the number of messages processed. Settings for SMS messages and delivery are kept and accessed via the `CSmsSettings` class.

SMS messages are typically handled when they arrive but are not explicitly retrieved as email messages are. (Recall the model for message delivery from Chapter 4: SMS messages are delivered via the "push" model.) SMS message receipt is typically done by system telephony and message servers, with received SMS messages placed in the inbox and any session observers notified as a result.

15.7.3 Fax Messages

Fax messages are handled by the fax MTM. This MTM is made up of a client-side MTM, which handles sending and receipt scheduling, along with a progress monitoring class and a settings class.

The fax client-side MTM is implemented by the `CFaxMtm-Client` class. This class implements specific operations for sending and receiving faxes and works with new or existing connections. Sending faxes means that outgoing messages are rendered into TIFF images and scheduled for delivery with the telephony server. Received faxes are kept in image format and placed in the message server inbox. While the `CFaxMtmClient` class is subclassed from `CBaseMtm` and `MEntryObserver` classes, some operations are not appropriate for fax message and are not implemented.

Fax message delivery progress is stored and accessed by the `TFaxSessionProgress` class. Information such as the current page being transmitted and the remote device's address are accessible. The MTM settings are accessed via the `TMTMFaxSettings` class.

15.7.4 BIO Messages

BIO messages are handled by Symbian OS using the familiar MTM structure. The BIO MTM is made up of a client-side MTM, a properties set class, and a progress class. In addition, a server-side MTM is an important component.

The client-side MTM is implemented by the `CBIOClientMtm` class. This class has an interface similar to what we have seen before with other client-side MTMs and provides specific support for BIO messages. Progress information can be obtained via the `TBioProgress` class for messaging operations.

The settings for BIO messages must be implemented in a special way. BIO messages are specifically *bearer independent,* that is, they assume no transport function. While BIO can travel over SMS, an infrared transport could just as easily be used. This means that some kind of structure for settings, transport information, and format must be built. In addition, the use of a BIO message is very open-ended. For example, some messages carry ringtones for phone handsets and some messages carry WAP files for a WAP browser. This structure must be accommodated by the BIO message system. This is complicated by the fact that some BIO settings for specific devices are typically proprietary.

Support for BIO messages and their properties is implemented through BIO Information Files (BIFs) and a BIO message database. BIFs hold BIO message properties and settings; they can be read or written using the `CBioInfoFileReader` and `CBioInfoFileWriter` classes. These files are constructed by the manufacturer of each Symbian device. Manipulation of the BIO database is done through the `CBIODatabase` class. Further analysis of these classes and BIFs are left to the reader.

15.8   Summary

In this chapter, we have discussed the Symbian OS messaging framework. Since messages vary widely in content but can be roughly categorized by form, this framework has been designed to be generic enough to handle all forms of messages but to allow specialization of message handling.

We reviewed the components of a message and outlined the structure of message type modules that implement each message type. Message type modules contain information about how to perform functions, such as editing, viewing and delivering a message for a specific message type. We then discussed the message server, the process that manages messaging stores and facilities, and detailed the ways that we interact with the message server to read and send email. We also discussed "send-as messaging", which is a convenient way to send messages through a simple interface, using functions common to all message types. We reviewed what it takes to communicate with the message server and receive a message. Finally, we reviewed some of the supplied definitions for preinstalled message types in Symbian OS version 6.1.

The next chapter details the HTML and WML content languages and their related delivery protocols.

16

Browsable Content Technologies

The World Wide Web had an inauspicious beginning. In the summer of 1991, Tim Berners-Lee of CERN released his "WWW Program" to the high-energy physics community, where it essentially flopped. He wrote up his work and submitted a paper describing the Web to a conference in 1991. The paper was promptly rejected. Initially written as a way to help his memory, the world of linked hypertext documents took off when Berners-Lee posted an article to the "alt.hypertext" newsgroups and some NeXT machine users got wind of what his idea could really do. Now, more than ten years later, the Web has seen some wild success and has spawned other "browsable" content technologies.

In this chapter, we will take a look at the support that Symbian OS gives to browsable content technologies, specifically HTTP and its small-display descendant WAP. Symbian OS treats HTTP as a member of the TCP/IP protocol family while building new infrastructure to handle elements of the WAP stack. Reviewing HTTP support reinforces our discussion of the TCP/IP stack; examining WAP support provides a good look at how a new technology fits into the Symbian communication architecture.

We will begin this chapter by looking at the support for HTTP in Symbian OS. We will then focus the rest of the chapter on WAP and the support for its suite of protocols in Symbian OS communication architecture. Support for WAP is implemented layer-by-layer, and we will examine each layer.

16.1 HTTP and HTML

To Symbian OS, HTTP is an application protocol supported by the TCP/IP transport infrastructure. There is no special handling of the protocol; there is no special class that encapsulates its functionality.

As a TCP-level protocol, HTTP requires connected sessions between the client and the server, and an implementation of an HTTP client assumes error-free, reliable transmission of data. Recall from Chapter 5 that HTTP is a text-based, stateless protocol that ties a simple client request format with a response from a Web page server in the form of a document typically written in HTML and packaged as a set of MIME objects.

The HTTP stack is shown in Figure 16.1. Symbian OS supports the layers of this stack, although not specifically for HTTP. The layers of the HTTP stack have support in various protocol modules; the tcpip.prt module supports the implementation of TCP/IP. There are no specific classes for TCP or IP data packets, because these are handled in the protocol module.

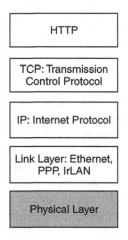

Figure 16.1 Protocol layers that support HTTP.

Transport of HTTP is done via sockets and is handled by the applications that implement the protocol. We demonstrated this type of transport in Chapter 12 with the Web page example.

Web pages are documents which are specified ("marked up") using HTML, a markup language based on SGML. It consists of a generic description of formatting by surrounding text with "tags" that describe the formatting that is needed. The display of HTML documents is done by a browser application that parses the HTML from a file and renders a set of formatted text in a document viewer. Since viewing HTML is an application-based activity, Symbian OS assumes applications will do this and has no built-in support for HTML viewing.

In summary, the transport of Web-based content is an application-based task that is supported by Symbian OS via existing TCP/IP implementations. The viewing of content is the responsibility of an application, and there is no supporting structure for HTML rendering.

> ## The Web Engine
>
> If you do a bit of poking around in the \Symbian\6.1\Quartz\ Epoc32\Include files, you will notice references to a Web engine. There are classes devoted to such an engine's implementation and a plug-in infrastructure that is built and supported by header files.
>
> These classes are supplied to support the Web browser that is supplied with Symbian OS version 6.1. It has a plug-in design that takes DLL modules to view documents of special content.
>
> Unfortunately, Symbian OS does not currently provide support for HTML viewers that can be embedded in applications and GUI objects

16.2 WAP

While HTTP is supported as a TCP/IP application protocol, the WAP suite of protocols poses a different problem for Symbian OS. As we discussed in Chapters 4 and 5 (see Figure 4.5 for the WAP stack details), WAP content is supported by a completely different protocol stack. Therefore, an entirely new protocol stack implementation had to be constructed from the bottom up.

16.2.1 Bearers

For WAP suite protocols, bearers constitute the very bottom of the stack, transporting data for the upper layers to use. The bearer layer in the WAP stack is analogous to a combination of the data link layer and the physical communication layer in a generic ISO stack model (see Figure 2.1). Bearers make up the transport infrastructure that gets WAP data packets to the WDP layer for processing. Examples of a bearer is a TCP/IP network; others are SMS messages, and CDMA/CDPD cellular transport.

Symbian OS supports two bearers: TCP/IP and SMS. Symbian OS supports both 7-bit and 8-bit SMS and, within these forms, the OS supports browsing messages and non-browsing messages. Figure 16.2 shows the relationships between the supported data forms. Browsing WAP content is an exercise that typically requires

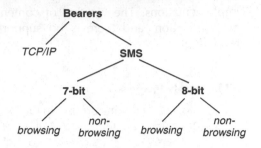

Figure 16.2 WAP bearer types.

quick access to links and rapid-fire downloads. Browsing WAP/SMS types of delivery messages have fewer requirements so as not to slow down the Symbian device with logging and other reporting activities.

It is important to realize here that browsing WAP content is different than browsing HTTP content. HTTP uses a "pull" model, i.e., the client opens a socket to the server, requests information, and the data flows back through the same socket. In a sense, the client reaches through a socket and pulls the information from the server. WAP content is handled differently; browsing WAP content over SMS uses both a "pull" and a "push" model. Although an initial request is sent from the browsing client, it is typical that WAP data will arrive via messages sent from the server to the client. The bearer will determine which type of content delivery is possible. Using a TCP/IP network, for instance, an application could enable a connected "pull" of WAP data; an SMS delivery system would dictate that a connectionless "push" should be used.

16.2.2   WAP Stack Support

Based on experience with transport protocols in Symbian OS, one would guess that support for the WAP stack would take the form of a new socket implementation. All of the other transport functions have been via sockets. However, support for the WAP stack is *modeled after* the socket implementation but is implemented by its own series of classes (analogous to socket types), because it needs to employ both pulling and pushing of data.

Figure 16.3 depicts the WAP stack with the classes that implement various portions of it.

The WAP session server

A WAP session is considered a resource that needs protection and management. So, in standard fashion, Symbian OS uses a server to

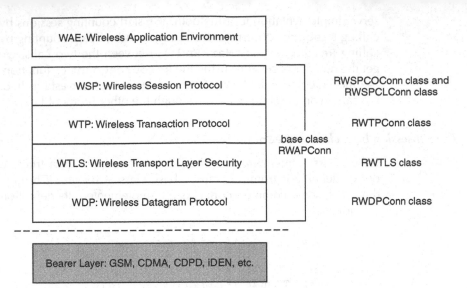

WAE: Wireless Application Environment	
WSP: Wireless Session Protocol	RWSPCOConn class and RWSPCLConn class
WTP: Wireless Transaction Protocol	RWTPConn class
WTLS: Wireless Transport Layer Security	RWTLS class
WDP: Wireless Datagram Protocol	RWDPConn class

base class RWAPConn

Bearer Layer: GSM, CDMA, CDPD, iDEN, etc.

Figure 16.3   Classes implementing the WAP stack.

manage the WAP resource. This server is analogous to the socket server; an application must first connect to the WAP session server before creating and opening a session across another protocol layer. To avoid confusion with the remote WAP server from which an application might retrieve WAP content, I will refer to this server as the *WAP session server*.

The RWAPServ class encapsulates the implementation of the WAP session server. The class definition is below:

```
class RWAPServ : public RSessionBase
{
  public:
    IMPORT_C RWAPServ();
    IMPORT_C TInt Connect(TInt aDefaultMessageSlots =
      KDefaultMessageSlots);
    IMPORT_C void ResourceCountMarkStart();
    IMPORT_C void ResourceCountMarkEnd();
    IMPORT_C TInt ResourceCount();
    IMPORT_C TVersion Version() const;
    IMPORT_C void Close();
};
```

The main functions here are Connect() and Close(); these open and terminate a WAP server session. The Version() function will return the current version of the WAP stack implementation. The remaining functions allow us to derive a count of connections to the WAP server; recall that we saw something similar in the SDP server implementation for Bluetooth. We start counting sessions by calling `ResourceCountMarkStart()`, and we stop counting by calling `ResourceCountMarkEnd()`. Between the two calls, we get the number of sessions using the `ResourceCount()` function.

Once a session with the WAP session server has been established, we can go on to set up sessions through the other protocol layers.

The subsession base class: `RWAPConn`

Other class implementations in the WAP support infrastructure derive definitions from a common base class: `RWPConn`. Through this class, some common concepts are implemented. Its definition is below:

```
class RWAPConn : public RSubSessionBase
{
  public:
    typedef TUint16 TPort;

    IMPORT_C virtual TInt Close();
    IMPORT_C class RWTLS Wtls();

    IMPORT_C void GetRemoteAddress(TDes8 &aAddress, TPort
&aPort) const;
    IMPORT_C void GetBearer(TBearer &aBearer) const;
    IMPORT_C TInt GetLocalPort(TPort &aPort) const;
    IMPORT_C void CancelAll();

  protected:
    TInt Open(RWAPServ &aServer,
              const TDesC8 &aRemoteHost,
              TPort aRemotePort,
              TPort aLocalPort,
              TBearer aBearer,
              TBool aSecureConn,
              TInt aFunction);
};
```

This class defines the basics for manipulating protocol sessions. We have `Open()` and `Close()` functions to start and terminate protocol sessions. We use `GetRemoteAddress()` and `GetLocalPort()` functions to derive the address and port of the remote partner and local port where the connection is made. There is a `CancelAll()` function that terminates and deletes any pending operations across a protocol session.

To open a WAP protocol session at any level, Symbian OS requires several pieces of information. These are all included in the `Open()` function definition. Note that subclasses of `RWAPConn` will overload this class definition for their own use. However, this definition contains all the information an Open() call needs:

- the WAP session server to use to open the port
- the address and port number of the remote service to which the protocol session is connecting
- the bearer the system is to use to make the connection
- whether or not this is to be a secure connection

If the connection is to be secure, the WTLS layer is created; a handle to this layer can be retrieved by the Wtls() function call.

From this base class definition, one can appreciate how closely the socket model has been followed. Protocol sessions are opened and closed like sockets, there are concepts of remote addresses and ports to connect to, we have the notion of canceling (draining) I/O operations before we close up. There are some differences here, namely, the idea of bearers and the optional use of a security layer in the protocol stack.

Implementing the WDP layer

The WDP layer lies just above the bearer layer and provides a general datagram transport service needed by upper layers in the stack. Its implementation is via the RWDPConn class. The definition is below:

```
class RWDPConn : public RWAPConn
  {
  public:
    IMPORT_C TInt Open(RWAPServ &aServer,
      const TDesC8 &aRemoteHost,
      TPort aRemotePort,
      TPort aLocalPort,
      TBearer aBearer, // an enum
      TBool aSecureConn);
    IMPORT_C TInt Open(RWAPServ &aServer,
      TPort aLocalPort);

    IMPORT_C void Recv(TDes8 &aRemoteAddress,
      TPckg<TPort> &aRemotePort,
      TDes8 &aBuffer,
      TRequestStatus &aStatus);
    IMPORT_C void CancelRecv();
    IMPORT_C TInt Send(const TDesC8 &aBuffer);
    IMPORT_C TInt SendTo(const TDesC8 &aRemoteAddress,
      TPort aRemotePort,
      const TDesC8 &aBuffer,
      TBearer aBearer);
```

```
IMPORT_C void RecvSize(
    TPckg<TUint16> &aDataSize,
    TRequestStatus &aStatus);
};
```

First notice that there are two versions of the Open() function: fully and not fully specified. The fully specified Open() can be used with the Send() function; because the information was supplied with the Open() function, the Send() function does not need destination information. The minimal Open() function is paired with the SendTo() function, which needs more information about the datagram destination. Note that the SendTo() function can be used for multiple destinations, whereas the Send() function sends data to only one destination.

To receive a datagram, we need to use the second version of the Open() function. The Recv() function will accept data but must specify from where the data is coming. The RecvSize() function waits for data of a specific length and immediately returns without performing I/O, allowing that data to be picked up by the Recv() function.

Finally, note that the sending functions are synchronous, and the receiving functions are asynchronous. The Recv() function is paired with a CancelRecv() as a receive operation cancellation function.

The RWDPConn class is used when sending WAP datagrams. This is not typically done; most WAP content is sent using WSP sessions.

Implementing the WSP layer

The WSP layer is implemented via two different classes. Like sockets at the TCP layers, WSP sessions can be connectionless or connected. A connectionless WSP session is suitable for the delivery of content requests and for the receipt of a single response. A connected WSP session is suitable for request and delivery over an error-free, reliable connection. These session types are analogous to connectionless and connected sockets. The biggest difference is that both WSP connection types must be made to accommodate both the push and pull models of data delivery.

Connectionless WSP sessions A connectionless WSP session is implemented by the RWSPCLConn class. I will break this class definition up a bit as we describe the class.

The Open() function is used to open a connectionless WSP session:

```
IMPORT_C TInt Open(RWAPServ &aServer,
      const TDesC8 &aRemoteHost,
      TPort aRemotePort,
      TPort aLocalPort,
      TBearer aBearer,
      TBool aSecureConn);
IMPORT_C TInt Open(RWAPServ &aServer, TPort aLocalPort);
```

As with the RWDPConn class, there are two versions of Open().
The first fully specifies both endpoints of the connection; the second
specifies only the local endpoint.

To use the pull approach to collecting content, we use the
UnitInvoke() and UnitWaitResults() functions below:

```
IMPORT_C TInt UnitInvoke(TFunction aFunction,
      const TDesC &aURI,
      const TDesC8 &aBody,
      const TDesC8 &aHeaders,
      TTransID aID);
IMPORT_C void UnitWaitResult(TDes8 &aBody,
      TDes8 &aHeaders,
      TTransID &aID,
      TWSPStatus &aWSPStatus,
      TRequestStatus &aRequestStatus);
   IMPORT_C void CancelUnitWaitResult();

   IMPORT_C TInt UnitWaitResult(TDes8 &aBody,
      TDes8 &aHeaders,
      TTransID &aID,
      TWSPStatus &aWSPStatus);
```

These functions come in synchronous and asynchronous versions,
with the asynchronous version accompanied by the appropriate
cancellation function. The UnitInvoke() function works like a
GET command for HTTP, i.e., it opens a connection to a remote WAP
server and sends both WAP headers and an optional content body.
In the above definition, the aURI parameter specifies the destination
(as an URI), and the body and WAP headers are sent as strings. The
return of the function will fill in the aID variable. The response
from this initial request is received using the UnitWaitResult()
function. This function returns the body and WAP headers from
the remote server's response. The aID value must match the initial
request's ID, and the status of the response is filled in when the data
is valid.

To wait for data to be pushed to a device, an application should
use a UnitWaitPush() function:

```
IMPORT_C void UnitWaitPush(TDes8 &aBody,
      TDes8 &aHeaders,
```

```
        TPushID &aID,
        TRequestStatus &aStatus);
IMPORT_C void CancelUnitWaitPush();
IMPORT_C TInt UnitWaitPush(TDes8 &aBody,
        TDes8 &aHeaders,
        TPushID &aID);
```

Again, this comes in two versions—synchronous and asynchronous—and a cancellation function is provided for the asynchronous version. When called, these functions wait for data to be pushed to the device. Upon their return, the body and WAP headers are filled in, along with an ID to identify the data.

There's More!

The definitions to the data classes we have just described are in the `\Symbian\6.1\Quartz\Epoc32\include` directory. Look up the definitions to classes like `TTransID`, `TWSPStatus`, and `TPushID` just to understand how the data is represented. These are found in the file `wapcli.h`. In addition to these, pay attention to the `TReturnCodes` enumerations as well as the multiple definitions that are defined inside this class

Connected WSP sessions A connected WSP session is implemented by the `RWSPCOConn` class. As before, opening a session is done with the `Open()` function:

```
IMPORT_C TInt Open(RWAPServ &aServer,
        const TDesC8 &aRemoteHost,
        TPort aRemotePort,
        TPort aLocalPort,
        TBearer aBearer,
        TBool aSecureConn);
```

There is only one version of `Open()`—the fully specified version. Like connected sockets, connected WTP sessions maintain a reliable connection over multiple data exchanges. So a specific target endpoint is required in the call.

Once created with `Open()`, a WTP session is connected to and disconnected from its endpoint using the following functions:

```
IMPORT_C TInt Connect(const TDesC8 &aClientHeaders,
                      class CCapCodec* aCap = 0);
IMPORT_C TInt Disconnect();
```

The `Connect()` function includes headers that are sent to the remote WAP server to set up the connected session and an optional set of "capabilities" through a codec. A codec is a software module that compresses data for transport and decompresses the data upon receipt (the name "codec" corresponds to "compressor/decompressor"). This CCapCodec structure includes properties that characterize the connection session, including the size of data packets, size of buffers for sending and receiving, protocol options, and the like.

The data exchange for a connected session is initiated by the following function:

```
IMPORT_C TInt CreateTransaction(TFunction aFunction,
    const TDesC &aURI,
    const TDesC8 &aHeaders,
    const TDesC8 &aBody,
    RWSPCOTrans &aTrans);
```

The parameters for this call are similar to those used with Unit-Invoke() functions for connectionless sessions, but there is some additional data: a description of the type of request that is being made must be provided in the aFunction variable), and an RWSP-COTrans object is returned. This latter object allows much more control over a connected session than a mere ID would.

Rather than the simple send/receive sequence that comprises a connectionless session, a connected session is characterized by a series of *events*, milestones in the exchange of data between both sides. These events drive a connected session. The GetEvent() function obtains the next event for processing:

```
IMPORT_C TInt GetEvent(TEvent &aEvent,
    RWSPCOTrans &aTrans) const;
IMPORT_C void GetEvent(TEvent &aEvent,
    RWSPCOTrans &aTrans,
    TRequestStatus &aStatus) const;
IMPORT_C void CancelGetEvent();
```

As usual, this type of function comes in synchronous and asynchronous versions, with the appropriate cancellation function. Sometimes several events are pending; if this is the case, the number of events can be obtained through the following function:

```
IMPORT_C TInt GetNrOfEvents(TUint &aNrOfEvents) const;
```

Once an event has arrived that has data attached to it, that data can be retrieved through the following function:

```
IMPORT_C TInt GetSessionData(TDes8 &aData,
    TSessionDataType aType) const;
```

This data is returned in a generic buffer, and the type of the data is available as well.

Given the above functions, the usual sequence for processing a connected session is as follows:

- Open a session to a specific endpoint.
- Connect the session through to the endpoint, setting the properties as necessary.
- Initiate a transaction with WAP headers and message content.
- Process events as they occur, exchanging data where necessary. This is much like processing connection states in an active object and may involve sending more data to the remote server.
- Close the session when the exchange is complete.

Several other operations are possible on connected sessions. These include suspending and resuming sessions, switching session bearers, and obtaining information about session progress.

There's More Here

There are many definitions for connected WSP sessions that we did not elaborate on. Look up the definition to the RWSPCOTrans class. Also, the TEvent class and the TBearer class, while applicable to more than RSPCOConn objects, make a lot of sense in this context. I recommend that you review them here.

Other WAP layers

Between the WDP and WSP layers, two other layers exist as support infrastructure. As applications using WAP content rarely manipulate these layers, I will not elaborate on them. However, for completeness, they should be mentioned.

The WTP layer is implemented by the RWTPConn class. This layer ensures the reliability necessary to support the WSP layer. Because of this, the definition of the class includes functions to initiate and acknowledge data packets that comprise upper layer sessions and functions to discover errors and gracefully recover from them. In addition, this layer has the only Read() and Write() in the stack implementation, indicating that it is in charge of the basic I/O operations for sessions.

The WTLS layer, sitting between the datagram delivery layers and the transaction layer, implements secure data encryption and provides an interface for managing secure connections. This layer is implemented by the RWTLS class. To maintain secure connections, this layer implements functions that engage in negotiation with the remote side to provide authentication and to exchange encryption keys and algorithm specifications. It uses certificates (implemented by the RCertificate class) to verify the identity and keys of remote servers. It then encrypts each transaction that goes through the WAP session server. Note that the WAP session server has a RWTLS class that it uses in its operation. This can be null if no security is desired.

Certificates

Certificates are used by the WAP security layer as a way to identify remote servers and to obtain their encryption keys. A certificate is a digital document that "vouches for" the computer system. It guarantees that the server is what it says it is and ensures that it is not an imposter trying to spoof its way in to hack at security. Certificates are typically issued by servers run by third parties that are assumed to be truthful and secure themselves. Certificates are issued by these third parties and maintained by each individual device or server. Certificates can be verified by contacting the issuer.

The class that implements certificate information is the RCertificate class. You can find this definition in the file \Symbian\6.1\Quartz\Epoc32\include\wapcli.h.

16.2.3 Viewing WAP Content

Once the WAP content has been obtained, it must still be displayed. Like HTML, Symbian OS provides no architectural support for WML content viewing. Version 6.1 comes with a WAP viewer, and there is WAP engine support, but there is no support for an embedded viewing of WML contents. An application is responsible for displaying the WAP contents and abiding by WAP properties.

16.3 Summary

This chapter has overviewed the support Symbian OS gives to browsable content technologies, specifically HTTP/HTML and WAP. HTTP is considered an application protocol that is supported by TCP/IP; as such, it is not supported in a specific way by Symbian OS. WAP, however, is a new technology with its own protocol implementations, and Symbian OS includes a complete implementation of the WAP stack. In both content situations, viewing the content is left to the application to implement; no support, such as embeddable viewers, is implemented in Symbian OS.

This chapter concludes the programming section of this book. In this past section, we have looked at how to communicate using Symbian devices over IrDA, through sockets, over Bluetooth and TCP/IP, through telephony and messaging technologies. We have also seen how Symbian OS supports Web (via HTTP and HTML) and WAP (through the WAP stack and WML) technologies. That's a wide range of possibilities for communication!

We have three more chapters to go, contained in the "Miscellaneous Topics" section. We will begin in the next chapter by examining the needs and support for device and PC synchronization.

Section 3

Miscellaneous Topics

17

Synchronization: PLP and SyncML

In Webster's dictionary, one of the definitions given for the word *synchronize* is "to ... arrange (events) to indicate coincidence or coexistence". This definition is very appropriate for the material in this chapter. The synchronization of devices is the process that arranges data objects to "indicate their coincidence" on both devices. Implementation of device synchronization is a black box to most people. We know the precondition for synchronization (i.e., that files and information might not be coincident) and the postcondition for synchronization (i.e., that files and information are indeed coincident). What happens between those two conditions has been somewhat of a mystery.

This chapter attempts to unravel this mystery to some extent. We will look at synchronization in general, and then concentrate on how the Symbian OS does synchronization. We will look at Psion Link Protocol (PLP) as the protocol currently used for synchronization, and we will examine a new method of synchronizing devices in SyncML. PLP represents Symbian's entry in the collection of proprietary protocols that are used for this task; SyncML represents the first attempt to standardize protocols for synchronization across devices and operating system manufacturers.

We will overview synchronization mechanics first. Once we understand the issues, we will look at some of the attempts in the industry and by Symbian to implement synchronization. We will then finish the chapter by focusing on PLP and SyncML.

17.1 Synchronization Mechanics

17.1.1 The Basics

The basic process of synchronization is easy to understand. Let's itemize this process:

- *Configuration phase:* Before we synchronize devices, we need to define *what gets synchronized*. Referring to our Webster's definition, we need to know *what data* have to be arranged and coincident between the devices. A typical collection of information that is synchronized might be one that consists of calendar information, to-do list items, email and other messages, and contact information.
- *Synchronization phase:* This phase is the one that is repeated constantly to make sure devices are in sync. Two devices are connected somehow, and applications are started on each one to facilitate the trading of data according to the configuration settings. Once the data objects have been arranged so that they are coincident, the two devices can be disconnected.

There are some aspects of synchronization that make it a unique process, distinguished from other data exchange processes (e.g., simple file transfer). First, synchronization is typically *automatic*, using the preset configuration to drive the exchange of data. Whenever the process is started, the same preconfigured series of steps is executed. Second, it often involves data format conversion. For example, to synchronize Agenda data on a Symbian OS device with a calendar application on a desktop computer, the Agenda data must be converted to a file of known format, say, Microsoft Outlook's format for calendar entries. That file must then be transferred to the desktop computer and converted into the format of the calendar application. Only then can each calendar entry be examined to see if it needs to be added to the calendar data set. Finally, in a synchronization exchange between two devices, both devices act as server and client. Requests for data are made by both sides, and both sides service data requests and send information back to the requestor.

17.1.2 Data Objects, Files, and Timestamps

Data objects are the items that are being transferred between the devices to be made coincident. It cannot be assumed that these items exist in a form that can be compared at any time. As stated above, file conversion may have to take place before information can be synchronized.

Note that *information* is synchronized, but *files* are the way that information is exchanged. The issue here is *granularity*, which is what the level of detail of synchronization is called. While files are exchanged (relatively coarse synchronization granularity), it is the individual entries within the files with which we are concerned (fine granularity).

One of the ways either side knows to synchronize information is by its *timestamp*. Differing timestamps in files are telltale signs that those files need to be synchronized. This is not, however, a simple copying of one file to replace another. Entries in each file are typically compared, and the information the files represent is merged together. That merged information is then sent to both devices as files to be installed as the new, synchronized information.

17.1.3 Communication Media

Any form of communication media that can be used to transfer data can be used to synchronize devices. As long as the medium enables bi-directional exchange, it is a usable medium.

The choice of synchronization media has a history. Early attempts at synchronization used serial cabled communication as a medium. This usage was expanded to include serial IR communication because the IR medium still worked as a serial medium. As communication, between devices was standardized, synchronization processes were also modularized to run over any communication medium that the two devices involved mutually supported. For example, many devices synchronize over USB connections using the same synchronization protocol implementations as they would for serial or network connections.

For most of their history, Symbian OS devices have used serial media. Most still do. As we will see, with the support developed for SyncML, the possibilities for synchronization media have expanded greatly.

17.1.4 Protocol Requirements

Many exchange protocols have been developed over the history of synchronizing devices. As these protocols have been designed, there has been a set of requirements developed that they try to satisfy.

The protocol must implement remote file handling. A synchronization client will need to browse the filesystem of the server. It may want to open files *on the server* and make the server read the contents, bringing data back to the client.

Implementations usually need to go beyond the mere copying of files. Extended functionality can include remote command execution and software package installation. It typically includes conditional copying or installation, based on timestamp comparison of source and destination objects.

The protocol must implement reliability and robust error recovery. This means that the protocol will likely be specified in layers, like most of the protocols we have seen. These layers implement a modular design, with each focusing on a different aspect of file transfer, new functionality, or robustness.

Finally, the protocol will need multiple implementations. One will usually exist in the basic protocols supported by the local operating system. Another implementation is needed for the synchronization destination, e.g., a desktop computer. Sometimes multiple implementations are required for multiple desktop operating systems. If a software development version is needed for testing purposes, another implementation is usually included in the SDK.

17.2   Some Early Attempts at Synchronization

There have been many synchronization protocols. Each has its own niche and application.

File transfer protocols can probably be considered to be the first attempts at synchronization systems. While early protocols like XMODEM were simply designed to move files, applications developed around other protocols implement rudimentary synchronization. For example, some applications that implement the File Transfer Protocol (FTP) for the TCP/IP suite have facilities for checking timestamps and conditionally transferring files based on time or previously existing files. Backup systems were early attempts at synchronization; while the file transfer was one-way, backups made a crude synchronization system work.

Early in its work with handheld devices, Psion saw the need for some kind of synchronization protocol. Early computers (for example, the Organiser II, which was made in 1984) used the popular implementations for exchange protocols (e.g., XMODEM and YMODEM) at 9600 baud. This software was for file transfer only. On the Series 3, a new protocol debuted—an early version of PLP—and, through various machines, matured into the PLP protocol we have today. Symbian adopted this protocol from Psion.

The software used to drive synchronization has undergone much change. In the early days desktop computers had implementations of XMODEM or YMODEM built into terminal emulation programs. When Psion included PLP in the Series 3, it provided some early synchronization applications. RCOM was the first software to implement synchronization; this application was a command line interpreter that could take commands from a file (and thus allowed scripting of file synchronization). This evolved into an application with a GUI called PsiWin. Psion then implemented the software driver side into a developer's kit and called it EPOC Connect. Psi-Win became the version of EPOC Connect "badged" by Psion. Symbian took over the development of this software and renamed it Symbian Connect.

17.3 PLP and Symbian Connect

The current state of the art in synchronization on Symbian OS devices is the combination of PLP and the Symbian Connect software. In this section, we will overview the implementation and support that the Symbian OS gives to this pair.

17.3.1 The Psion Link Protocol

We gave a brief overview of PLP in Chapter 4; see Figure 4.3. PLP is specifically designed to use either the serial or the IR port. Its serial configuration uses hardware handshaking and a frame format of 8 bits, with 1 stop bit and no parity.

On top of the physical layer, PLP has a three-layer design. The link layer implements reliable transport of data, implementing error recovery via the retransmission of data frames. The Network Control Protocol (NCP) layer implements data stream multiplexing over this link layer. The NCP layer also implements flow control over each service's data stream. The Services layer implements the various services used by the remote device: software management, file manipulation and synchronization of files.

PLP allows the remote device to manipulate files on the local device and manage software installation. The Services layer implements the functionality needed to perform synchronization tasks. There are several servers that run at this layer to field and answer requests from clients.

- The *Link* server is started first and is used to communicate with the NCP layer. It starts the other servers as needed.

- The *Remote Protocol Command Service (RPCS)* server answers commands sent from the remote device. It supports general operations, such as launching and terminating processes. On some early devices, the RPCS server was not present by default; it was added by synchronization software upon usage.

- The *Remote File Services (RFSV)* server provides a remote interface that behaves similarly to local file accesses; files must be opened before they can be read or written, and a sequential file pointer is maintained for each open file. A current directory is also maintained, allowing use of relative file names.

- The *Generic Custom Service (GENCSERV)* server is used by some designers to implement specialized services. For example, Ericsson implements a GENCSERV server that provides access to a device's contacts database. This is currently used on the Ericsson R380 phone, the first "one-box" phone.

It is the purpose of the NCP layer to multiplex data streams to and from each of these servers. Incoming data streams are first directed to the Link server, which makes sure the correct server is registered and running. Services layer packets include the name of the server they need to access; names for the servers differ slightly depending on the version of the OS and the model of the device.

17.3.2   Using PLP with Symbian Connect

A Symbian OS device will synchronize with a synchronization server; this server is typically a desktop computer running Microsoft Windows. The desktop computer must run software that can use the link protocol and drive the synchronization process; Symbian provides Symbian Connect for this purpose.

Through Symbian Connect, a software structure like that in Figure 17.1 is built. On the right side, data flows from the Symbian device—through its own PLP connection engine—to a server on the remote computer. This server sets up a connection and passes data to the connection engine, which is used by a desktop application

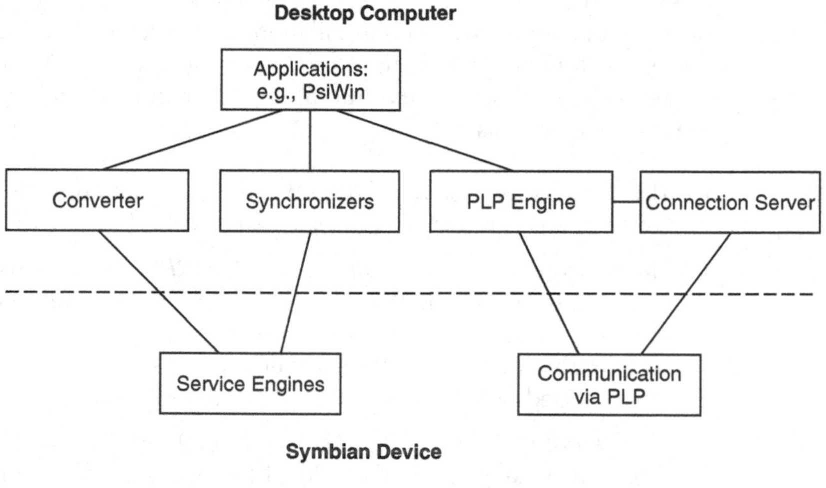

Figure 17.1   Symbian Connect synchronization structure.

to move data back and forth. When data moves between the two computers, synchronization services (using timestamps, file transfer, etc) and conversion services (converting files between computer application formats) are used.

This process requires that PLP clients and servers exist on both sides. On the Symbian OS device side, these functions are typically built into an application, typically called a "desktop link". On the desktop computer side, this is implemented by Symbian Connect.

The Symbian Connectivity Software Development Kit

To write applications that run on a desktop computer and use PLP to control a Symbian OS device, you need the Symbian Connectivity SDK. This is a collection of software, libraries, and source code examples that support the creation of software that can service and manipulate PLP. You can pick this up from Symbian's developer Web site.

Note that this SDK is only for computers that run Microsoft Windows

---

17.4 SyncML

17.4.1 Proprietary is Problematic

Although PLP works well as a synchronization protocol, and is available for developers to use, it is a proprietary protocol. Its design is guarded information by Symbian, and official implementations exist only for Symbian OS devices and Symbian-OS-device-to-PC software. (Unofficial implementations are available for other operating systems; for example, Linux has an open source PLP implementation not sponsored by Symbian.)

Proprietary systems can restrict users. Indeed, while synchronization works well with Symbian Connect, Symbian OS devices are also restricted by Symbian Connect. For example, the only medium that is implemented for synchronization is serial communication; network synchronization would be a great benefit, as would synchronization with devices running other handheld operating systems. Along with Symbian, other manufacturers of other handheld devices also face this dilemma: each handheld operating system uses proprietary protocols for synchronization and is limited by the implementation of protocols by its manufacturer.

SyncML is an attempt to solve this problem. SyncML is the result of an initiative supported by a consortium of handheld device hardware and software companies. This consortium sought to create a single, common synchronization protocol and format specification that all its members would support. Several hundred companies support this initiative, with Symbian as one of the charter sponsors of the initiative.

SyncML support is expected to be implemented by large numbers of the consortium members in their products in 2002.

17.4.2 SyncML Characteristics

The benefits of using a single synchronization platform for different devices are many. Using a single implementation of desktop computer software (which can be developed by third parties), devices from many vendors can synchronize their data.

SyncML's design is broad enough that devices are now limited by their own capabilities—not that of the synchronization protocol. A wide variety of media can be used: serial, Bluetooth, and Ethernet networks. New and interesting services can be implemented—imagine a "synchronization service provider" that can be used over the Internet.

The designers of SyncML had to grapple with several criteria:

- *The system must support current, popular data formats*. These include the standard vCard and vCalendar data formats that we have seen in this book, as well as collaborative formats such as email.

- *The system must support binary data formats*. Synchronization can include the exchange of executable code or databases—that is, data objects that do not have a neat textual representation.

- *The system must be extensible*. As new data formats are designed, the SyncML system must extend to accommodate these as well.

- *The system should build on existing transport technologies*. Current transport methods include serial communication and networking, as well as transport protocols like HTTP, SMTP, and WSP that ride on top of these other methods. The system should embrace all of these technologies.

The consensus in designing SyncML was that the system should not mandate data formats. It should be centered on format *description* rather than specific format *implementation*. The consensus was also that the data transport should work in layers that are as high as possible in a protocol stack—i.e., transport should not be restricted, but applications should embrace as many transport methods as possible.

To implement these criteria, SyncML is based on Extended Markup Language (XML). XML is a data description language that can be used to describe any kind of structured data stream and how application software (such as browsers) are to deal with it. It has been suggested that XML will replace HTML as the language for describing Web pages. This would be possible, because HTML is one of the basic structured streams that XML specifies and recognizes. Other examples might be database records, scientific data to be visualized in a browser, and (of course) synchronization data such as vCalendar and vCard format entries. Naturally, future data formats, which do not exist today, can be specified with XML as well.

Consider an example. Assume that we want to transfer a contact to a synchronization server. As part of a larger SyncML data stream, we might represent the contact data as a vCard and transfer that vCard as the SyncML format in Figure 17.2. Let's make a few observations about this example:

```
<Add>
    <CmdID>12345</CmdID>
    <Cred>
        <Meta>
            <Type xmlns="syncml:metinf">syncml:auth-md5</Type>
            <Format xmlns="syncml:metinf">b64</Format>
        </Meta>
        <Data>MJJkNDI2x7ZjNjgwMTNiYWZk455yN2JjMjNlZDM4YzENCg==</Data>
    </Cred>
    <Meta>
        <Format xmlns="syncml:metinf">chr</Format>
        <Type xmlns="syncml:metinf">text/x-vcard</Type>
    </Meta>
    <Item>
        <Source>
            <LocURI>./card</LocURI>
        </Source>
        <Data>BEGIN:VCARD
         VERSION:2.1
         FN:Mike Jipping
         N:Jipping;Mike
         TEL;WORK;VOICE:+1-616-555-1234
         TEL;WORK;FAX:+1-616-555-4321
         EMAIL;INTERNET:mike@jipping.com
         END:VCARD
        </Data>
    </Item>
</Add>
```

Figure 17.2 Example SyncML vCard representation.

- Note that the format is full of bracketed tags, like HTML and its parent SGML. As in HTML, tags are used to delineate sections of the specification. In the example, we have four main sections: `CmdID`, `Cred`, `Meta`, and `Item`.

- The `CmdID` gives the code of the function being used in the current operation (e.g., `Add`).
- The `Cred` section gives the authentication information. In this example, the credentials are given using an MD5 hash algorithm for encryption and base 64 encoding.
- The `Meta` section gives details about the data structuring. In this example, we are using character format (`chr`) with a type encoding of a vCard (`text/x-vcard`).
- The `Item` section gives the actual vCard specification. In this example, we have specified the source of the vCard (the `<Source>` tag) and then given the vCard data (the `<Data>` tag).

In addition to a data description language, SyncML specifies a common, universal data transfer protocol. The SyncML standard specifies that many protocols can transfer SyncML data. However, it also specifies a specific synchronization protocol that can tunnel through existing protocols. Supporters are also free to use their own proprietary protocols to support the data transfer if they wish.

Figure 17.3 holds a diagram of the protocol stack for SyncML. Synchronization applications communicate with each other through SyncML, via its data formatting and its universal data transfer protocol. The SyncML data format is then transmitted over some

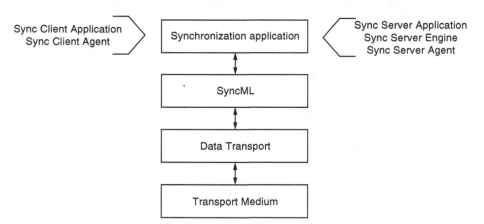

Figure 17.3   SyncML protocol stack.

transport protocol and medium to the remote device, which passes the received data through SyncML and incorporates the result.

Note that protocols may—in fact, most certainly will—encapsulate the SyncML data in other packages for transport. Certainly, data packets are wrapped by protocol data packets as they move through protocol layers. SyncML data will probably be formatted as MIME objects for use in email. There have also been suggestions that, on devices with restricted resources or limited bandwidth, SyncML be encoded in a binary format (e.g., WAP Binary XML (WBXML), a binary format for transmission over WAP protocols). This binary encoding would reduce the size of the data as well as the length of the transmission time.

More Information

More information about SyncML is available from Internet sources. The core site for SyncML is *http://www.syncml.org*. In addition, the many manufacturers that back SyncML have information on their sites that encourage more learning and software development. Nokia, for example, has an extensive segment of their site dedicated to SyncML (see *http://www.forum.nokia.com/main/1,6668,1'47,00.html*).

17.4.3   Support for SyncML

Specifications for SyncML are very new. Originally planned for late 2000, the specifications were officially published in mid-2001. Implementations have started surfacing during 2001. For example, Nokia has included SyncML support in some of its newest phones (e.g., the 9210 and 7650).

Recall that SyncML is both a data format and a data protocol. One would imagine that SyncML support would take the form of a socket and, as the data protocol is implemented, that is the form it will likely take. However, most of the effort for SyncML support has been concentrated on the data format, and this takes the form of library support for format conversion.

In version 6.1 of the Symbian OS, there is no support delivered with the distribution. However, support can be added later; for example, Nokia has delivered extensions to its emulators that upgrade them to support SyncML.

Upgrade Your Emulator

If you want to upgrade your emulator installations to run SyncML, check this book's support Web site for pointers to SyncML applications: Nokia's SyncML client for both the 9210 and 7650 emulators, and Symbian's upgrade for their reference emulator implementation

17.5   Summary

In this chapter, we have highlighted device synchronization. We reviewed the issues and the history of synchronization. We dug into Symbian's current support of PLP and Symbian Connect as their current synchronization solution, and we overviewed SyncML as the next implementation of synchronization. SyncML represents the future of this area and will be supported in upcoming releases of the Symbian OS.

The next chapter looks in detail at the Symbian OS communications database which is used to store persistent communication settings for devices and applications.

18

The Communications Database

If one could "configure" a social engagement much like one can configure a computer system, going to a party would be a whole lot easier. If this were the case, one could simply set up a central area with personal details. Anyone entering the party would check this information center first and all the initial details about meeting someone would be taken care of straight away. While people would still scramble to figure out what to chat about, this would cut down on repeating your name and occupation for each new person you meet.

This is the idea behind the use of a communications database to centrally store all communication configurations for a Symbian OS device. The database stores those common items that must be repeated for each application that uses communication. For instance, each TCP/IP application must know about your ISP, and each SMS messaging application must know about the service center number you want to use. As the lifespan of this database extends beyond each application's execution time, it can be referenced for the common configuration items that it holds for all implementations in the communications architecture.

We will discuss this communications database in this chapter. We will start by reviewing some issues that configuration of communication involves. We will then spend the majority of the chapter reviewing the API for accessing and manipulating the communications database.

18.1 Configuration and the Communications Database

Configuration issues have dogged computer systems for a long time. Configuration settings must be persistent and must outlast the execution of any single application. At the same time, many applications must be able to access configuration settings and alter them, hopefully through a common, efficient interface. Sometimes applications make changes that should be permanent; sometimes changes should be temporary and thus be discarded before an application terminates.

These aspects of configuration have resulted in different functions of storing and maintaining settings on different systems. The Unix operating system, for example, takes the lowest common denominator approach. Unix configuration settings are kept in files, stored on accessible disks, in readable textual format with no rules as to how to specify settings (i.e., there is no standard API). Humans and applications can read configuration files and alter them easily. The Unix approach specifies that since any application should be able to read text files, text storage is the best (i.e., simplest) function. Microsoft has taken a more organized, proprietary approach in Windows. The Windows registry is a hierarchical, highly organized way of keeping configuration settings. With the registry, an application works with settings from a category hierarchy (e.g., categories like HKEY_LOCAL_MACHINE/SOFTWARE/Psion/PsiWin) in key/value pairs. Microsoft provides an API for programmer access to this registry and tools for users and administrators to access it. Still other operating systems store crucial information in system-maintained tables, available only to applications that make system calls to retrieve this information from the OS kernel (e.g., older VAX systems running Open VMS).

After considering these different ways of storing information, the Symbian OS designers made several important design decisions about settings for communication resources. First, they decided that settings should be applied on a system-wide basis for all applications. Using this idea, a configuration editor could be used to affect all applications (e.g., the Control Panel on some Symbian OS devices). Second, they decided that configuration information should be visible and changeable by all applications. Finally, they decided to store configuration information in a database form, accessible through an API that uses a database context. This meant that they could implement it via included database mechanisms and that the API would be familiar to many Symbian OS programmers.

18.2   The Communications Database API

Symbian OS database implementation is based on a standard database management system (DBMS) implementation. While I will explain a bit about DBMS concepts, I will not be defining them in detail. It is helpful here to be familiar with concepts such as database tables, views, and record selection. These comprise a large part of the DBMS implementation.

18.2.1 Database Structure

The communications database is structured as a standard Symbian OS relational database, managed through DBMS procedures. As a single database, it holds several data tables. Each data table is manipulated by constructing a view of the table and working with its records through that view. The tables contained in the communications database are listed in Table 18.1, along with the names used to access them. Tables without names (listed with N/A as the name in Table 18.1) are accessed using special function calls that we will discuss later.

Therefore, to access the communications database, you must know which table you need to access and how you want to access it. The standard way to access this structure is through the following steps:

- Create a new database object.
- Use this database object to create a view of a data table.
- Select a record—either by creating a new record or by finding an existing one.
- Manipulate this record—read from or write to it as needed.
- Commit any changes made to the record.
- When completed, delete the view and database objects.

18.2.2 Communications Database Classes

The communications database is implemented via the CComms-Database class. In turn, this class is derived from the CComms-DatabaseBase class. Together, these classes define a very large number of functions which I will summarize here.

Review the Communications Database Definition

Take some time to review the definitions setup for the communications database. In the \Symbian\6.1\Quartz\Epoc32\Include directory, pay specific attention to the cdbcols.h file for table-naming macros and to the commsdb.h file for class definitions.

Table 18.1 Communications database tables

Table	Table Name	Description
Incoming Connection Preferences	N/A	Order ranking for IAP settings for incoming connections
Outgoing Connection Preferences	N/A	Order ranking for IAP settings for outgoing connections
Global Settings	N/A	Miscellaneous settings that govern most connection configurations
Internet Access Point	IAP	The settings used to access the Internet (e.g., which modem)
Outgoing ISP	DialOutISP	Connection settings for the ISP used for outgoing messages
Incoming ISP	DialInISP	Connection settings for the ISP used for incoming messages
Outgoing GPRS Provider	OutgoingGPRS	Settings used for the GPRS provider for outgoing data
Incoming GPRS Provider	IncomingGPRS	Settings used for the GPRS provider for incoming data
Default GPRS Provider	DefaultGPRS	Default settings for a GPRS provider
Modem List	Modems	A list of modems available on the device and their settings
Location List	Locations	A list of phone settings for various locations
Charge Cards	ChargeCard	A list of charging settings used to make long distance phone calls
Proxy List	Proxies	A list of HTTP proxy servers and their settings
WAP Access Point List	WAPAccessPoint	A list of sites to access WAP data
WAP IP Bearers	WAPIPBearer	A subset of the WAP access point list that are IP bearers, including their IP settings
WAP SMS Bearers	WAPSMSBearer	A subset of the WAP access point list that are SMS bearers, including their settings
Bluetooth Device List	BTDeviceTable	A list of Bluetooth devices available
Bluetooth Default Settings	BTDefaultTable	The default settings used for a Bluetooth device
Bluetooth Security Settings	BTSecurityTable	Security settings for Bluetooth devices

Creating the database object

New instances of the CCommsDatabase class are created with the NewL() functions, defined below:

```
IMPORT_C static CCommsDatabase* NewL(
    TCommDbDatabaseType aType);
```

```
IMPORT_C static CCommsDatabase* NewL(
    TCommDbDatabaseType aType,
    TCommDbOpeningFunction &aOpeningFunction);
```

These two functions must be given the type of database that is to be created. `TCommDbDatabaseType` is an enumeration, giving three types of databases: an Internet Access Provider database, an Internet Service Provider database, and a generic, unspecified type of database. An IAP database is identical to an ISP database, except that the former provides information about providers of Internet access, and the latter does not include these. However, these distinctions are moot in version 6.1 of Symbian OS, because the ISP database has merged into the IAP database. The second function also requires a specification of the way the system is to open the database: creating it, copying it, or opening an existing one.

Creating a view of the database

Once a database object has been created, the next step is to create a view of a data table. A table view is encapsulated by the `CCommsDbTableView` class. We can get an instance of this class in several ways. The easiest way is to get it using a `CCommsDatabase` object, using one of the functions defined below:

```
IMPORT_C CCommsDbTableView* OpenTableLC (
    const TDesC &aTableName);
IMPORT_C CCommsDbTableView* OpenViewLC (
    const TDesC &aTableName, const TDesC &aSqlQuery);
```

The first function takes the name of the table we need to open and creates a view that makes all records in the table accessible. The name of the table is one from Table 18.1 (which can be found in the constants in the `cdbcols.h` file). The second function uses the name of the table to open an SQL query to select specific records out of the table that we are opening. Structured Query Language (SQL) is a standard DBMS manipulation language and is the language that Symbian OS uses to manage its database systems.

As an example, let's say that we want to list all the charge cards that are stored in the communications database. We would open the database and create a view of the `ChargeCard` table that would give us all table entries. We could do this in the following way:

```
void CDB::ViewEntries()
{
    CCommsDatabase *db;
    CCommsDbTableView *view;
```

```
    TInt result, count;
    TBuf<40> Name, AcctNumber, Pin;
    // Open the database and get a table
    db = CCommsDatabase::NewL(EDatabaseTypeIAP);
    view = db->OpenTableLC(TPtrC(CHARGECARD));

    // ... more code to view all entries

    delete view;
    delete db;
}
```

We will fill in the commented-out portion shortly. Using a view created with this code, the program could display the output shown in Figure 18.1.

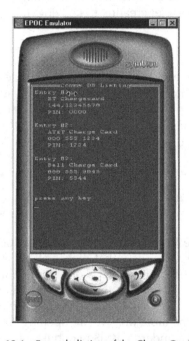

Figure 18.1   Example listing of the ChargeCard table.

Now let's say that we wanted to only view entries with non-zero PINs. We could substitute the `OpenTableLC()` call with a `OpenViewLC()` call, which requires the use of SQL. This function needs an SQL view query, which is generated by an SQL `SELECT` statement. This statement has the following general form:

```
SELECT  selection-spec FROM  table-name
                [WHERE  condition] [ORDER BY  sort-spec]
```

The *selection-spec* field is either a list of record fields or a "*" to select all fields. The *table-name* is the name of the table with which we are concerned. The *condition* is a Boolean condition that will be used to select specific records. The *sort-spec* is a list of fields that are used as sorting keys on which to sort the resulting records. For example, to view all entries except those with PINs equal to "0000", we could replace the OpenTableLC() call with the function call below:

```
view = db->OpenViewLC(TPtrC(CHARGECARD),
           _L("SELECT * FROM ChargeCard WHERE Pin <> '0000'"));
```

In this code, we specify the ChargeCard table, but we add an SQL statement to view only the entries we want. The result of using this to define our view is in Figure 18.2.

Figure 18.2 Example listing of ChargeCard table records whose PIN () 0000.

I should make two points about this use of an SQL statement:

- Notice we give the table name *twice*: once in the first parameter and once in the SQL statement. This is unavoidable; leaving either one out causes a system panic.
- Those who are used to writing SQL for relational database queries will want to terminate this SQL statement with a semi-colon (this is standard syntax). However, this statement *should*

not have a terminating semicolon; inserting one will cause a system panic.

Using SQL in this way is the most flexible way to select and order database table entries. If you do not want to wrestle with SQL statements, however, there are more ways to open a view and select records. These functions still use SQL to query the communications database, but they do not require the programmer to understand SQL, just to be able to use a simple API.

```
IMPORT_C CCommsDbTableView* OpenViewMatchingUintLC(
    const TDesC &aTableName, const TDesC &aColumnToMatch,
    TUint32 aValueToMatch);
IMPORT_C CCommsDbTableView* OpenViewMatchingBoolLC(
    const TDesC &aTableName,const TDesC &aColumnToMatch,
    TBool aValueToMatch);
IMPORT_C CCommsDbTableView* OpenViewMatchingTextLC(
    const TDesC &aTableName, const TDesC &aColumnToMatch,
    const TDesC8 &aValueToMatch);
IMPORT_C CCommsDbTableView* OpenViewMatchingTextLC(
    const TDesC &aTableName, const TDesC &aColumnToMatch,
    const TDesC16 &aValueToMatch);
```

Each of these functions requires a table name as the first parameter. The second parameter is the name of the column that we want to perform the selection over. The third parameter is the value to match—an integer, Boolean, or string (8-bit ASCII or 16-bit Unicode). Note that each function performs a straight equality match. Unfortunately, this means that a selection like that in our example above would not be possible with these functions; they cannot specify inequality (e.g., ``...WHERE PIN <> `0000'''``).

Using SQL for Selections

If you know SQL, it is by far the best way to select records from the communications (or any Symbian OS) database. It is the most flexible query mechanism and can streamline a search for items. The SQL used by the Symbian OS DBMS has a few small differences from conventional SQL. I have already highlighted differences in semicolon usage, and wildcards in the WHERE clause use ``*'' instead of ``%''. Using SQL for searching minimizes the coding effort for the search process; you can find records with SQL for which you would have to implement many lines of code in an application without it.

SQL is worth learning if you do not know it already. Two books worth reading to learn SQL are *Beginning SQL Programming* by

18.2.3   Accessing and Reading Records

Once we have established a view as an object of the `CComms-DbTableView` class, we need to find the records we want to manipulate. Three functions are provided to navigate through a view's records. They are defined below:

```
IMPORT_C TInt GotoFirstRecord();
IMPORT_C TInt GotoNextRecord();
IMPORT_C TInt GotoPreviousRecord();
```

These allow us to find the first record in a view, then to move to the next or previous record based on a current record position. Should any of these functions find that it cannot navigate as requested, it will return the `KErrNotFound` error code. The database system maintains the concept of a "current record position". All record operations are performed on the record at the current record position. Note that there is no specific class that represents a communications database record.

Record data is read column-by-column, using one of the `CCommsDbTableView` functions below:

```
IMPORT_C void ReadUintL(const TDesC &aColumn,
    TUint32 &aValue);
IMPORT_C void ReadBoolL(const TDesC &aColumn,
    TBool &aValue);
IMPORT_C void ReadTextL(const TDesC &aColumn,
    TDes8 &aValue);
IMPORT_C void ReadTextL(const TDesC &aColumn,
    TDes16 &aValue);
IMPORT_C HBufC* ReadLongTextLC(const TDesC &aColumn);
```

These functions read integer, Boolean or string data, from the column whose name is given as the first parameter, into the variable given as the second. For string reads, there are three versions: one that reads data as 8-bit ASCII values, one that reads data as 16-bit Unicode values; and one that will read a value of any length into a string. While the variables in the `ReadTextL()` functions are bounded in size (they are preallocated), the `ReadLongTextLC()` function reads a column value into the heap and returns a pointer to where the results are stored. In the latter case, the function takes care of string allocation.

Now we can complete our example that prints ChargeCard table entries. The complete function definition is given below:

```
void CDB::ViewEntries()
{
    CCommsDatabase *db;
    CCommsDbTableView *view;
    TInt result, count;
    TBuf<40> Name, AcctNumber, Pin;


    // Open the database and get a table
    db = CCommsDatabase::NewL(EDatabaseTypeIAP);
    view = db->OpenTableLC(TPtrC(CHARGECARD));


    // Walk through each record, retrieve fields and print
    count = 1;
    result = view->GotoFirstRecord();
    while (result == KErrNone) {
        view->ReadTextL(TPtrC(COMMDB_NAME), Name);
        view->ReadTextL(TPtrC(CHARGECARD_ACCOUNT_NUMBER),
                        AcctNumber);
        view->ReadTextL(TPtrC(CHARGECARD_PIN), Pin);
        console->Printf(_L("Entry #%d:\n %S\n %S\n PIN: %S\n\n"),
            count++, &Name, &AcctNumber, &Pin);
        result = view->GotoNextRecord();
    }


    delete view;
    delete db;
}
```

In the code above, note that I use standard defined macros for the names of the fields in the ChargeCard database.

18.2.4   Creating and Editing Records

New database records are inserted at the current record position through a call to the CCommsDbTableView function defined below:

```
TInt InsertRecord(TUint32 &aId);
```

This function will make all preparations for inserting a record and make that record the one at the current record position. The ID of this new record is returned in the parameter.

To write into entries, we first need to indicate our intentions. For new records, we can use the `InsertRecord()` function defined above. For existing records, we need the function defined below:

```
TInt UpdateRecord();
```

A panic will be raised if any writes are made to a database record without first calling `InsertRecord()` or `UpdateRecord()`. One of these must be called for each set of changes made to an existing record.

To actually modify a record, we need to use one of the functions defined below:

```
IMPORT_C void WriteUintL(const TDesC &aColumn,
    const TUint32 &aValue);
IMPORT_C void WriteBoolL(const TDesC &aColumn,
    const TBool &aValue);
IMPORT_C void WriteTextL(const TDesC &aColumn,
    const TDesC8 &aValue);
IMPORT_C void WriteTextL(const TDesC &aColumn,
    const TDesC16 &aValue);
IMPORT_C void WriteLongTextL(const TDesC &aColumn,
    const TDesC &aValue);
IMPORT_C void SetNullL(const TDesC &aColumn);
```

The forms here are analogous to those used to read from entries, in that writing is done by entering specific values into specific columns. The name of the column is given as a string for the first parameter and the value to be written is given as the second. As with reading, we can write using three data types: integer, Boolean, and string. Strings can be written in 8-bit and 16-bit forms, and long, unlimited strings allocated from the heap may be written using the `WriteLongTextL()` function. A specific column may be made to be null (i.e., having *no* value, as opposed to a blank value) by the `SetNullL()` function.

When changes to a record have been completed, these changes need to be committed to the database. Commitment of changes is done on a record-by-record basis; we cannot commit changes to several records at once. We commit changes by calling the function defined below:

```
IMPORT_C TInt PutRecordChanges(TBool aHidden = EFalse,
    TBool aReadOnly = EFalse);
```

This call allows some tailoring to be done to the record as it is committed to the database. The record can be designated as hidden; it can also be entered as read-only. These attributes are retained until the next commitment of changes to it in the database. Prior to closing access to the database, changes to a record can be cancelled by using the following function:

```
void CancelRecordChanges();
```

This is effective for both new (started with InsertRecord()) and existing records (started with UpdateRecord()).

As an example, let's say we continue our crusade against zero PINs. We want to change all PINs in the ChargeCard table that are 0000 to have the value '4321'. We could use the code fragment below to do this:

```
view = db->OpenViewLC(TPtrC(CHARGECARD),
_L("SELECT * FROM ChargeCard WHERE Pin = '0000'"));
result = view->GotoFirstRecord();
while (result == KErrNone) {
   view->UpdateRecord();
   view->WriteTextL(TPtrC(CHARGECARD_PIN), _L("4321"));
   view->PutRecordChanges();
   result = view->GotoNextRecord();
}
```

18.2.5   Using Transactions

There are times when we should be concerned that allowing multiple users to simultaneously access the communications database might cause problems. For example, if a process is reading the entries that another process is changing, the reader might get the wrong information. Transactions help to avoid these situations.

A *transaction* is a set of statements that is guaranteed to run *atomically*. This means that a transaction will either run from start to finish with no interference from other processes or it will not be run at all. This is useful for both database readers and writers; readers can be assured of no changes during a read, and writers can be assured that the written data will be used as a unit with no half-completed writes conveying bad information.

The CCommsDatabaseBase class provides functions to implement transactions. A transaction is bracketed by the functions defined below:

```
IMPORT_C TInt BeginTransaction();
IMPORT_C TInt CommitTransaction();
```

Any statement between the two functions above is assumed to be part of the transaction. The system implements the transaction as follows:

- The use of the `BeginTransaction()` function causes the system to try to obtain a *read-lock* on the database. This type of lock is shared by readers and, while only read operations are being used, multiple read-locks may coexist on the database.

- At the time the first write operation is used, the system converts the read-lock obtained by the process to a *write-lock*. Write-locks are exclusive, and no read- or write-locks may coexist with a write-lock.

- When the `CommitTransaction()` function is used, the lock held by the process committing the transaction is removed, and any changes made during the transaction are committed to the database.

If a write-lock is already held by another user when a `BeginTransaction()` call tries to obtain a read-lock, the function call will return a `KErrLocked` error code. Note that changes to the database made during a transaction still require additional `PutRecordChanges()` calls; the `CommitTransaction()` function will not take care of operation commitment.

It is possible to *rollback* changes—that is, reverse them—if a transaction is terminated with the following function:

```
IMPORT_C void RollbackTransaction();
```

This function call is used in place of calling `CommitTransaction()`. It causes all changes to the database to be discarded and removes any locks.

Information about transactions and locking status can obtained by the following functions:

```
IMPORT_C TBool InTransaction();
IMPORT_C TBool IsDatabaseWriteLockedL();
```

If a transaction is in progress—determined by whether a process has made a `BeginTransaction()` call—then the `InTransaction()` function will return an `ETrue` value. If the database has been write-locked by a process, the `IsDatabaseWriteLockedL()` will return an `ETrue` value.

Let's rework our anti-zero-PIN example one more time. This time, we will change the way we select records, and we will group all changes in a transaction. The code is below:

```
view = db->OpenViewMatchingTextLC(TPtrC(CHARGECARD),
    _L("Pin"), _L("0000"));
db->BeginTransaction();
result = view->GotoFirstRecord();
while (result == KErrNone) {
```

```
              view->UpdateRecord();
              view->WriteTextL(TPtrC(CHARGECARD_PIN), _L("4321"));
              view->PutRecordChanges();
              result = view->GotoNextRecord();
          }
          db->CommitTransaction();
```

During this change to the `ChargeCard` table, no readers or writers can access the database.

18.2.6 Special Purpose Tables

Table 18.1 lists the tables in the communications database. While you are encouraged to explore all of them, and most are self-explanatory, there are a few that need further explanation.

The connection preferences tables contain information about the ordering of Internet Access Points (IAPs) in a connection sequence. These IAPs are tried in order until a connection succeeds. There is a sequence specified for incoming connections and for outgoing connections. The information in the table contains a ranking of the IAP in the sequence, the type of bearer that should be used, a determination of how to interact with the user about this IAP (e.g., conversing with the user through a dialog before connecting or connecting automatically), and the direction of the connection. Connection preference tables are represented by their own class (the `CCommsDbConnectionPrefTableView` class); this class has its own functions to open and view each table as well as to browse each table in a specific order.

There is a special table that holds "global" settings. These are settings that govern all connection attempts. They are miscellaneous settings like the number of dial attempts and whether a device accepts incoming GPRS connections. To use these settings, no view needs to be established; a table is opened automatically when the communications database object is created. Global settings can be read, written, and cleared using the function definitions below:

```
IMPORT_C void GetGlobalSettingL(const TDesC &aSetting,
    TUint32 &aValue);
IMPORT_C void GetGlobalSettingL(const  TDesC &aSetting,
    TDes &aValue);
IMPORT_C void SetGlobalSettingL(const TDesC &aSetting,
    TUint32 aValue);
IMPORT_C void SetGlobalSettingL(const TDesC  &aSetting,
    const TDesC &aValue);
IMPORT_C void ClearGlobalSettingL(const TDesC &aSetting);
```

Settings have either integer or string values. Each function takes the name of the setting to access as the first parameter. Get-GlobalSettingL() fills the second parameter; SetGlobalSettingL() takes the new value from the second parameter.

18.2.7   Other Functionality

In addition to the large core of operations that we have covered, there are a few more concepts that we need to deal with before we leave communications databases. We will overview them here.

Deleting records

No set of operations would be complete without the ability to delete. Deleting records is accomplished by the following function:

```
IMPORT_C TInt DeleteRecord();
```

As with other database changes, deleting a record must be committed to the database by calling PutRecordChanges().

Notification of changes

Applications can be notified by the system when changes are made to the communications database. Notification involves waiting for the system to send a signal, and this kind of situation naturally calls for an active object. As with other active object scenarios, notification of database events requires that an active object makes a request and uses SetActive() to return control to the operating system. This notification request is made via the CCommsDatabaseBase function below:

```
IMPORT_C TInt RequestNotification(TRequestStatus &aStatus);
```

As is the standard operating procedure, this asynchronous call includes a status variable through which we can receive database update information. This request can be cancelled through the function below:

```
IMPORT_C void CancelRequestNotification();
```

Upon notification of a database event, the type of change that occurred is denoted in the value of the status variable passed the request function. The value of this variable is defined by the enumerators of the `RDbNotifier::TEvent` structure.

Hidden records

Records can be designated as hidden in the communications database. Hidden records do not show up in normal record selections. To allow hidden records to be selected, an application must call the `CCommsDatabaseBase` function below:

```
IMPORT_C void ShowHiddenRecords();
```

Records are designated as hidden when the `PutRecordChanges()` function is called. Including the first parameter with an ETrue value will make this designation.

Specialized functions

There are a few functions in the class collection for the communications database that are not specifically tied to tables or setting, but are useful nonetheless.

- The functions below resolve phone numbers:

```
IMPORT_C static void ResolvePhoneNumberL(
    TDesC &aNumber, TDes &aDialString,
    TParseMode aDialParseMode,
TUint32 aLocationId, TUint32 aChargecardId);
IMPORT_C void ResolvePhoneNumberFromDatabaseL(
    TDesC &aNumber, TDes &aDialString,
    TParseMode aDialParseMode,
TUint32 aLocationId, TUint32 aChargecardId);
```

These functions from the `CCommsDatabaseBase` class will take a phone number in the first parameter and translate it into the second parameter, using the specific parsing function, dialing location and charge card given in the rest of the parameters.

- Each table can have a *template record*, a record that is copied to a new record whenever one is created. This is useful for establishing default values in records. Template records are implemented by their own class (the `CCommsDbTemplateRecord` class) and are manipulated in the same way standard communications database records are manipulated.

- The communications database uses the idea of *override settings*. These settings are *(tablename, columnname, value)* triples that override the settings in the communications database for a single connection only. These settings are implemented by their own class (the `CCommDbOverrideSettings` class). The use of these settings provides a way to change a single configuration set without changing the database.

18.3   Summary

This chapter has dealt with the Symbian OS communications database, the database which holds the configuration settings for Symbian OS communication systems. These settings are to be persistent between application executions and can be changed by applications. We discussed configuration issues and spent most of the chapter reviewing the API for manipulating the communications database.

The next chapter is the final chapter in this book. In it, we discuss the future of communications support on Symbian OS.

19

Looking Ahead

The computer field is strewn with empty predictions by intelligent people. Thomas Watson, when he was chairman of IBM, said in 1945 that "there is a world market for maybe five computers". Ken Olsen, then the president and founder of Digital Equipment Corporation, said in 1977 "There is no reason why anyone would want a computer in the home". Even Bill Gates, founder of Microsoft, said about a computer's memory capacity, "640 K should be enough for anybody". He said that in 1981.

Nevertheless, I am going to finish this book by looking into the future and making a few predictions. We have spent this book looking at Symbian OS version 6.1. At this writing (January 2002), Symbian OS version 7.0 is being launched. These new development efforts will undoubtedly test the communication architecture by implementing new ways to use communication technology. New media, new protocols, and new forms of content will likely be incorporated in hardware and software for Symbian OS devices.

This chapter looks at what is possible for future implementation. There are some obvious technologies; we will see these first. Then there are some technologies way out there on the horizon. We will mention these in closing.

19.1 The Next Step: GPRS

Symbian OS version 7.0 contains support for GPRS integrated into the messaging infrastructure. There is some support in version 6.1.

19.1.1 What is GPRS?

General Packet Radio Service (GPRS) is a bridge protocol, implemented for 2.5G networks. Second generation (2G) networks are in common use today, allowing technologies such as GSM to implement voice and data transport. Third generation (3G) networks are several years off; they require new and expensive equipment. 2.5G networks upgrade the speed of 2G networks while avoiding the high price tag of 3G networks. GPRS is one of the services provided by 2.5G networks.

GPRS is a data-only enhancement to GSM. Where GSM provides both voice and data transport, GPRS provides only data transport. Recall from Chapter 4 that GSM uses Time Division Multiplexing (TDM) to place digitized voice or data information into fixed size packets that get transferred in fixed time slots. Currently, this multiplexing is done over a set of circuits; each circuit represents a voice or data channel. Although the data is sent in packets, the circuits are multiplexed in order. This means that if nothing is sent over a circuit, then that slot in the multiplexed data stream is empty. GPRS uses true packet switching; all data is sent via packets exactly when they are ready. The time slots are still fixed, but each will contain a data packet if there is one available. The stream resembles a network, and network concepts such as packet reassembly and fragmentation are applicable to GPRS.

GPRS reduces overhead and increases the utilization of slots in the multiplexed stream. It takes on properties of a network—i.e., it is always on and supports concepts like virtual connections. Data over GPRS also move much faster; the upper bound on data speed over GPRS is 171.2 Kbps, versus 19.2 Kbps for GSM. This upper bound depends on the maximum number of timeslots used for GPRS packets (eight slots is the maximum); initial implementations will likely fall back to using two or three slots, thereby reducing the speed practically possible.

GPRS also transitions users from the restrictions and costs of a dial-up model of Internet access to the benefits of "always-on" network-style access. Users who use dial-up technologies like GSM are used to a delay for connection time, slower access times, and a cost model that charges for the duration of the connection. GPRS is always on and connection time is vastly reduced. The cost model for GPRS is to charge for data sent or received. This means that normal use—like reading and understanding a Web page—will potentially cost much less with GPRS.

There are downsides to using GPRS. Because it takes more timeslots than other technologies, it does not share the frequencies as well and therefore consumes more resources. Other communication methods—voice and 2G data can transmit in parallel with GPRS—can be squeezed out by too much GPRS traffic. In addition, the use of several timeslots at once increases the probability that packets will be lost or corrupted by assembly errors. This results in greater overhead and reduced data throughput.

It is important here to reiterate that GPRS is a stopgap measure. It is intended to upgrade 2G networks by using the same equipment with new protocols. In doing so, it paves the way for 3G network implementation.

19.1.2 Using GPRS

In order to take advantage of GPRS, users need several different technologies to come together:

- *A user must have a GPRS-enabled phone and/or computer.* Existing GSM or TDMA devices do not support GPRS.

- *A user must subscribe to a carrier service that implements GPRS.* GPRS-enabled service is just now (in 2002) being implemented and is in its infancy.

- *GPRS must be enabled for a particular service.* Because data and voice services can be run in parallel with GPRS, it is possible that a user will have voice service and not data service. Users need to be specifically enabled for GPRS data use.

- *There must be a GPRS-enabled destination.* In addition to mobile devices, Internet destinations are reachable through GPRS (we call these "GPRS-enabled").

It is important to think of GPRS as analogous to TCP/IP or WAP and not equivalent to something like GSM. Web pages are accessible over GPRS, for example, as are other data services, like email and printing protocols.

19.1.3 Symbian OS Support for GPRS

The support that Symbian OS needs to give to GPRS is minimal. Currently, version 6.1 treats GPRS in the same way as it handles GSM: both are considered to be call-oriented connection media. In version 6.1, devices can receive SMS over GPRS, and GPRS is integrated into ETel. However, it is not yet viewed like a network protocol; there are no PRT modules implemented yet. This means programmers cannot use GPRS for data link layer transport and users with GPRS data service cannot use it transparently as they would services like network transport. These will undoubtedly be coming in future versions.

Currently, there are only 4,294,967,296 possible IP addresses. While this may seem like a lot, when you take out the reserved addresses (e.g, for a local host or multicasting) and the addresses used for broadcasting, the actual number that can be assigned to devices is substantially reduced. If you consider how many devices might possibly be assigned an IP address (e.g., it is estimated that there were 860 million mobile phones worldwide at the end of 2001, and that this number will double in five years), this number dries up quickly. Even with schemes like dynamic address assignment, IP numbers are starting to become scarce.

Most of today's Internet uses version 4 of the Internet Protocol (IPv4). IPv4 is now nearly twenty years old and has been remarkably resilient in spite of its age. But recently, it has developed some problems. First and foremost, there is the growing shortage of IPv4 addresses. Second, as more devices proliferate across many different carriers, routing algorithms have grown in complexity and have tested the bounds of IPv4 routing capability. Third, more protocols on more devices have pushed the limits of fixed headers in IP packets. Finally, issues of autoconfiguration and self-renumbering have cropped up as beneficial to system administrators and users alike.

Internet Protocol version 6 (IPv6) has been designed to address these situations and more. The most noticeable change with IPv6 is the size of its addresses. IPv6 addresses are 128 bits wide, versus 32 bits for IPv4. The notation is a colon-delimited notation, such as A:B:C:D:E:F:G:H, where each letter is a 16-bit quantity. This address space now contains 2^{128} addresses, or 3.4×10^{38}. Because the address space is so large, we can create additional addressing hierarchies. IPv4 addresses are split into network ID and host ID portions. IPv6 could add a new level of Internet Service Provider to these existing levels. IPv6 routing might first route a packet according to the ISP ID, then route to a network within the ISP, and finally route to a host.

IPv6 also specifies a flexible header format to packets. Many headers are optional and can be omitted. This accommodates both lower-bandwidth networks and networks with large capacity that want more features built into each packet. IPv6 is open-ended with its protocol definition. More protocols can be added in the future and can be incorporated into the protocol structure; underlying network hardware could change without harming the protocol stack. IPv6 also includes support for the autoconfiguration and dynamic renumbering of a machine's address. A new machine could join an IPv6 network by assigning itself an address and changing that address on the fly as it participates in network traffic. IPv6 has also been specified to incorporate other protocols' addressing schemes.

To use IPv6 on a network, all devices on that network must be using IPv6. Unfortunately, IPv4 is incompatible with IPv6. IPv6 can incorporate some IPv4 features—e.g., an IPv4 address is also an IPv6 address—but many facets of IPv4 do not translate to IPv6. So, new network equipment, new drivers and new software are all required to take advantage of the new IP mechanism.

Fortunately, Symbian OS version 6.1 is IPv6 aware. Many of the APIs that have network interfaces can work with both IPv4 and IPv6. The protocol modules still need to be upgraded; however, compatibility can be easily reached with the inclusion of a future `tcpip.prt` implementation.

19.3   Other Future Technologies

It is a very safe prediction that GPRS and IPv6 will be incorporated in future versions of Symbian OS. There are other communication technologies being developed whose future is uncertain and therefore whose support from Symbian OS is not a given.

19.3.1   MMS: Multimedia Messaging Service

A message—as we have discussed it in this book—is usually a text-centered object with data attachments. These data attachments can be any type of object and are accessed by using a viewer for the attachment. The model for this type of messaging is one that centers on text messages with connected multimedia pieces that must be detached and viewed.

A new standard for messages takes the opposite viewpoint. The Multimedia Messaging Service (MMS) lets users send and receive messages with formatted text, graphics, images and audio and video clips. The model for an MMS message is a data stream rather than a set of text. It supports image formats (e.g., GIF and JPEG formats), video formats (e.g., MPEG 4) and audio formats (like MP3).

In the MMS model, messages can come from many different sources. They can be downloaded to a device from a WAP site, transferred via an attached device (such as a digital camera) or received as an MMS message. MMS messages can be sent either to another MMS-enabled mobile phone or converted to email and sent to an e-mail address.

The MMS model does not specify transport but, for many formats, it is dependent on networks with high transmission speeds. GPRS and 3G technologies (see Section 19.3.3) are necessary for most uses. GSM can be adapted to support MMS, but the slow data rate of the technology will restrict the formats that can be sent or received. WAP is used for transport over GSM.

Several companies have begun to implement MMS compatible devices. The Nokia 7650 is MMS-capable and the Series 60 development platform for Symbian OS has MMS support built in. Ericsson's T68 phone has MMS support and the company also has adapters that will make non-MMS phones able to receive MMS messages.

19.3.2   i-Mode Service

i-mode is a communication suite dedicated to allowing mobile phone access to Internet protocols. It is wildly popular in Japan but currently only in Japan. In October, 2001, there were over 27 million i-mode subscribers, and this number was increasing by about 40,000 per day. There were about 60 million mobile users in Japan, which means that i-mode accounted for about 47% of mobile phone usage. At the moment 99.999% of i-mode users are Japanese. Since i-mode has only been in use since early 1999, these numbers are quite impressive.

i-mode was invented and is currently supported by NTT DoCoMo, a subsidiary of NTT, Japan's national telephone carrier. At the present time, NTT DoCoMo is the sole carrier of i-mode data.

Just as GPRS is a packet-switched extension of a GSM or TDMA phone system, i-mode is the packet-switched extension to NTT DoCoMo's ordinary mobile phone system. As with GPRS, i-mode is "always on". This means that it is (in part) a data link layer carrier with unique properties for use on mobile phones. For example, packet sizes are fixed at 128 bytes. Overhead reduction is important, because the current speed of i-mode is only 9600 bps.

i-mode also addresses content. i-mode uses cHTML (compact HTML), a subset of HTML that represents a new HTML standard. In addition to HTML tags, i-mode defines additional tags that are used only in i-mode microbrowsers. For example, there are new HTML tags that can define a link that dials a phone number when it is clicked and ones that identify Web pages as i-mode pages. There are also many special characters used in i-mode phones, such as symbols for kisses and hot spring baths.

A comparison between i-mode and conventional phone services like WAP is not simple. At the present time, WAP is implemented over a call-based carrier while i-mode is implemented over a data link network carrier. WAP uses WML for its contents, while i-mode uses cHTML (which is perhaps easier to learn). However, when a comparison is made between WAP using GPRS and i-mode, the two are much closer in function. Currently, GPRS has the transfer speed advantage over i-mode.

Whatever promise i-mode shows in its popularity and usefulness is hampered by its proprietary nature. At the present, NTT DoCoMo is the sole implementor of i-mode, and there have been no attempts to make i-mode a standard. Until this changes, it is unlikely that we will see i-mode in wide use outside of Japan.

19.3.3 3G Mobile Phone Service

One of the constant pressures on mobile communication providers is for faster transmission speeds. Digital transmission over current 2G networks is bounded by 19.2 Kbps; GPRS running over 2.5G networks has a theoretical upper limit of 171.2 Kbps. While 2.5G is an improvement, it does not approach the speeds necessary for many of the applications planned for mobile communications. Video streaming, for example, needs network-level bandwidth.

Third generation (3G) mobile radio communications will help meet these bandwidth needs. 3G networks will provide data in speeds up to 2 Mbps. For 3G communication, GSM and GPRS protocols of the past will be replaced with Universal Mobile Telecommunication System (UTMS) protocols. UTMS is a radio communication standard that provides two different transmission implementations:

- *Frequency Division Duplex (FDD)* is a method that uses two radio frequencies to transmit data: a *downlink* from the provider to the client and an *uplink* from the client to the provider. This method is best used in larger broadcast cells for general purpose use. The maximum data speed in FDD environments is 384 Kbps.

- *Time Division Duplex (TDD)* uses a single frequency, transmitting down and uplinks in fixed time slots. Less effort is spent maintaining a pair of frequencies, but there are higher error and transmission rates. Therefore, TDD must be used in much smaller cells, where the receiver is closer to the transmitter and is not moving. In these environments, data rates approach 2 Mbps.

TDD has a further advantage in that it can be asymmetric in transmission. The amount of data in the uplink can be very different to the downlink; the 2 Mbps bandwidth would be filled by whatever side needed to transmit the most. This means that TDD is better suited for contexts where a simple request results in a large download of data (e.g., requesting a video or audio stream).

While it is possible to run GPRS over existing GSM equipment, UTMS requires entirely new installations. To implement 3G networks, providers are going to have to roll out brand new services to brand new customer equipment. New phone handsets that support UTMS will be needed. However, once the equipment is in place, new, all-digital services can be used. Voice-over-IP (VOIP) services that encode analog voice transmission for sending out over IP networks can be enabled. Services that implement IP networking over UTMS carriers will support efforts like VOIP. Messaging services over high speed connections now take on new meaning when the carrier services approach network speeds.

3G networks will increase call capacity, provide network services to handheld devices, and increase transmission speed. However, to Symbian OS, it will be the carrier that lies underneath much of the communication architecture. The biggest change for Symbian OS designers to consider will be how 3G will affect services and applications which are already supported. If we can send data at 384 Kbps in an always-on network context, how does that affect SMS messaging? Do we really want short messages in this context? How does this affect SMS-based data, like WAP content? Providing services in an environment where the quality of networks change will also be challenging. More expensive 3G networks will probably only be available initially in dense population centers with 2G and 2.5G network coverage elsewhere. Providing consistent application service through service changes and interruptions will be extremely difficult.

19.4   Summary

The word "uncertain" is a good way to summarize future technologies. This chapter muses about a few technologies of the future and how Symbian OS might support them. However, the future is prone to change. While GPRS and IPv6 are almost certain to be used in the future, other technologies change as they are implemented. Only time will tell.

Appendix

Developer Resources and Bibliography

Download the code for the examples in this book from *http://www.symbian.com/books/socp/socp-support.html*.

Documentation for the various releases of Symbian OS can be found in the SDKs for each release.

White papers on all aspects of Symbian OS can be found at *http://www.symbian.com/developer/techlib*.

Symbian Web Sites

Corporate: *http://www.symbian.com*
Developer resources: *http://www.symbian.com/developer*

Symbian Partner Developer Web Sites

Ericsson: *http://www.ericsson.com/developers*
Nokia: *http://www.forum.nokia.com*
NTT DoCoMo: *http://www.nttdocomo.com*

Chapter-by-chapter resource guide

Chapter 1 An Introduction

Allin, J., *et al.*, *Wireless Java for Symbian Devices*, John Wiley and Sons, Ltd., 2001.

The ENIAC: *http://ftp.arl.mil/mike/comphist/eniac-story.html*
Nokia phones: *http://www.forum.nokia.com*

Chapter 2 An Introduction to the Symbian Communication Architecture

Pottruck, D.S. and Pearce, T., *Clicks and Mortar*, Jossey-Bass Publishers, 2000.

Chapter 4 Transport Technologies

Comer, D.E, *Internetworking with TCP/IP: Principles, Protocols, and Architectures*, Volume 1, Fourth Ed., Prentice Hall, 2000.

Tutorials on RS232:   *http://www.arcelect.com/rs232.htm*
                       http://www.sangoma.com/signal.htm
Network cabling: *http://www.techfest.com/networking/lan/ethernet5.htm*
IrDA standards: *http://www.irda.org*
Bluetooth protocol
    standards: *http://www.bluetooth.org*

Chapter 5 A Look at Content Technologies

Email standards (including
    receipt and delivery):   *http://www.ietf.org*
SMS messaging: *http://www.iec.org/online/tutorials/wire˙sms/*
vCard and vCalendar
    formats: *http://www.imc.org*
Fax protocol standards: *http://www.faqs.org/rfcs/rfc804.html*
HTTP and related
    standards: *http://www.ietf.org*
HTML standards: *http://www.w3c.org*
WAP protocol standards: *http://www.wapforum.org*

Chapter 6 Security and Communication

Denning, D.E., *Information Warfare and Security*, Addison Wesley, 1999.
Kaufman, C., Perlman, R., and Speciner, M., *Network Security: Private Communication in a Public World*, Prentice Hall, 1995.

Security attack information: *http://www.cert.org*

Chapter 8 Serial Communications

Tasker, M., *et al.*, *Professional Symbian Programming*, Wrox Press, 2000.

Chapter 10 Using Sockets

Stevens, W.R., *UNIX Network Programming*, Prentice Hall, 1990.

General socket programming:
http://www.uwo.ca/its/doc/courses/notes/socket/
http://compnetworking.about.com/library/weekly/
aa083100a.htm
http://world.std.com/ jimf/papers/sockets/sockets.html
http://py-howto.sourceforge.net/sockets/sockets.html

Chapter 12 Communicating with TCP/IP

IP address classes and routing: *http://www.ralphb.net/IPSubnet/*
Network Time Protocol: *http://www.eecis.udel.edu/ntp/*

Chapter 17 Synchronization: PLP and SyncML

SyncML: *http://www.syncml.org*
Developing with SyncML: *http://www.nokia/com/syncml*
http://www.forum.nokia.com/main/
1,6668,1`47,00.html

Chapter 18 The Communications Database

Bowman, J., Emerson, S., and Darnovsky, M., *The Practical SQL Handbook*, Addison Wesley, 2001.
Kaufman, J., Matsik, B., and Spencer, K., *Beginning SQL Programming*, Wrox Press, 2000.

Chapter 19 Looking Ahead

GPRS: *http://www.gsmworld.com/technology/gprs.html*
IPv6: *http://www.ipv6.org*
MMS: *http://www.ericsson.com/mms/*
http://forum.nokia.com/main/1,6668,1`2`7,00.html
i-mode: *http://www.eurotechnology.com/imode/faq.html*
3G networks: *http://www.3gnewsroom.com*

Index